WOMEN COMPOSERS

Music through the Ages

WOMEN COMPOSERS

Music through the Ages

EDITED BY

SYLVIA GLICKMAN
AND
MARTHA FURMAN SCHLEIFER

Volume 2

Composers Born 1600–1699

G.K. HALL & Co.
An Imprint of Simon & Schuster Macmillan
NEW YORK

PRENTICE HALL INTERNATIONAL
LONDON   MEXICO CITY   NEW DELHI   SINGAPORE   SYDNEY   TORONTO

G.K. Hall and Co.
An Imprint of Simon & Schuster Macmillan
1633 Broadway
New York, NY 10019

Music engraving by Lejoy & Goodpeak Co.

Library of Congress Catalog Number: 95-24552

Printed in the United States of America

Printing number:
   2   3   4   5   6   7   8   9   10

Library of Congress Cataloging-in-Publication Data
Women composers : music through the ages / edited by Sylvia Glickman
    and Martha Furman Schleifer
        1 score.
        ". . . annotated, modern performance scores from the ninth through
the twentieth centuries also contain . . . explanatory essays . . ."
        Contents: v. 1. Composers born before 1599
        v. 2. Composers born 1600–1699
        Includes bibliographical references and index.
        ISBN 0-8161-0926-5 (v. 1)
        1. Music. 2. Women composers' music. 3. Women composers-
Biography. I. Schleifer, Martha Furman. II. Glickman, Sylvia.
        M2.W88 1995   95-24552
                                                                    CIP
                                                                     M

ISBN 0-8161-0563-4 (v. 2)

This paper meets the requirements of ANSI/NISO Z39.48-1992 (Permanence of Paper).

Contents of Volume 2

Composers Born 1600–1699

Series Introduction

Women Composers: Music through the Ages

Women's contribution to the arts and humanities has been the subject of an explosion of interest in recent years. Historically, there has been a deep-rooted prejudice against women composers. Those who created music in the earliest eras were either women in convents, aristocrats, or members of professional musical families. In the seventeenth century performer-composers (primarily singers) began to emerge, joining the groups that preceded them. The Italian *ospedali,* actually orphanages and hostels for the indigent, offered music instruction to their resident children as a way of helping them toward later employment. However, few examples of compositions by women educated there exist, as the emphasis was on musical performance. During the eighteenth century women appeared in public concerts and salons as soloists and composers. Many wrote music in appropriate small forms, but the unusual women ventured further and produced operas and orchestral and choral works. In the nineteenth century new public, secular conservatories (some an outgrowth of the *ospedali*) provided educational opportunities for women, although it was not until the end of the century that they were allowed into music theory or composition classes. A dramatic shift in musical activity from the private to the public sphere took place in the early twentieth century. Accepted into the labor force, women play in orchestras, appear professionally in public, and, with all restrictions in conservatories lifted, now are exhibiting a burst of creative musical activity that demands acceptance by society.

Ignoring the creative output of women has denied them ongoing support for centuries. Imaginative, memorable music survived, however, because it was worthy of preservation, and we are now in the process of rediscovering it. *Women Composers: Music through the Ages* is a new, valuable resource for the modern scholar, performer, teacher, student, and the general public. Until recently this music was scattered, often inaccessible, underexplored, and therefore infrequently performed. This series remedies these circumstances and reveals hidden riches. International in scope, the twelve volumes of annotated, modern performance scores from the ninth through the twentieth centuries also contain explanatory essays that illuminate the scores.

Women Composers: Music through the Ages is organized in chronological order. Volume 1 includes composers born before 1599. Volume 2 includes those born between 1600 and 1699. The eighteenth century volumes (3, 4, and 5), nineteenth (6, 7, and 8) and twentieth (9, 10, 11, and 12) are divided by genre (instrumental music, vocal music, and mixed combinations). The last of the twentieth-century volumes is devoted to experimental music.

This series makes no attempt to be comprehensive; it includes music that exemplifies the exceptional woman composer. The traditional separation between male and female creators, indeed, the omission of the work of women in music history books, tacitly implied that their compositions were inferior. These volumes will prove otherwise.

All music, prepared from original materials, edited and corrected by experts, carefully differentiates between the original and the performance editions. Marks in brackets are editorial and figured-bass realizations, in reduced-size notes, are the suggestions of the contributors. All music is newly engraved to ensure clarity and ease of use for classroom and performance. (Performance parts for scores included in this collection are available through the Hildegard Publishing Company.)

We want to express our gratitude to all the contributors for their expertise and their efforts in helping to create this unique series. We thank Robert Kendrick for his careful reading of the manuscripts of Volumes 1 and 2 and for his useful suggestions.

Our warmest thanks are to our families and to our husbands, Dr. Charles R. Schleifer and Dr. Harvey Glickman, for their caring support which helped to make this series a reality.

Sylvia Glickman
Martha Furman Schleifer

Introduction to Volume 2

The composers included in Volume II of *Women Composers: Music through the Ages* were born between 1600 and 1699. Some were singers or instrumentalists who had lengthy performing careers at courts or in convents, but many of them published their music at an early age and then disappeared from public view. Often their music was published before marriage or, in the case of nuns, before their final vows.

Francesca Campana was a composer, a keyboard player, and one of Rome's finest singers. Her collection, *Arie a una, due, e tre voci*, published in 1629 when she was a young woman, includes twelve pieces in a variety of styles. Three works from that collection included here reflect the diversity of her output. Barbara Strozzi, a well-known virtuoso singer, published eight books of music that include about one hundred pieces, primarily for voice. As a daughter of the poet Giulio Strozzi, she had access to Venetian intellectuals and artists, enabling her to study with the composer Francesco Cavalli and to pursue an active performing career. Antonia Bembo, another singer and student of Francesco Cavalli, wrote music that combined stylistic traits of her native Venice and her adopted country, France, with texts in three languages. The three early works from her first book of vocal compositions are included here: an Italian aria, a Latin motet, and a French air. The French virtuoso harpsichordist Elizabeth-Claude Jacquet de la Guerre began her career as a child prodigy. She composed works for voice, chamber groups, and solo instruments. La Guerre served in the court of Louis XIV and was praised for the sophisticated level of her musical thinking. German princess Sophie Elisabeth, Duchess of Brunswick and Lüneburg, also led a privileged life. Although a very religious woman, she wrote music for and participated in court festivities. In addition, she was a prodigious writer of religious poetry. The first woman in English history to publish music under her own name was Mary Harvey, the Lady Dering. Her three extant songs, two of which are included here, are settings of poetry by her husband, Edward Dering, a Parliamentary politician. This volume also includes an unusual example of music notation from Diacinta Fedele's collection of Italian *villanelle*, published in 1628. The folk poetry is accompanied by *alfabeto* tablature to be strummed on the Spanish guitar.

Many women composers in the seventeenth century were nuns. Isabella Leonarda was recognized as a singer and composer in the Ursuline convent, which she entered in 1636, and where music was an important aspect of the celebrated festivals. Leonarda's published works, of which nearly two hundred survive, span a period of sixty years; most of her compositions appeared after she was fifty years old. Maria Xaveria Peruchona, another Italian nun who joined an Ursuline convent, published only one collection of music when she was about twenty-three years old. She is more typical of women composers of the time. Chiara Margarita Cozzolani, on the other hand, left the largest and most varied oeuvre of seventeenth-century Milanese nuns who composed music. More is known about her life than that of other Italian nun composers of the period. She published four collections of music between 1640 and 1650. The works included here exemplify her use of dialogue, a popular style in Milan. Rosa Giacinta Badalla, like Cozzolani, was a nun from the San Radegonda monastery. Very little is known about her life except that her *Motetti a voce sola* was published in Venice when she was just over twenty years old. The life of Bianca Maria Meda, a Benedictine nun, is also a mystery. *Cari musici*, which opens her only preserved work, is a fairly elaborate example of the late seventeenth-century solo motet. It displays virtuosity and a personal expression of her devotion. Maria Francesca Nascinbeni is representative of those talented young women who composed some music and were never heard from afterward. All that is known of her life is the information on the title pages and prefaces of her two volumes of music published in 1674. The composers Caterina Benedetta Gratianini, Camilla de Rossi, and Maria Margherita Grimani were from Northern Italy. They share the unusual accomplishment of having had their works performed in Vienna during their lifetimes.

Sylvia Glickman
Martha Furman Schleifer

Francesca Campana

(ca. 1605/1610–1665)

THOMASIN LAMAY

In an impassioned letter of December 3, 1633, the poet Fulvio Testi described Francesca Campana as a brilliant composer, keyboard player, and singer.[1] He particularly praised her vocal abilities and found her to be one of Rome's finest performers. Since the city then boasted the considerable talents of singers Anna Maria Cesi, Adriana Basile, and Basile's young daughters, Leonora and Caterina, Campana must have been an exceptional virtuosa. Testi penned his accolade four years after Campana published her *Arie a una, due, e tre voci*. Also in 1629, her publisher Robletti included one of her two-part madrigals and a solo aria in his collection *Le Risonante sfere* (most of which is now lost). Although she was still a young woman and records attest that she performed until at least 1640,[2] Campana published no other works.

Her brief foray into the public world of publishing characterized the efforts of most women composers of that time.[3] Of Campana's predecessors, only Madalena Casulana published more than one complete collection.[4] The reputation of her contemporary, Francesca Caccini, rested primarily on her published opera, *La liberazione di Ruggiero* (1625), although she had previously produced *Primo libro delle musiche* in 1618. All other female composers of the period produced single collections or pieces within collections.[5] Their publications appeared early in their careers, after which many of those women disappeared from public view and documents. This was perhaps in part because they viewed themselves as virtuose and wrote music for their own purposes. Many singers, such as Adriana Basile, were known to have performed their own compositions but never to have published them.[6] With the exception of Paola Massarenghi, who is documented only as a composer, all female composers of the period were singers and instrumentalists who had active performing careers either in convents or at court. They were trained to perform, however, and not to compose. Those who did publish generally did not do so after marriage (Francesca Caccini was a notable exception). Con-

versely, their male contemporaries made their way primarily as composers, directors, and instrumentalists. While historical documents record many male singers, Giulio Caccini is one of the few virtuosi who composed and performed his own works.[7] Women may have preferred the performance experience to the compositional one since their discomfort with the sexual implications of madrigal texts might have been mitigated by interpolating or reworking traditional mythologies to include feminine perspectives.[8] This was less easily achieved on paper, where violation of standard transmission became a permanent record and therefore less acceptable to publishers and patrons.[9]

Few documents survive regarding Campana's early life. Eitner situates her originally in Florence,[10] but all other sources place her in Rome from birth, as the daughter of the Roman Andrea Campana.[11] She married Giovan Carlo Rossi, youngest brother of the celebrated composer Luigi Rossi, sometime after 1633 (Testi's letter of that year implies that she was then unmarried). Her husband was an organist and occasional composer who came to Rome in 1630 to work with his brother. It appears from the scanty documentation available that Campana and her husband led somewhat independent lives, even if she did not publish after marriage. Giovan Carlo was born in 1617, her junior at least by some margin. He followed job opportunities provided by his brother, while Campana maintained her own performance career at least until 1640.[12] There is no record that they had children. When Rossi worked for the king in Paris from 1661 to 1666, Campana did not accompany him, perhaps for health reasons as she died in Rome during his absence in July of 1665. The notary papers regarding her death use only her unmarried name and state that their household included an excellent music library, several instruments, and paintings by Leonardo da Vinci, Raphael, and Salvatore Rossi.[13] Campana was surrounded by resources with which to further her musical career, but no documents survive under her name or her husband's that describe her activities after 1640.

Campana's collection offers twelve pieces in a variety of styles. Most overtly, she explored what Edith Borroff described as polar texture.[14] In the late sixteenth and early seventeenth centuries, interest in the solo voice and its affective power eclipsed the Renaissance fascination for equally voiced polyphonic madrigals. The polar-textured madrigal was conceived as a solo whose important musical line was balanced by accompanying lines, with special reference to the bottom. The polarity of bottom and top lines gave dramatic vitality to the voice and structural vitality to the instrument, in what Borroff described as "a motivating fusion of separate functions."[15] The structural voice around which the multivoiced madrigal had been constructed was replaced by a harmonic element, which required that certain chords be heard as discrete vertical elements, not as the result of specific linear interactions.

The polar style emerged most prominently at the turn of the century in the monodies of Giulio Caccini, the accompanied motets of Lodovico Grossi de Viadana, and the continuo madrigals of Monteverdi.[16] This new musical repertory must have informed Campana's training as a singer and composer. Her works, favoring the solo voice, most nearly resemble Caccini's monodies in musical detail. She also organized her collection similarly to Caccini's *Nuove Musiche*, alternating virtuosic madrigals with simpler strophic canzonettas. Of the *Arie's* twelve pieces, eight are solos, two are duets, and two madrigals are for three voices. All pieces except the last, the three-voice madrigal *Occhi belli, occhi amati,* employ figured bass, though unlike Caccini, Campana did not specify the figures. Only single notes appear in the bass, and the realization derives in part from melodic implications (whether the third would be raised or lowered) and also from a semicodified system of rules that had begun to circulate following the works of Viadana and Caccini.[17] Most consistently, theorists and composers stressed the harmonic function of the bass, which should never cover or detract from the voice. Each written bass note without figure required the addition of the third and fifth to complete the harmony. The octave was necessary only to accent special words or cadences. The accompaniment was not obliged to avoid consecutive fifths or octaves.[18] All notes in the bass that were sharped required the sixth rather than the fifth and never the octave (a B-natural in the bass seems often to function in the same way). Accidentals were not to be carried over to the end of the measure unless specified, nor were they to be added unless indicated or required by the solo line. If the solo was for soprano, accompaniment was placed in the upper registers so that the voice could be heard; further, the accompaniment never doubled the soprano.

Over this harmonic framework, the vocal part projected the music's *affetto,* or emotional property, through what Giulio Caccini described as *musica recitativa,* or speaking in tones. This was achieved through a semideclamatory setting of certain words, a flexible approach to rhythm and tempo, and a sensitive cadential reflection of the poem's structure. The singer's other obligation was to delight the senses with well-placed ornaments, which most composers of early monody elected to specify in the score.[19]

The three pieces selected from Campana's *Arie* for this book reflect the diversity of her output. *Semplicetto augellin,* which opens the collection, is a through-composed four-part solo madrigal with figured bass and a virtuosic soprano line written in *musica recitativa.* Each of the four parts is related through a flexible bass, which is not repeated exactly for each stanza but does maintain the same opening and closing pitches and the same general pitch sequences; the first and third, and second and fourth stanzas have identical closing cadences. For the vocal line, Campana frequently used slurs above the printed notes to indicate a vocal connection between pitches (for example, in mm. 18, 36, 48, and 53).[20] She also placed rests in the middle of words (mm. 30 or 47), a madrigalism that had been employed by others, such as Monteverdi, to emphasize the paradoxical implication of the text. Campana's ornaments delight the ear and fall on appropriate words and cadences, but the *affetto* derives equally from the harmonies. The realized bass, with its preponderance of minor thirds and lowered leading tones, casts a musical shadow over the poem's textual lament.

S'io ti guardo ti sdegni is in the less virtuosic canzonetta style. Seventh in the collection and also its centerpiece, it is a typical madrigal text with one exception: it is written from the perspective of one old enough to have "white tresses." The issues of loss and frustration commonly explored in the madrigal repertoire are expressed by a person bereft of the benefits of youthful appearance. This poignant reflection of one loved but cast aside, perhaps for someone younger, borrows from traditional vocabulary but is most probably expressed from a feminine perspective.[21] Alternating sections in triple meter present a single unornamented verse (a "grieving" verse) with instances of coloration in the bass. The duple sections are composed in the more elaborate *musica recitativa.* The direct and highly personal expression of text is underscored by the simple minor harmonies of the bass.

Occhi belli, occhi amati, the final piece in the collection, is a through-composed madrigal for three equal voices and no figured bass, in the style of the Roman *concerto delle donne.*[22] Unlike their North Italian contemporaries, composers of the Roman style often wrote for two sopranos and bass rather than for three sopranos. The popular Roman three-voice villanella was typically composed with two canto voices and bass without continuo. The later three-voice virtuosic repertory often added continuo, which usually doubled the bass. Campana's bass line explores an extensive lower range, but it is also equally integrated and virtuosic and was probably meant to be sung. Many of the cadences in this piece are somewhat unusual. The strong cadences are frequently open octaves (mm. 6, 22, 29, 33, 44, and the final cadence), suggesting no emotional or harmonic resolution. Campana also includes harmonic cadences that do not coincide with melodic resolutions for the bass (mm. 36–37) or cadences where one voice resolves both textually and harmonically after the other two (mm. 18–19). In m. 37, the bass line's movement down to G undermines what appeared to be a D-major cadence. Similarly, in m. 19, the second canto's failure to resolve before the first canto moves on renders the cadence impotent. The only strong cadence in the piece that is not an open octave occurs in mm. 24–25, where a major third preceded by its dominant A-major chord informs the word *morte*. This seems an unlikely choice for the only clearly defined cadence in the madrigal, unless one realizes that the expected death did not in fact occur.[23] While Campana seemed more comfortable with the solo aria, this somewhat elusive madrigal, given pride of place at the close of her collection, suggests an effort to grapple with a style and text popularized, if not always understood, by *concerti delle donne*.

Campana's published works probably represent only a fraction of the music she composed and performed. It is evident in the dedication of the *Arie* that she recognized her special position as a published virtuosa. In offering the collection to Signor Luigi Gonzaga, she commented that the world would accuse her of too much daring in publishing but would at least commend her for her choice of dedicatee.[24] Like many virtuose, the details of her career are sadly incomplete. Yet her collection reveals a highly competent musician whose contributions to her own time were undoubtedly far greater than her published legacy.

Notes

1. *Fulvio Testi: Lettere,* ed. Maria Luisa Doglio (Bari, 1967), I:495. The letter is addressed to Francesco I of Modena.

2. Alberto Cametti, "Alcuni documenti inediti su la vita di Luigi Rossi compositore di musica (1597–1653)," *SIMG* 14 (1912–13):23.

3. For a complete list of published Italian women composers from 1566 to 1700, see Jane Bowers, "The Emergence of Women Composers in Italy, 1566–1700," in *Women Making Music: The Western Art Tradition, 1150–1950,* ed. Jane Bowers and Judith Tick (Urbana: University of Illinois Press, 1986), pp. 116–66.

4. Casulana published two books of madrigals for four voices (1568 and 1570) and a collection for five voices (1583). A selection of her works appears in *Women Composers: Music through the Ages, vol. 1.* Caterina Assandra may have also published two collections. Her surviving *Motetti* of 1609 are designated as her *opera seconda,* suggesting that they were preceded by another volume now lost. One of her works appears in *Women Composers: Music through the Ages, vol. 1.* Also Vittoria and Raphaela Aleotti, probably the same person, published a collection of madrigals as well as a book of

motets, both in 1593. A selection of Aleotti's works is also included in *Women Composers: Music through the Ages, vol. 1.*

5. Cesarina Ricci's *Primo libro de madrigali a cinque voci* (1597) was her only publication. Unfortunately only the lower three-voice parts survive, but they demonstrate considerable compositional skill. Many other examples are included in *Women Composers: Music through the Ages, vol. 1:* Paola Massarenghi's only published madrigal; Lucia Quinciani's single piece, "Udite lagrimosi spirti" (1611); Claudia Sessa's two published madrigals of 1613; Sulpitia Cesis's collection, *Motetti spirituali* (1619); and Lucretia Orsina Vizana's *Componimenti musicale* (1623). Diacinta Fedele's *Scelta di vilanelle napolitane* of 1628 was her only published work (see Chapter 8 below).

6. Basile (ca. 1580–ca. 1640) was an exceptional mezzo-soprano and instrumentalist. During her tenure in Mantua under Duke Vincenzo Gonzaga, she is documented to have received a salary greater than Monteverdi's. Although the latter may have envied her considerable wages, several of his surviving letters attest to her musical excellence and describe her also as a fine composer. This writer acknowledges Susan Parisi's work on archival documents regarding Basile in Mantua.

7. Caccini is a notable exception to this male paradigm in that he was known both for his compositions and for his virtuoso singing skills. His immediate contemporaries, such as Monteverdi, Quagliati, Cifra, and de Monte all produced quantities of vocal music but were not virtuosi themselves. Filippo Vitali, who composed vocal music, was a singer in church choirs but did not perform as a secular virtuoso.

8. The poet and virtuosa Gaspara Stampa, who made her living in the palazzi and academies of Venice during the 1540s and 1550s, has no surviving published music. Her published poetry, however, suggests a lively enthusiasm for the female side of storytelling. For example, she borrowed from the Ovidian tale of Philomela and Procne, a myth often reworked in madrigal texts by her male contemporaries, such as the poet Sannazzaro. Stampa turned the poem into a discussion of rape, while male poets avoided the rape that initiated the story and instead focused upon the punishment of the two women who devised to kill the rapist. One can only imagine that her performances of traditional repertoire may have included similar reevaluations. For further discussion, see Ann Rosalind Jones. "New Songs for the Swallow: Ovid's Philomela in Tullia d'Aragona and Gaspara Stampa" in *Refiguring Women, Perspectives on Gender and the Italian Renaissance,* ed. Marilyn Migiel and Juliana Schiesari (Ithaca: Cornell University Press, 1991), pp. 263–77.

9. This is not to suggest that women who did publish their music failed to challenge traditional structures and stories. Paola Massarenghi's only published madrigal, *Quando spiega l'insegn'al sommo padre,* employs a purposeful misappropriation of the adjective *saggio* in the phrase *saggio duce* ("wise leader"). The adjective should be masculine to modify the masculine noun *duce,* but Massarenghi rewrote it as *saggia,* thus rendering the leader of the poem feminine (see *Women Composers: Music through the Ages, vol. 1*). Suzanne Cusick's recent analysis of Francesca Caccini's *La liberazione di Ruggiero* explains how that composer worked within the general theme of political allegory to explore relationships of gender to power and especially, given the cultural proscriptions against

women's speech, how Caccini dealt with the relationship of women to the restorative power of rhetoric (see "Of Women, Music, and Power: A Model from Seicento Florence," in *Musicology and Difference: Gender and Sexuality in Music Scholarship,* ed. Ruth Solie [Berkeley: University of California Press, 1993], pp. 281–304).

10. Robert Eitner, *Biographisch-Bibliographisches Quellen-Lexikon der Musiker und Musikgelehrten. . . .* (1898; reprint, New York: Musurgia, 1947), II:296. He gives no source for this information.

11. A. Cametti, "Alcuni documenti," 23; and A. Ghislanzoni, *Luigi Rossi: biografia e analisi delle composizioni* (Milan, 1954), p. 167.

12. A. Cametti, "Alcuni documenti," p. 23.

13. Ibid. Some of these possessions were inherited from the estate of Luigi Rossi, who died in 1653.

14. Edith Borroff, *The Music of the Baroque* (Dubuque: William C. Brown Co., 1970), pp. 3–5.

15. Ibid., p. 5.

16. The Mantuan cathedral director Lodovico Grossi Viadana published his *Cento concerti ecclesiastici* in 1602; the collection is credited as being the first to use structured harmonies and figured bass. Also in 1602, the Florentine Giulio Caccini published his first collection of *Nuove Musiche,* which employed figured bass as well as written embellishments to prevent singers from improvising in such a way as to impede harmonic and textual clarity. Monteverdi first introduced harmonic accompaniment to the multivoiced madrigal in the six so-called continuo madrigals that concluded his *Libro quinto* of 1605. His subsequent publications included a variety of accompanied solos and madrigals.

17. Campana was not the only early practitioner of figured bass who did not use actual figures. It was common at that time for composers to use only single bass notes. Viadana explained figured bass, but his own basses were unfigured. Similarly, Francesca Caccini's *Primo libro* features an unfigured bass. Only Giulio Caccini, Jacopo Peri, and Emilio de Cavalieri consistently utilized figures. By the time of Campana's *Arie,* there had been several theoretical writings on the use of figures. Most commonly known were Agostino Agazzari's *Del sonare sopra il basso* (1607), Francesco Bianciardi's *Breve regola per imparare a sonare sopra il basso* (1607), Adriano Banchieri's *Conclusioni del suono dell'organo* (1608), and Michael Praetorius' *Syntagma musicum* (1619). The general rules discussed below were derived from these writings, and used also in this editor's realization of Campana's basses. For further discussion and translation, see Franck Thomas Arnold, *The Art of Accompaniment from a Thorough-Bass as Practised in the 17th and 18th Centuries* (Oxford: Oxford University Press, 1931).

18. The permitting of consecutive fifths and octaves became known as Viadana's "Ninth Rule" and accounts for the characteristic variations in sound between early and late Baroque continuos. See Arnold, *Art of Accompaniment,* p. 18.

19. Such composed ornamentation was common primarily to this early Baroque period; both late Renaissance and later Baroque composers relied to some extent on the performer's knowledge of correct practice in supplying passage work. Early seventeenth-century composers were often preoccupied with controlled declamation of both text and ornament. This effort at control is interesting in that it came at a time when especially the female virtuose had gained significant influence on both vocal and compositional techniques. Anthony Newcomb thoroughly documents this in his study of the rise of virtuose, their access to professional status, and their importance in musical circles. See Anthony Newcomb, *The Madrigal at Ferrara, 1579–1597* (Princeton: Princeton University Press, 1980). During the 1580s until the mid-seventeenth century, groups of *concerti delle donne,* or singing women, emerged for the first time as professional performers, recruited and paid by courts, not because of their aristocratic birth but because of their talent. These women became both musical and social centerpieces at court as well as in convents, such as S. Vito in Ferrara, S. Martino in Naples, and S. Agata near Milan. Such highly acclaimed composers as Wert, Luzzaschi, Marenzio, and Monteverdi adjusted their compositional styles to incorporate features that had been developed by the virtuose. Yet the late Renaissance virtuosa was also largely free to embellish in performance and thus to participate in a virtuosic rhetorical dialogue. That skill had formerly been reserved for men. It seems no coincidence that controlled monody emerged alongside the flourishing *concerti delle donne,* whose tradition continued in many cities well into the Baroque period. Most music composed for female virtuose was published between 1600 and 1640 and includes both composed ornamentation and music that could be embellished. See Susan C. Cook and Thomasin K. LaMay, *Virtuose in Italy, 1600–1640* (New York: Garland Press, 1984).

20. In the original partbooks, the indication for a slur resembles that of a tie. Campana always placed the tie below the pitch, and the slur above.

21. This is not to suggest that men could or would not consider that issue sensitively, but women of that era were socially much less mobile than men and would have been unlikely to contemplate leaving an older spouse.

22. While there are some similarities, the music composed for *concerti delle donne* by Roman composers or composers with strong Roman ties differs from the Northern Italian counterpart. For a lengthy comparison of these two styles, see Susan C. Cook and Thomasin K. LaMay, *Virtuose in Italy,* pp. 53–85. Apart from Campana, the primary composers of the Roman repertoire were Giovanni Anerio, Antonio Cifra, Paolo Quagliati, Raffaello Rontani, and Filippo Vitali, all of whom produced many volumes of music for virtuose.

23. As I continue to work on music by Renaissance women, their choices of text and cadence emerge as powerful tools that stand in contrast to conventional devices of male composers. The word *morte* elicited very specific cadential and harmonic effects for women. Since the word had sexual implications, the absence of death might also imply the absence of a sexual act or its successful completion.

24. All'illustrissimo et eccellentissimo Signor, il Signor Don Luigi Gonzaga, Principe del Sacro Romano Imperio e di Castiglione, Marchese di Medole, Signore della Rocca di Solferino, Libero Barone nel Regno di Boemia, e Grande di Germania e di Spagna.

Nell'esporre alla vista del mondo il primo libro delle mie *Arie,* lo consacro a Vostra Eccellenza perche se nella publicatione saro forse accusata per troppo ardita, dovero essere almeno commendata per giuditiosa nella dedicatione, mentre col patrocinio di un tanto Principe acquisto a' miei componimenti merito singolare, e gli procuro nel titolo quella luce che Vostra Eccellenza porta negli splendori delle due glorie. Il nome di Lei sara il piu cospicuo ornamento di queste carte, le quali per tributo della mia osservanza offerisco a Vostra Eccellenza con altretanta devotione, quanta ho certezza che Ella sia per gradirle con incomparabil benignita, che ha luogo cosi principale fra l'altre eminentissime virtu sue; e Le fo humilissima reverenza.

In Roma, al 1 ottobre 1629.

To the most illustrious and most excellent Signor, Signor Don Luigi Gonzaga, Prince of the Sacred Roman Empire and of Castiglione, Marquis of Medole, Lord of the fortress of Solferino, Free Baron in the kingdom of Bohemia, and Grandee of Germany and Spain.

In presenting my first book of *Arie* to the view of the world, I dedicate it to Your Excellence, because, should I be accused of being too daring for publishing it, at least I must be commended as judicious for the dedication, since, with the patronage of such a Prince, I acquire singular merit for my compositions, and in the dedication I secure for them that fame which Your Excellence bears in the splendor of his glory. Your name will be the most conspicuous ornament of these pages, which I offer to Your Excellence as a token of my respect, with an equal measure of devotion and certainty that you will accept them with incomparable kindness, which has such an outstanding place among your other most eminent virtues; and I pay you my most humble respects.

From Rome, the first of October, 1629.

Bibliography

Arnold, Franck Thomas. *The Art of Accompaniment from a Thorough-Bass as Practised in the 17th and 18th Centuries.* Oxford: Oxford University Press, 1931.

Borroff, Edith. *The Music of the Baroque.* Dubuque: William C. Brown, Co., 1970.

Bowers, Jane. "Women Composers in Italy, 1566–1700." In *Women Making Music: The Western Art Tradition, 1150–1950,* edited by Jane Bowers and Judith Tick, 116–66. Chicago: University of Illinois Press, 1982.

Cametti, Alberto. "Alcuni documenti inediti su la vita di Luigi Rossi compositore di musica (1597–1653)," *SMIG* 14 (1912–1913): 23.

Cook, Susan C., and Thomasin K. LaMay. *Virtuose in Italy, 1600–1640.* New York: Garland Press, 1984.

Cusick, Suzanne G. "Of Women, Music, and Power: A Model from Seicento Florence." In *Musicology and Difference: Gender and Sexuality in Music Scholarship,* edited by Ruth Solie, 281–304. Berkeley: University of California Press, 1993.

Eitner, Robert. *Biographisch-Bibliographisches Quellen-Lexikon der Musiker und Musikgelehrten,* II:296. Reprint, New York: Musurgia, 1898.

Jones, Ann Rosalind. "New Songs for the Swallow: Ovid's Philomela in Tullia d'Aragona and Gaspara Stampa." In *Refiguring Women: Perspectives on Gender and the Italian Renaissance,* edited by Marilyn Migiel and Juliana Schiesari, 263–77. Ithaca: Cornell University Press, 1991.

Newcomb, Anthony. *The Madrigal at Ferrara, 1579–1597.* Princeton: Princeton University Press, 1980.

Testi, Fulvio. *Fulvio Testi: Lettere.* Edited by Maria Luisa Doglio. Bari, 1967.

Discography

The solo aria *Fanciulla vezzosa* is recorded on *La Musica: 16th and 17th Century Music.* New York: Leonarda, 1985. The piece is listed on the recording as *Pargoletta, vezzosetta.*

Critical Notes

Two libraries possess the surviving partbooks for Campana's *Arie:* the Biblioteca Apostolica Vaticana in Rome and the Bibliothèque Nationale in Paris. The two sources are identical. These transcriptions were made from the Bibliothèque Nationale source, from a microfilm supplied to the University of Michigan.

There are no concordant settings for any of the *Arie,* nor does Campana indicate a poet, which suggests that she may have supplied at least some of the texts herself. The English translations are transcribed by Professor Nello Barbieri, Binghamton, New York. For these translations, punctuation, capitalization, and accents have been provided according to modern Italian; the original Italian, including original spellings, has been used for text underlay.

Clefs and pitches have been modernized and barlines added to conform with current practice. The minim has been transcribed as a quarter note. No accidentals have been added or deleted from the original source with three exceptions, all in the madrigal *Occhi belli.* In the original source, m. 31, the A-flat is repeated for all three notes of the first canto; this is redundant in modern practice. In m. 32, first canto, the B is given a natural sign, as is the E in the first canto of m. 35. These are unnecessary in modern notation and have been omitted.

The bass has been realized as simply as possible, in accordance with the principles outlined in this text. The third and fifth have been supplied for all bass pitches that do not have accidentals. The third and sixth are given to raised or lowered pitches. Octaves are used only at cadences. Passing notes have been left unfigured. The general cautions of early seventeenth-century continuo practice suggest not covering the voice or adding accidentals unless indicated. Campana would have played her own accompaniment, and even with those proscriptions in mind, these *arie* would have been intensely personal expressions. An artistic performance might have included some interpretive gesture, depending on the instrument used. Since Campana did not specify major or minor chords with figures, this also left some freedom to the performer. In an effort not to be interpretive, this edition has used minor thirds unless the soprano line includes an accidental that should be matched in the bass. This conforms to the notion that accidentals should not be added, and the minor mode suits the textual content.

There are currently no other published editions of Campana's work.

Semplicetto augellin che mentre canti

Semplicetto augellin che mentre canti
chiami l'arcier che ti percuota il petto
torna, deh torna a celebrar tuoi vanti
dentro alle frondi del natio Boschetto.

2 a.p.
Che ove il mondo superbo ha gl'habitanti
pieni d'inganno e di malvagio affetto
quanto spiegherai tù più dolci canti
tanto men troverai fido ricetto.

3 a.p.
Misero tu non sai quanti lacciuoli
portando invidia alla tua lieta forte
si nascondan fra i rami ove tu voli.

4 a.p.
Vattene via dalle mentite scorte
che non puoi miser se non ti muoli
o salvar libertade o fuggir morte.

Naive little bird, by singing
you call the archer to strike your breast;
go back, pray, go back to celebrate your talents
inside the branches of your native woods.

For, when the arrogant world is inhabited by people
full of deceit and evil passions,
the more you unfold sweet songs
the less you will find a safe shelter.

Poor thing, you do not know how many snares
envious of your merry state,
hide among the branches where you fly.

Flee from false companions,
because unless you fly away, O wretched one, you can
neither keep your freedom, nor escape death.

S'io ti guardo ti sdegni

S'io ti guardo ti sdegni
s'io ti parlo tu fuggi.
E sdegnosa e fugace ogn'hor mi struggi.
Se m'odii perchè vedi
pallido il volto e già canuto il crine.
Non dispregiar mio ben
le pellegrine bellezze che possidei
che se ciaschuna è nel mio core impressa.
Disprezzando il mio core
sprezzi te stessa.

Vorrai cruda sprezzare
i ligustri, e le Rose
che nel sen,
ne le guancie amor compose.
Vorrai forse schermire
lo splendor de begl'occhi, dove suole
di mezza note ancor ardere il Sole,
Nò, Nò, perchè languire.
Tu faresti il mio cor, pieno di sdegno
quasi di tua beltà, recitto indegno.

If I look at you, you resent it;
if I talk to you, you flee
and, resentful and fugitive, you always wear me out.
If you hate me because you see
that my face is pale and my hair already gray,
do not despise, my love, the singular
beauties you possess,
because if each of them is imprinted on my heart,
by despising my heart
you despise yourself.

Will you, O cruel one, despise
the privets and the roses
that Love put in your breast, in your cheeks?
Will you perhaps sneer at
the splendor of those beautiful eyes, where
at midnight the sun is still wont to burn?
No, no, because you would cause
my heart to languish, full of resentment
as if an unworthy abode of your beauty.

Occhi belli, occhi amati

Occhi belli, occhi amati
mentre inferno d'Amor fissi vi mirro.
Deh perchè vi chiudete occhi spietati
Ah forse per pietà del mio martiro
Chiudete del bel guardo à me le porte
ond'io non guinga à morte.
Mà senza voi mirar
morrò mi ancora.
Già di duol vengo meno
deh scoprite ò bei rai
pri mach'io mora
per bear la mia morte il bel sereno.

Beautiful eyes, beloved eyes,
while, sick with love, I fixedly gaze on you,
alas, merciless eyes, why do you close?
Ah, perhaps out of pity for my torments
you close the doors of your beautiful sight to me,
so that I will not come to death.
But if I cannot look at you,
I will die nevertheless:
already I am fainting for grief.
O lovely rays, before I die,
pray unveil your beautiful splendor
in order to gladden my death.

Semplicetto augellin

Francesca Campana
Thomasin LaMay, editor

Seconda parte: "Che ove il mondo superbo"

Terza parte: "Misero tu non sai"

Quattro parte : "Vattene via dalle mentite scorte"

se non ti muo — — li. O sal-

var li-ber-ta — — de o fug-gir mor — — te

o sal-var li-ber-ta — de o sal-var li-ber-

ta-de o fug — — gir mor — te.

S'io ti guardo ti sdegni

Francesca Campana
Thomasin LaMay, editor

gi.

Se m'o - dii per - chè ve - di

pal - li - do il vol - to e già ca - nu - to il

cri - ne. non dis - preg - giar - - - -

- - mio ben le pel - le gri - ne bel -

lez - ze che pos - sie - di che se cia - scu - na è

nel mio co - re im - pres - sa. Dis - prez - zan - do il mio

core dis - prez - zan - do il mio core sprez -

- zi sprez - zi te stes - - sa.

Occhi belli

Francesca Campana
Thomasin LaMay, editor

Sophie Elisabeth, Duchess of Brunswick and Lüneburg

(1613–1676)[1]

KARL WILHELM GECK

Among the German princesses of the seventeenth century, one of the most interesting was Sophie Elisabeth, Duchess of Brunswick and Lüneburg. Born in Güstrow on August 20, 1613, she was the oldest daughter of Duke Johann Albrecht II of Mecklenburg-Güstrow (1590–1636) and Duchess Margarete Elisabeth (1584–1616). The latter died when the princess was only three years old, and Johann Albrecht, who had meanwhile turned away from the Lutheran Church and become a Calvinist, remarried in 1618. His highly gifted second wife, Elisabeth (1596–1625), was the daughter of Landgrave Moritz of Hessen-Kassel, who had spotted the genius of Heinrich Schütz. Elisabeth, who was versed in foreign languages, engaged in writing, sang, played several instruments, and probably composed music.[2] Very likely she was the person who most influenced Sophie Elisabeth's education. It was she who saw to it that Joh(an)n Stanley, one of several English instrumentalists for whom the Güstrow court orchestra was noted, gave the young princess lute lessons, and to an astonishing extent Sophie Elisabeth's later accomplishments reflect those of her stepmother. Sophie Elisabeth's second stepmother, Eleonore Marie of Anhalt-Bernburg, whom Johann Albrecht married in 1626, was a Calvinist princess similarly well educated whose talents also included music. Probably because of Eleonore, the princess became a member of the Académie des Loyales in 1629 since she had been the head of this society of educated Calvinist noblewomen since 1627. The main purposes of the Académie were the cultivation of interest in foreign languages (especially French and Italian), fancywork, music, and literature. The first of Sophie Elisabeth's three surviving music manuscripts in the Herzog August Bibliothek, Wolfenbüttel, a collection of French songs begun in 1633, is probably the immediate result of her membership. Prior to this early attempt at composing music, the princess had suf-

fered a severe hardship when in 1628, as a result of the Thirty Years' War, the ducal family had been expelled from Mecklenburg. It is more likely that Sophie Elisabeth spent the entire three or more years of her exile in Anhalt, the homeland of her stepmother, Eleonore Marie, and not mainly at the Kassel court, which hitherto has generally been assumed.

In 1635 Sophie Elisabeth became the third wife of the scholarly bibliophile Duke August the Younger of Brunswick and Lüneburg, thirty-four years her senior. As Wolfenbüttel, capital of the duchy that August was about to inherit, was occupied by imperial troops, the couple took residence in the neighboring city of Brunswick. Here Sophie Elisabeth, who now had four stepchildren (among them Anton Ulrich, later a significant poet), gave birth to her own children—Ferdinand Albrecht (1636), Marie Elisabeth (1638), and Christian Franz (1639), who died shortly thereafter. In 1638 August established a court orchestra with Stefan Körner as Kapellmeister, and between 1639 and 1646 a first series of court festivities in the vanguard of opera emerged: at least two ballets and four plays interspersed with vocal music, all devised by the poet and philologist Justus Georg Schottelius, instructor to several of the ducal children. Sophie Elisabeth provided at least two of these works with music, the plays *Friedens Sieg* (1642, the only court festivity of this period whose music has survived) and *Die Gebuhrt unsers Heylandes* (1645).

Around 1644, after the move to the Wolfenbüttel castle, the court orchestra had deteriorated, and the Duchess, evidently responsible for the necessary reorganization, consulted Heinrich Schütz, who was temporarily residing in Brunswick. She also asked him to look over some (hitherto unidentified) "arias" that she had composed, and he stated that his "modest instruction" had resulted in notable improvement.[3] Sophie Elisabeth's surviving music, originating in Wolfenbüttel, was composed after 1646. Her small sacred concertos and continuo songs included in the other two music manuscripts, as well as the tunes she wrote for Joachim von Glasenapp's printed song collection *Vinetum evangelicum* (1651), are expressions of remarkable piety. At least from 1650 on, this piety induced the Duchess to read the entire Bible each year according to a strict schedule and to write several stanzas daily of religious verse, a practice she probably continued during the rest of her life. Sophie Elisabeth was evidently more prolific as a writer than as a composer. A comprehensive study of her handwritten, purely literary output, which includes about 2,600 pages of religious poetry, the translation of parts of a novel by Honoré d'Urfé, and a play, does not yet exist.

Her strong religious interest did not deter Sophie Elisabeth from shaping the second series of court festivities, which paved the way for the rise of opera. For the wedding of a stepdaughter in 1653 and her husband's birthdays in 1654, 1655, and 1656, she devised the masquerades *Götter Bancket, Der Natur Banquet, Der Minervae Banqvet,* and *Glükwünschende Waarsagung und Ankunft der Königin Nicaulae*[4] and took a leading role in every one of them. Except for the *Götter Bancket,* each of these masquerades encompassed at least one theatrical entertainment with music. *Der Natur Banquet* closed with the only established contemporary performance of Staden's and Harsdörffer's *Seelewig,* the earliest extant German opera (1644). *Der Minervae Banqvet* ended with the *Ballet der Zeit,* for which Sophie Elisabeth perhaps composed two songs, and included her *Glückwünschende Freüdensdarstellung,* the only festivity aside from *Friedens Sieg* with music by her still extant. The *Glükwünschende Waarsagung* closed with the *Vorstellung und Glükwünschung der 7. Planeten,* a parody of Staden's and Harsdörffer's *Tugendsterne.*

In 1655 the court orchestra once more needed reorganization, and Sophie Elisabeth again consulted Schütz, who procured several good musicians, above all Kapellmeister Johann Jacob Löwe von Eisenach. In 1656 Prince Anton Ulrich returned from his grand tour. He was strongly influenced by the splendid theatrical performances he had attended in Paris and succeeded his stepmother as spiritus rector of the Wolfenbüttel court festivities, apparently writing the texts of at least seven operas and six ballets performed between 1656 and 1663. The transition to opera and full-scale ballet had been effected, not least of all thanks to Löwe, who very likely composed the bulk of the (lost) music, whereas Sophie Elisabeth, who in this phase of the court festivities seems to have restricted herself to the role of patroness, probably only contributed a few peripheral songs. However, during these years she must have set a considerable number of Anton Ulrich's sacred songs to music. They were published under the title *ChristFürstliches Davids-Harpfen-Spiel* in 1667, the year after her husband had died, and were printed again in 1670. She then moved to Lü-

chow, where she led a quiet and pious life, making her residence an asylum for the poor and persecuted and probably never ceasing to compose sacred songs.

Sophie Elisabeth's surviving compositions are to be found almost exclusively in her music manuscripts Ms. I, II and III, in the published collections of the sacred songs *Vinetum evangelicum* and *ChristFürstliches Davids-Harpfen-Spiel,* and in the court festivities *Friedens Sieg* and *Glückwünschende Freüdensdarstellung.*

Ms. I, begun in November 1633 and probably completed at the onset of the following decade, is an early and obviously autodidactic attempt at composition in which Sophie Elisabeth concentrated on arrangement and parody. Almost three-quarters of the 115 French songs are *airs de cour,* which the duchess copied out of books one to five (1608–1614) of Gabriel Bataille's *Airs de différents autheurs.* In doing so, she substituted for the original lute accompaniment a self-created thoroughbass, which quite often reveals technical flaws (for example, parallel fifths) and clearly shows that she had not yet reached the relative technical skill demonstrated in *Friedens Sieg.* Most of the remaining songs seem to be *airs de cour* copied from unknown sources or dance tunes supplemented with a text. In several instances the melody may have been created by the duchess or assembled by her from dance citations.

Unlike Ms. I and III, most of Ms. II, which contains mainly sacred concertos, is not in Sophie Elisabeth's handwriting. Of the twenty-two compositions, only the four pieces in her own hand can be attributed to her. These include a continuo song with additional viole di gamba accompaniment, which the duchess dedicated to her husband for his birthday in 1653 (a published version also exists), and three small sacred concertos for solo voice and basso continuo that date from 1647. Of these, the expressive setting of Paul Fleming's poem "Was acht ich diesen Leib" is much more convincing than the two psalm compositions, which clearly show Sophie Elisabeth's limitations with regard to structuring and voice leading.

At least fifty-two of the seventy-five pieces from Ms. III, written between 1647 and 1655, are by the duchess. For the most part these are continuo songs for solo voice, generally sacred in character; but they also include the small sacred concerto *Vom Himmel kommt der Trost* that originated in 1649. The piece, which opens with a distinctive gesture repeated in the manner of a motto, gains validity especially through its expressive diction, achieved by the use of rhetoric figures (note the *katabasis* in measures 18/19–22). The division of the text into two parts (earthly futility vs. heavenly hope) is underlined musically through the change to triple meter. Despite occasional shortcomings in the declamation of the text, this piece constitutes one of Sophie Elisabeth's best compositions. It is her last sacred concerto on record. She probably found this genre too demanding and devoted herself more and more to sacred songs in which she increasingly employed the expressive style of her small sacred concertos.

An early example is the music to Anton Ulrich von Braunschweig's *Will meine Seel sich nimmer mehr abgeben*. Its monodic character is based foremost on the syncopation in line 1, the recitative formulation in line 3, the threnodic outburst in line 4, the *climax* in lines 5 to 7, and the chromatic transition to the concluding line. Like the other nine musical settings of song texts by Anton Ulrich in Ms. III, *Will meine Seel* was incorporated into the Prince's published song collection *Christ-Fürstliches Davids-Harpfen-Spiel* (1667), whose sixty settings for solo voice and thoroughbass (sixty-three in the second edition) "were for the most part conceived by a female personage of equally high birth" (Sophie Elisabeth).[5]

The tendency towards expressive, rhythmically animated sacred songs for private worship continues here, with the duchess approaching monody in several instances more strongly than in the older collection. On the other hand, the variety of the music forms a wide spectrum reaching from the monodic song to the simple, triple-metered dance song. Thus it leads without a break to *Vinetum evangelicum* (source of *Als ein Exempel, auch zur Gab*), specifically to the second edition (1651) of Joachim von Glasenapp's collection of lection-based songs (*Perikopenlieder*), which in contrast to the first edition (1647) was supplied with music notes. The 106 settings—in reality eighty-three, since there were twenty-three instances of repetitious use—are the result of an interesting coauthorship: the melodies were by the duchess, the thoroughbasses by her husband. The latter are figured in greater detail and bear witness to a more intensive technical schooling than comparable continuo parts written by Sophie Elisabeth. The melodies can be divided into three main categories: forty-four show affinity to the Geneva Psalter and thus are an expression of Sophie Elisabeth's Calvinist convictions; twenty-two are related to the Lutheran chorales originally assigned by Glasenapp (*Töne*);[6] seventeen are influenced by the triple-meter dances galliarde, sarabande or courante (for instance, the tune of *Als ein Exempel, auch zur Gab,* which resembles John Dowland's famous *Earl of Essex's Galliard*). Like all melodies in the collection, it displays a certain leaning towards *Kirchenstyl:* a frugal use of melisma, confinement for the most part to the minim and semibreve, and employment of a relatively large main note value (minim).

Friedens Sieg, which was composed to celebrate the Goslar Preliminary Peace Agreement (1642) and performed several times in connection with the Peace of Westphalia (1648), is, contrary to assertions in scholarly literature, neither an opera nor a ballet. Rather it is a play in prose that incorporates processional elements (*Festzug*), dance, and—of special interest with regard to the rise of opera—the singing of character roles. The latter takes place within the strophic songs set to music by the duchess, which illustrate or loosen up the spoken action. There are eighteen vocal and four instru-mental settings that constitute ten song compositions, in part for solo voice, in part for ensemble. The most interesting of these are the four dialogue songs, because through simple means they offer a considerable measure of musical drama. Of these, the highlight is the song of the four War Horrors (Death, Hunger, Poverty, and Injustice) in the second act. Its distinctiveness shows up especially clearly in the music of strophes 1, 3, and 5: not only is all discourse marked by musical contrasts, but the composer also managed to give the four figures individual features by means of musical rhetoric (for instance, Hunger is personified by the extensive use of the rest figure *suspiratio*). The two dialogue settings, defined by their strong text emphases, are complemented by the ensemble settings of strophes 2 and 4, which through their rhythmic drive and homophonic style call to mind Gastoldi's popular *Balletti* (1591) and their German posterity.

Sophie Elisabeth's *Glückwünschende Freüdensdarstellung,* which was first staged on the birthday of her husband in 1652, is neither an opera nor a ballet, but a song pageant (*Gesangsaufzug*) in the sense of Georg Philipp Harsdörffer's *Von der Welt Eitelkeit* and *Die Tugendsterne*. Scenes 1–4, which are devoted to the four life stages of her celebrated husband, correspond to the analogous seasons and consist of a commentating continuo song with an introductory sinfonia. In each song, the type of voice corresponds to the stage of life in question (for example, childhood, represented by spring, is sung by a soprano). Even more interesting is the fifth and last scene. It begins with a commentating solo continuo song while an angel crowns Duke August with a wreath. Preceded also by an introductory sinfonia, the "angel chorus" for choir, continuo, and four instruments that appropriately concludes the play is Sophie Elisabeth's only surviving large-scale concerto setting. The strength of this piece with its numerous textural contrasts lies in its convincing overall structure with an even- and an odd-measured part—corresponding to the text's four trochaic and two amphibrachic verses—and the charm of its melodic ideas. However, the duchess does not always succeed in developing them into adequate compositional sections. Her difficulties in composing for several voices polyphonically over longer intervals may be seen in the occasional awkwardness of the instrumental voices in Part I and in the stagnant harmony of the only noteworthy imitative passage beginning at measure 8. If Chrysander's opinion of 1863 proves itself to be surprisingly up-to-date—"the ideas of the final choir would have been worthy of a better treatment and development"[7]—the duchess, nevertheless used her resources for a considerable achievement. Of all her surviving compositions, the angel chorus is not only by far the most ambitious but also one of the best.

Sophie Elisabeth is one of the earliest documented German women composers since the Middle Ages and evidently the first one whose music was published to a large extent during her lifetime. The following incentives likely contributed to her desire to compose: the influence of her stepmothers and of the Académie des Loyales; encouragement from her husband; the mental vacuum caused by the Thirty Years' War, which made cultural activities of noblewomen desirable; and later, her urge to make music a part of her worship. As a composer, Sophie Elisabeth was influenced most by the genres of song and dance and by the expressive diction encountered in, for example, Schütz's *Kleine geistliche Konzerte*. Her limited technical abilities indicate that she was, on the whole, an autodidact and benefitted at most occasionally from such instruction by Schütz as mentioned above. However, in most of her music she was able to make up for these shortcomings through imagination and talent. Schütz's statement that Sophie Elisabeth was "a princess incomparably perfect in all other royal virtues, but especially in the noble profession of music" is certainly to be seen in this context.

Notes

1. Dedicated to Virginia Leila Geck, the author's dear mother, who helped him express himself in English and translated the texts of the music examples.

2. Claudia Knispel, who comes to the conclusion that Elisabeth did not compose (*Das Lautenbuch der Elisabeth von Hessen,* p. 35), was not aware of a contemporary source that supports this ability; see Karl Wilhelm Geck, *Sophie Elisabeth Herzogin zu Braunschweig und Lüneburg (1613–1676) als Musikerin.* Saarbrücker Studien zur Musikwissenschaft, n.s., vol. 6 (Saarbrücken: Saarbrücker Druckerei und Verlag, 1992), p. 25.

3. *Letters and Documents of Heinrich Schütz 1656–1672: An Annotated Translation,* trans. Gina Spagnoli, Studies in Music, 106 (Ann Arbor: UMI Research Press, 1989), p. 242.

4. With one exception (*Götter Bancket*), the relevant texts are to be found in Sophie Elisabeth, *Dichtungen,* ed. Hans-Gert Roloff, vol. 1, Europäische Hochschulschriften, 1/329 (Frankfurt am Main: Peter D. Lang, 1980).

5. [English translation of this quotation from the preface is by the author.] The collection includes several instances of parody (see Gudrun Busch, "Herzogin Sophie Elisabeth und die Musik der Lieder in den Singspielen Herzog Anton Ulrichs zu Braunschweig und Lüneburg," in *Studien zum deutschen weltlichen Kunstlied des 17. und 18. Jahrhunderts,* ed. Gudrun Busch and Anthony J. Harper, Chloe, vol. 12 (Amsterdam: Rodopi, 1992), passim; and Geck, *Sophie Elisabeth,* pp. 232–34: two song texts have settings from *Seelewig;* because of their unusual strophic form, at least four others reveal themselves as parodies on arias from operas of Anton Ulrich.

6. Glasenapp had written his songs by replacing texts belonging to well-known hymn tunes. The designation for such tunes was *Töne.* In twenty-two instances, Sophie Elisabeth exchanged the *Töne* specified by Glasenapp for related, though newly composed, melodies.

7. Friedrich Chrysander, "Geschichte der Braunschweig-Wolfenbüttelschen Capelle und Oper vom 16. bis zum 18. Jahrhundert," *Jahrbücher für musikalische Wissenschaft 1* (1863), p. 173. [English translation is by the author.]

Bibliography
Sources with music by Sophie Elisabeth

Herzog August Bibliothek, Wolfenbüttel (henceforth HAB): Cod. Guelf. 52 Noviss. 8°, Cod. Guelf. 11a Noviss. 2°, Cod. Guelf. 11 Noviss. 2° [cited as Ms. I, II and III].

Anton Ulrich, Duke of Brunswick and Lüneburg. *ChristFürstliches Davids-Harpfen-Spiel.* N.p. [printed by Christoph Gerhard, Nürnberg], 1667. Facs. ed.: New York: Johnson Repr. Corp., 1969. 2nd ed.: n.p. [printed by Paul Weiß, Wolfenbüttel], 1670. [HAB: T1 8b]

Glasenapp, Joachim von: *Vinetum evangelicum.* 2nd ed. N.p. [printed by Johann and Heinrich Stern, Wolfenbüttel], 1651. [HAB: 817.81 Theol.]

Schottelius, Justus Georg. *Neu erfundenes Freuden Spiel genandt FriedensSieg.* Wolfenbüttel: Conrad Buno, 1648. [HAB: Lo 6992] 2nd ed.: Brunswick: Gottfried Müller, 1649. [Yale University Library, New Haven, Collection of German Baroque Literature] The Niedersächsische Staatsarchiv, Wolfenbüttel, possesses a contemporary German keyboard tablature containing most of the play's music: 1 Alt 22 No. 227.

Sophie Elisabeth, Duchess of Brunswick and Lüneburg. *Glückwünschende Freüdensdarstellung.* N.p. [printed by Johann and Heinrich Stern, Lüneburg], 1652. [HAB: Gn 2° Sammelband 3 (1)] Facs. ed.: Bircher, Martin, and Bürger, Thomas, eds. *Alles mit Bedacht: Barockes Fürstenlob auf Herzog August (1579–1666) in Wort, Bild und Musik.* Wolfenbüttel: HAB, 1979, pp. 114–28. 2nd ed.: n.p. [printed by Johann and Heinrich Stern, Wolfenbüttel], 1655. [HAB: Gn 2° Sammelband 3 (11)]

Works cited

Busch, Gudrun. "Herzogin Sophie Elisabeth und die Musik der Lieder in den Singspielen Herzog Anton Ulrichs zu Braunschweig und Lüneburg." In *Studien zum deutschen weltlichen Kunstlied des 17. und 18. Jahrhunderts,* pp. 127–182. Edited by Gudrun Busch and Anthony J. Harper. Chloe, vol. 12. Amsterdam: Ed. Rodopi, 1992.

Chrysander, Friedrich. "Geschichte der Braunschweig-Wolfenbüttelschen Capelle und Oper vom 16. bis zum 18. Jahrhundert." *Jahrbücher für musikalische Wissenschaft 1* (1863), pp. 147–286.

Geck, Karl Wilhelm. *Sophie Elisabeth Herzogin zu Braunschweig und Lüneburg (1613–1676) als Musikerin.* Saarbrücker Studien zur Musikwissenschaft, n.s., vol. 6. Saarbrücken: Saarbrücker Druckerei und Verlag, 1992. Includes incipit catalog (pp. 470–528).

Knispel, Claudia. *Das Lautenbuch der Elisabeth von Hessen.* Frankfurt am Main: Haag & Herchen, 1994.

Schütz, Heinrich. *Letters and Documents of Heinrich Schütz, 1656–1672: An Annotated Translation.* Translated by Gina Spagnoli. Studies in Music, no. 106. Ann Arbor: UMI Research Press, 1989.

Sophie Elisabeth, Duchess of Brunswick and Lüneburg. *Dichtungen.* Edited by Hans-Gert Roloff. Vol. 1: *Spiele.* Europäische Hochschulschriften, series 1, vol. 329. Frankfurt am Main: Peter D. Lang, 1980.

Sources and Editorial Comments

All figured bass realizations in this edition are by the author.

Vom Himmel kommt der Trost

The meter requires "Trost wird dir sonst werden," line one; the meter requires "mein einz'ger Trost," line three. HAB: Cod. Guelf. 11 Noviss. 2°, leaves 28^v/29^r (autograph score dated May 31, 1649).

Will meine Seel sich nimmer mehr abgeben

Read "nicht," stanza one, line four; read "vor," stanza six, line six, as in stanza seven, line six.
1. HAB: Cod. Guelf. 11 Noviss. 2°, leaves 35^v/36^r (autograph score dated December 22, 1652).
2. *ChristFürstliches Davids-Harpfen-Spiel,* 1667, pp. 89–94.
3. *ChristFürstliches Davids-Harpfen-Spiel,* 1670, pp. 96–101.

The edition follows source 3, which is the most reliable one. Source 2 is identical except for the time signature c and the missing bar line between measures 18 and 19. The manuscript version in-cludes two instances of incorrect note values in the bass. Its text consists of only six stanzas; the central stanza is missing.

Als ein Exempel, auch zur Gab

Like the other song texts in *Vinetum evangelicum,* this one is laden with biblical references identified by footnotes. These have been omitted in this edition. *Vinetum evangelicum,* 1651, p. 52 f.

Song of the War Horrors (Ich, der häßlich bleiche Tod, etc.)

1. *FriedensSieg,* 1648, p. 98 f. (text) and leaf between (score).
2. *FriedensSieg,* 1649, p. 98 f. (text) and preceding leaf (score).
3. Niedersächsisches Staatsarchiv, Wolfenbüttel: 1 Alt 22 No. 227, leaves 8^v-10^v (text and tablature).

The edition follows sources 1 and 2, which employ the same music engraving. The tablature version includes a wrong note (second stanza, measure 2, fourth voice: G instead of E) but otherwise is almost identical. In one instance (second stanza, measure 5, third voice), it was used for the purpose of clarifying an all but illegible passage.

Sinfonia and Angel Chorus (Dieses ist das Fürstenhaus)

1. *Freüdensdarstellung,* 1652, pp. 13–16.
2. *Freüdensdarstellung,* 1655, pp. 15–18.

The edition follows source 1. Source 2 is a newly set copy of source 1, which adds several mistakes to the ones in the earlier source.

All spelling and punctuation has been modernized by the author.

I. *Vom Himmel kommt der Trost*

Vom Himmel kommt der Trost, kein Trost, der wird dir sonst werden,
Du hastest, wie du willst, von der trostlosen Erden.
Mein Trost, mein einziger Trost, ist Gott, und der allein.
Wer Trost bei diesem sucht, der kann nicht elend sein.
(author unknown)

From heaven comes comfort; you will receive no other consolation,
However much you hasten from this cheerless earth.
My consolation, my only consolation, is God and He alone.
Who finds solace in Him cannot be miserable.

II. *Will meine Seel sich nimmermehr abgeben*

1 Will meine Seel sich nimmermehr abgeben
Von ihrer Sorg? Wird sie nie besser leben?
Soll sie wohl sonder End mit Trübsal schwanger gehn?
Nein, nein, ihr Schmerze wird nit ohne Ziel bestehn.
Weil sich alles enden soll,
Was hier auf dieser Welt,
Wird sich auch noch wenden wohl
Mein Leid, wann's Gott gefällt.

Will my soul never be released
From its cares? Will it never know a more fulfilled existence?
Must it forever be paired with sorrow?
Nay, nay, its pain will not continue aimlessly.
Since all in time will cease
Which here we have on earth
So, too, my pain will end
Whene'er it please the Lord.

2 Muß guter Tag' allhier ich nicht genießen,
Wohl dir, o Seel! Laß dir das nicht verdrießen.
Wer hie mit Tränen sät und bauet so sein Feld,
Wird fröhlich ernten ein die Frucht in jener Welt.
Weil sich alles enden soll,
Was Gott hier hat beschert,
Wird sich auch noch wenden wohl
Mein Leid auf dieser Erd.

3 Wer hie betrübt, in Gott wird fröhlich werden.
Nur Christi Kreuz soll sein dein Trost auf Erden:
Dabei erkennet man ein Herz, so Gott beliebt,
Wann Er es in die Press' des scharfen Kreuzes gibt.
Weil sich alles enden soll,
Was hie ist zubereit',
Wird sich auch noch wenden wohl
Mein Leid zu rechter Zeit.

4 Dein Jesus sagt: Wer will mein Jünger heißen,
Der folge mir, der mag sich nur befleißen,
Daß er sein Kreuz auf sich ja lege mit Geduld,
So bleibet er bei mir und erbet meine Huld.
Weil sich alles enden soll
Und nicht währt immerdar,
Wird sich auch noch wenden wohl
Mein Leid und mein Gefahr.

5 Gleich wie das Gold, gereinigt in den Flammen,
Bewähret wird, wann es kommt oft zusammen,
Also wird auch ein Mensch geläutert von der Sünd,
Das Feur des Kreuzes macht die Seel zu Gottes Kind.

Weil sich alles enden soll
Noch vor dem letzten Tag,
Wird sich auch noch wenden wohl
Mein Leid und meine Plag.

6 Faß einen Mut, mein abgemattes Herze!
Bei Gottes Feur zünd an des Glaubens Kerze:
Es läutert dich ganz wohl und macht dich sündenrein,
Daß deine Seele kann sich schwingen himmelein.
Weil sich alles enden soll
Noch für der Ewigkeit,
Wird sich auch noch wenden wohl
Mein Leid in lauter Freud.

7 Dank deinem Gott, der dir das Kreuz bescheret,
Denn solches dir vor vielen Sünden wehret.
Wer immer fröhlich lebt, denkt nicht an seinen Gott,
Die Trübsal lehret dich das Beten in der Not.
Weil sich alles enden soll
Noch vor der Ewigkeit,
Wird sich auch noch wenden wohl
Mein Leid in lauter Freud.

(Anton Ulrich, Duke of Brunswick and Lüneburg)

If life here on this earth is not to be enjoyed,
Take courage, oh my soul! Let this not trouble you.
Who here his field does sow and cultivate with tears
Will reap its fruit with joy there in the world to come.
Since all in time will cease
That comes to us from God,
So, too, will end some day
My pain upon this earth.

Who is sad here will be joyful in the Lord.
Alone the cross of Christ is to comfort you on earth:
Thereby may a heart be known as beloved by God
When He lets it be hard pressed by the sharp edges of the Cross.
Since all in time will cease
That here can come to pass
So, too, will change some day
My pain in its good time.

Your Jesus says, he who would be called my disciple,
Let him follow me; let him strive
To bear his cross with fortitude.
So shall he remain in me and be heir to my grace.
Since all in time will cease
And not forever last,
So, too, will change some day
My pain and jeopardy.

Just as gold refined in the flames
Is gathered up as quickly as it is purified,
So will a human being be purified from its sin,
The searing flame of the Cross transforms the soul
into a child of God.
Since all in time will cease
Before the Judgement Day
So, too, will end for sure
My pain and trials here.

Take courage, my worn-out heart!
Light up your candle of faith with the Lord's fire.
It will purify you completely and make you free of sin
So that your soul can soar heavenwards.
Since all in time will cease
Before eternity
So, too, will be transformed
My grief to purest joy.

Be thankful to your God for giving you your cross,
For such has sheltered you from falling into sin.
Who leads a carefree life forgets to think of God
But sorrow teaches prayer in our need.
Since all in time will cease
Before eternity
So, too, will be transformed
My grief to purest joy.

III. *Als ein Exempel, auch zur Gab*

1 Als ein Exempel, auch zur Gab,
Ich meinen Herren Christum hab.
Er ist zur Gab uns frei geschenkt,
Für unser Sünd ans Kreuz gehenkt,

2 Auch zum Exempel als ein Licht
Und Lebens-Richtschnur aufgericht,
Allhie uns Ruh zu schaffen fleucht,
Daß Fliehen frei, zugleich bezeugt,

3 Oft für Tyrannen dieser Welt;
Uns ist ein ander Haus bestellt,
Da wir nach allen Angstbeschwerd'n
In stolzer Ruhe wohnen werd'n.

(Joachim von Glasenapp)

As an example and a gift
I have my Lord Jesus Christ,
He was given to us freely
And hanged on the cross for our sins,

Also for our example
He was set up as a light to point us on our way,
Fled there to give us peace,
thereby testifying that fleeing

From the tyrants of this world often bespeaks freedom.
A different dwelling is set aside for us;
After all anxieties
We shall live there in proud peace.

IV. *Ich, der häßlich bleiche Tod*

Song of the War Horrors

1 *Tod:* Ich, der häßlich bleiche Tod.
Hunger: Ich, die schwarze Hungersnot.
Armut: Ich, die Armut, bittres Leid.
Ungerechtigkeit: Ich, die Ungerechtigkeit.

2 Wir sein Töchter unsers Krieges,
Lohn und Wirkung seines Sieges,
Uns erzeugt das Kriegesglück,
Wir des Krieges Meisterstück.

3 *Tod:* Ich erwürge. *Hunger:* Ich verschmachte.
Armut: Ich sehr drücke. *Ungerechtigkeit:* Ich verachte.
Tod: Ich zerhaue. *Hunger:* Ich zergehe.
Armut: Ich stets quäle. *Ungerechtigkeit:* Ich nicht stehe.

4 Kommt der Krieg, so kommen wir,
Plagen stets mit steter Gier.
O ihr Menschen lernet Krieg,
Nur uns vieren bleibt der Sieg.

5 *Tod:* Mir, dem häßlich bleichen Tod,
Hunger: Und der schwarzen Hungersnot.
Armut: Mir, der Armut, bittren Leid,
Ungerechtigkeit: Und der Ungerechtigkeit.

(Justus Georg Schottelius)

Death: I am hideous, pale Death.
Hunger: I am bleakest Starvation.
Poverty: I am Poverty, bitter Misery.
Injustice: I am Injustice.

We are the daughters of our war,
The reward and consequence of its triumph.
We were sired by war's vicissitudes,
We are war's masterpieces.

Death: I strangle. *Hunger:* I am consumed.
Poverty: I oppress. *Injustice:* I scorn.
Death: I wreak havoc. *Hunger:* I disintegrate.
Poverty: I plague unceasingly. *Injustice:* I have no backbone.

If there comes war, so we come, too,
Torturing always with constant greed.
Oh, mankind, learn to know war,
Victory belongs exclusively to us four.

Death: To me, hideous, pale Death,
Hunger: And to bleakest Starvation,
Poverty: To me, Poverty, bitter Misery,
Injustice: And to Injustice.

V. *Dieses ist das Fürstenhaus*

Dieses ist das Fürstenhaus
Und das Schloß der Frömmigkeit,
Da wir ziehen nimmer aus,
Sondern bleiben allezeit
Und über euch, Herzog Augusten zu freuen,
Und bringen euch immermehr Gutes von neuen.

(Sophie Elisabeth, Duchess of Brunswick und Lüneburg)

This is the House of the Prince
And the Palace of Piety
Which we nevermore will leave
But will remain in forever
Hovering over you to please Duke August
And bestow increasing good upon you ever more.

Vom Himmel kommt der Trost
(Trost bei Gott allein)

Sophie Elisabeth
Karl Wilhelm Geck, editor

* Original time signature for measures 26 ff. : 3.

Will meine Seel sich nimmer mehr abgeben
(Kreuztrost)

Sophie Elisabeth
Karl Wilhelm Geck, editor

Will mei - ne Seel sich nim - mer - mehr.

— ab - ge - ben Von ih - rer Sorg? Wird sie nie

[#]

bes - ser___ le - ben? Soll sie wohl son - der End mit

Trüb - sal schwan - ger gehn? Nein, nein, ihr Schmer - ze wird___

[#]

Als ein Exempel, auch zur Gab

Sophie Elisabeth
Karl Wilhelm Geck, editor

Song of the War Horrors
(Ich, der häßlich bleiche Tod)

Sophie Elisabeth
Karl Wilhelm Geck, editor

1. Ich, der häß - lich blei - che Tod. Ich, die

schwar - ze Hun - gers - not. Ich, die Ar - mut,

bitt - res Leid. Ich, die Un - ge rech - tig - keit.

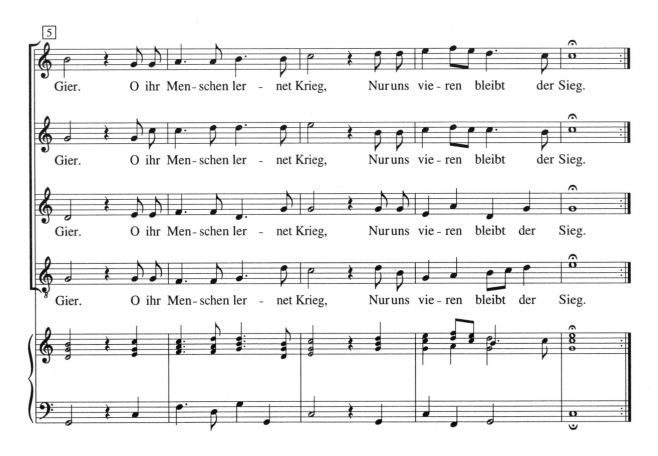

Dieses ist das Fürstenhaus
(Sinfonia and Angel Chorus)

Sophie Elisabeth
Karl Wilhelm Geck, editor

Da wir zie - hen nim - mer, nim-mer, nim-mer, da wir zie-hen nim - mer___ aus, Son-dern

Da wir zie - hen nim - mer, da wir zie-hen nim - mer aus,

Da wir zie - hen nim - mer, nim - mer aus,

Da wir zie - hen nim - mer ___ aus,

* Both sources read b flat.

* Original time signature for measures 15ff. : 3.

* In both sources this note is repeated three times instead of once, which makes the measure too long.

* In both sources the last two notes of this measure are f f[sic].

Barbara Strozzi

(ca. 1619–ca. 1664)

RANDALL WONG

Barbara Strozzi (ca. 1619–ca. 1664) was one of the most important composers of Italian cantatas of the seventeenth century as well as one of the principal female composers of the Baroque period. Extremely prolific, Strozzi published eight books of music that include about one hundred pieces primarily for solo voice. By any account this was an exceptionally large number of publications. The fact that Strozzi was a woman composer whose works were published makes her even more extraordinary.

Barbara Strozzi attended the meetings of the *Accademia degli Unisoni,* a group of the Venetian intelligentsia. Though probably not an actual member, Strozzi frequently was the hostess, presenting her own works as musical entertainment. As the adopted, and presumably illegitimate, daughter of the poet Giulio Strozzi, Barbara was given access to a society of intellectuals and artists that was denied most other women. It is undoubtedly this special social status that enabled Strozzi to pursue a career in music and to study with the composer Francesco Cavalli.

There are contemporary accounts of Strozzi's abilities as a singer; she is referred to as *la virtuossima Cantatrice* in the dedications of Niccolo Fontei's *Bizzarrie poetiche,* books 1 and 2 (1635, 1636). Barbara was also reputedly a visual centerpiece for the gatherings of the *Accademia;* given the contemporary association of the arts with licentiousness, she may have been a courtesan as well. There are contemporary satirical letters castigating Strozzi's morals and chastity: "It is a fine thing to distribute the flowers after already having surrendered the fruit."[1] One satirical barb even accused of her of having relationships with a castrato, thus avoiding pregnancy.

Barbara was unusually sensitive to the nuances of text, probably influenced by her literary father. Her handling of musical form was imaginative and highly developed, which mirrors the shifting affects in her poetic texts. She was equally adept at dramatic musical *recitativi* and mellifluous *arie.*

Strozzi was an extraordinarily gifted composer; her last three books in particular show her to be a true master of larger formal organization. Only a very few individual cantatas, arias, and madrigals exist in modern editions; none of the complete books have yet appeared. The two cantatas from Strozzi's *Arie,* op. 8, were selected for this publication because of their musical excellence and maturity.

Arie, op. 8, is the last of Strozzi's published works. It is dedicated to the Palatinate princess, Sophia of Braunschweig and Lüneberg; despite the dedication, she never received the patronage and financial security that she sought. The original was published in Venice by Magni [detto Gardano] in 1664 and is now housed in Bologna at the library of the Accademia Filarmonica. The copy used in the preparation of this edition is a facsimile reprint published in Bologna by Antiquae Musicae Italicae Studiosi, 1970. The original is an ottavo oblong and contains a mistake in pagination; page numbers 17 through 24 are repeated. The book contains six *arie,* five *cantate,* and one *serenata (con violini)* for soprano voice. The texts are exclusively secular, with all but the first dealing with love as the subject matter. Half the texts include attributions.

The Music

In Italian cantatas of the mid-seventeenth century, the strict division into *aria* and *recitativo (semplice* or *secco)* characteristic of later secular vocal music is not yet rigidly defined. *Arias* during that time were a musical setting of generally regular poetic units in a closed musical structure. The form was either bipartite (AB), tripartite (ABA), strophic, or elaborations built from these basic units (ABA ACA ADA, ABA CA DA, and so forth). The *aria da capo* as we know it today was a development of the second half of the seventeenth century, and Strozzi's *arie* are not based on this restricted, later premise. *Recitativo* comes closer to our modern notion of recitative, a style and musical unit mirroring the inflections of natural speech. Strozzi's music continues in the tradition of the seventeenth-century *stile recitativo,* which originated in the monodies of Caccini and became a highly developed art-form in the *lamenti* of D'India and Monteverdi. Strozzi divides her works into *aria-recitativo* sections that flow from one to the other without rigid boundaries. This fluidity is most evident in her longer cantatas and laments where there is larger scope for an imaginative handling of formal structure.

Strozzi composed with a large palette of subtle gradations of recitative. The *stile recitative* or *recitativo cantando* is by definition a more "sung" or "heightened" style of recitative than that found in the late seventeenth- or eighteenth-century cantata. This *cantando* style itself is varied, running the gamut from dramatic and declamatory outbursts to vocal depictions of winds and flight. Op. 8, no. 4 also contains the musical description *parlando,* implying a more conversational or *recitativo parlando* style; while these instances are brief, we can see in them the seeds of the later *recitativo secco* or *semplice.*

In addition to the formal *aria* sections are numerous *ariosi.* The word *arioso* is itself misleading and rather vaguely defined. Margaret Murata writes, "When a bit of music appears that is melodic and regular, but not a complete closed piece, it can be called an *arioso* passage."[2] The *ariosi* are melodically in the style of the *arie* (tuneful and sequential) but lack the closed formal structure and proportions of the *aria.* The use of *arioso* to denote a style poised between *aria* and *recitativo* is subjective and open to varying interpretation. Strozzi's *ariosi* are never more than one or two lines of text.

Strozzi's melodic style in *aria, recitativo,* and *arioso* is that of common practice for the mid-seventeenth century. However, she frequently employs a high degree of melodic and unprepared dissonance akin to the mannerist works of the first quarter of the seventeenth century as, for instance, those of Sigismondo D'India. When prompted by extreme emotions in the texts, the melodic intervals frequently become large and jagged.

Strozzi's mellifluous and lyric melodic style in the *aria/arioso* is very similar to that of Cavalli and is most apparent in her triple-metered sections. The *arie/ariosi* contain frequent affective suspensions, appoggiaturas, sequences, and easily recognizable melodic contours. Strozzi also employs a high degree of madrigalism or word-painting similar to that in the works of D'India and Monteverdi, on such words as *sospiri* (sighs) and *fuggia* (flew).

Strozzi's harmonic language is predominantly modal; harmonic movement in her work is not governed by the polarities of tonic and dominant. Chordal progressions tend towards harmonizations of stepwise (that is, modal) movement. Cadential relationships of the fifth (I–V, ii–vi, for example) function as punctuation and represent strictly localized events; there are no large-scale tonic-dominant

tonal schemes in which cadences assume a structural significance.

The Poetry

In her choice of poetic texts, Strozzi was very much a product of her time and environment. The poems are all of a Marinist[3] bent, employing bizarre and luxuriant imagery, obscure metaphors, multiple clauses within clauses, as well as the resulting erratic syntax, to express emotions. Five poems have attributions; the remaining texts were probably by Strozzi herself. As the adopted daughter of the poet and librettist Giulio Strozzi, it is likely that she would be well educated in the arts of poetry and literature.

Eleven of the twelve op. 8 texts deal with the subject of love; ten of these are about love's misery, while the last deals with love cynically. While this is a narrow aspect of love, Strozzi treats it with variety and with all the multicolored emotional shadings that a Marinist text would provide.

The Marinist texts are erratic in both rhyme and scansion. The poems frequently break out of their rhyme scheme or meter, as if the poetic structure inhibited the expression of overwhelming emotion. The result alternates between "normal" units of meter and rhyme and blank verse. Divisions into poetic lines are frequently ambiguous. Strozzi does not closely coordinate poetic and musical forms; she moves freely between the various forms of recitative, aria, and arioso, regardless of poetic divisions. Occasionally, but inconsistently, poetic and musical structures coincide.

The Selections

The first six cantatas in op. 6 have irregular poetic structures. The most extreme of these is *L'Astratto,* no. 4 with text by Giuseppe Artale. In this extended cantata, the *ariosi* take on a theatrical significance, representing incomplete or aborted efforts at true *arie.* The text is remarkable for its dramatic conceit; the protagonist/singer tries to express his love in song, but every time he attempts an aria he abruptly ends it, not finding the correct expression for his emotions. It is not until the end that he manages to sing an actual two-strophed aria, followed by his decision to stop singing because he has already sung too much. The distraught emotionality of this quasi-operatic solo *scena* mirrors Artale's irregular poetic structure. Strozzi utilizes abrupt shifts of meter, tempo, tessitura, and tonal area, which results in a nearly expressionistic and schizophrenic musical setting.

The multiplicity of affect and fragmentation of tempi, meter, style, and textual phrase is unusual and extreme even for a period whose hallmark is frequently bizarreness of expression; it would be difficult to find a parallel example among the works of Strozzi's contemporaries. Composers of the subsequent generation would not continue such experiments in expressionistic formal structures but would evolve towards the rigid *aria-recit-aria* scheme of the late seventeenth and eighteenth centuries.

Rhyme Scheme and Syllables[4]

[*recitativo cantando*] Voglio sì, vo cantar,	a	6
forse cantando trovar	a	7
pace potessi [*arioso: 4/4*] al mio tormento;	b	11
ha d'opprimere il duol forza [*recit. cantando* concento.	b	11
[*recitativo parlando*] Si, si, pensiero aspetta;	★	7
[*arioso: 3*] a sonar comintiamo	c	7
[*recit. parlando*] e a nostro senso una canzon troviamo.	c	11
[*arioso—aborted aria: 3*] "Hebbi il core legato un dì d'un bel crin . . ."	★	11
[*recit. parlando*] la stracerei! Subito ch'apre un foglio	d	11
[*recit. cantando*] sento mi raccorda il mio cordoglio.	d	10
[*recit cantando—aborted aria: 3*] "Fuggia la notte e sol spiegava intorno"	e	11
[*recit. parlando*] Eh! Si confonde qui la nott'e'l giorno.	e	11
[*arioso—aborted aria: 3*] "Volate o furie e conducete	★	10
un miserabile al foco eterno . . ."	f	10
[*recit. parlando*] ma che fò nell'inferno?	f	7
[*arioso—aborted aria: 4/4*] "Al tuo ciel vago desio	★	8
spiega l'ale e vanne . . ."	★	6
[*recit. parlando*] a fè che quel che ti compose	★	9
poco sapea del amoroso strale;	g	11
[*arioso: 6/8*] desiderio d'amante in ciel non sale.	g	11
[*arioso—aborted aria: 3*] "Goderò sotto la luna . . ."	h	8
[*recit. parlando*] hor questa si ch'è peggio,	★	7
[*arioso: 6/8*] sa il destin degl' amanti e vuol fortuna	h	11
[*recit. cantando*] Misero i guai m' han da me stesso stratto,	★	11
e cercando un soggetto	i	8
per volerlo dir sol cento n'ho detto.	i	11
[*aria: 3*] "Chi nel carcere d'un crine	j	8
i desiri ha prigionieri,	k	8
per sue crude aspre mine	j	8
ne men suoi sono i pensieri.	k	8
Chi ad un vago alto splendore	l	8
diè fedel la libertà	m	7
schiavo alfin tutto d'amore	l	8
ne men sua la mente avrà."	m	7

[*recit. cantando*] Quind'io misero e stolto	n	8
[*arioso: 6/8*] non volendo cantar, cantato ho molto.	n	11

The serenata *Hor che Apollo,* has a more formal structure. The appellation *serenata* is misleading; rather than the quasi-dramatic *serenata* of the later Baroque (as, for example, those by Alessandro Scarlatti or Handel), *Hor che Apollo* is an "artistic" or "elevated" form of an evening serenade sung from beneath the balcony of one's beloved (by Venetian tradition, sung from a boat). The rhyme schemes are comparatively conventional; the versification is more regular than *L'Astratto* but does not conform to a classical model. Within the vocal sections, the borders between *aria, arietta*—sections that possess the formal structures and closures but not the musical and textual proportions of a true *aria—arioso,* and *recitativo* are less distinct than in *L'Astratto.*

Rhyme Scheme and Syllables

sinfonia

[*recitativo (cantando)*]		
Hor che Apollo è à Theti in seno	a	8
[*arioso 4/4*] e il mio sol stà in grembo al sonno,	b	8
[*arioso 4/4*] hor ch'à lui pensand'io peno	a	8
ne posar gl'occhi miei ponno.	b	8
[*recit*] À questo albergo per sfogar il duolo	c	11
[*arietta: 3*] vengo piangente, innamorato, e solo.	c	11

ritornello

[*recit*] Si, filli questo core	d	7
[*arioso: 3*] che per Amor si more,	d	7
à te vien supplicante,	e	7
de tuoi bei lumi amante.	e	7

ritornello

[*aria: 3*] Mira al pie tante catene	f	8
lucidissima ma mia stella,	g	9
e se duolti ch'io stia in pene	f	9
sì men cruda ò pur men bella.	g	8

ritornello (ut supra)

[*aria: 3*] Se men cruda pietade havrò	h	8
del mio servir saprò che m'ami,	i	9
e se men bella io frangerò	h	8
i legami.	i	4

ritornello

[*aria: 3*] Vedi al core quante spine	j	8
tu mi dai vermiglia rosa,	k	8
sdegni mie rouine	j	8
sì men fiera, ò men vezzosa.	k	8
[*arioso (concitato)*] Mà isfogatevi,	l	[3][5]
spriggionatevi,	l	[3]

[*arietta:* 3] miei sospir, stio già comprendo	m	8
che di me ride filli anco dormendo.	m	11

ritornello

[*recit*] Ride de miei lamenti	★	7
certo, questa crudele	n	7
e sprezza i preghi miei, le mie querele.	n	11
[*aria*] Deggio per ciò partir senza conforto	o	11
se vivo non mi vuoi, mi vedrai morto.	o	11

[*ritornello*]

[*aria:* 3/1] Mentre altrove il piè s'invia,	p	8
io ti lascio in dolce oblio.	q	8
Parto filli, parto, anima mia,	p	11
questo sia l'ultimo à Dio.	q	8

Performance Practice

Voice

The majority of Strozzi's works were written for solo soprano; only four of her published cantatas are for other vocal ranges. Her solo soprano works and those dedicated to her by Nicolò Fontei demonstrate a general range of d′ to a″ with occasional excursions below the staff and a general working tessitura of f′ to f″.[6] Given that Strozzi was a noted *virtuosa* it can be assumed that she performed them herself;[7] it is also more than likely that she provided her own instrumental accompaniment, presumably on a lute or archlute. In modern performance, most sopranos and mezzos would easily negotiate the range. A greater challenge would be to sing not only extremely florid passages but very sustained sections as well, in manner appropriate to the historical style. A controlled vibrato and an ability to vary subtle gradations of dynamics and phrasing are required. Strozzi is always extremely sensitive to nuances of text expression, and her works require a similar sensitivity from the performer.

Conforming to contemporary poetic convention, the texts of op. 8 are from the viewpoint of a male protagonist, but the cantatas are intended for a soprano voice. There is no particular reason why they could not be transposed down an octave and sung by a tenor. There is no compelling reason that transpositions should be avoided; this was certainly contemporary practice, and the pitch itself was not yet completely standardized.

Basso Continuo and the Realization

Most of Strozzi's solo cantatas were meant to be performed in intimate surroundings, such as at meetings of the Accademia degli unisoni; it is possible that Strozzi accompanied herself. "When monodies were performed in an intimate setting, a chordal instrument alone provided all the needed support."[8] Although the lute family probably provided the original basso continuo accompaniment for Strozzi's work, a harpsichord or even (double or triple) harp might also be an appropriate choice; an organ would be a less likely accompaniment as it would not have been originally available for home performance. The addition of a sustained bass instrument (viola da gamba, cello, or dulcian), outside of a church or theater, was generally a later development. In modern performance, the best guide to the choice of instrument(s) would be the performance venue; there are certainly practical circumstances that would support the addition of a sustained bass or supplemental chordal instrument. In the *serenata Hor che Apollo,* a bass instrument would be a desirable addition to balance the two violins.

Strozzi's works are heavily weighted towards the text, and any realization drawing attention to itself would be inappropriate. Generally a straightforward and uncomplicated realization that avoided countermelodies would be suitable. If Strozzi did indeed accompany herself, it would be difficult to imagine her devising elaborate accompaniments for such textually sensitive music.

Bass figures are rare in op. 8, and the chords implied are primarily triadic—including nonfunctional 6/4 chords—despite the unusual horizontal chromaticisms of the bass line. A realization involving chords of sevenths and ninths, apart from those with dominant functions, would be at odds with Strozzi's harmonic idiom. It must be remembered that the voice is frequently dissonant to the bass and the continuo player should not try to rationalize such dissonances with a complex chord (accounting for and doubling the note in the voice). As an example, in the final portion of *Hor che Apollo,* fully scored for voice, two violins, and continuo, there are no such complex harmonies.[9]

The bass realizations of this edition are in no way meant for actual performance; they are merely one possible and plausible way of interpreting the largely unfigured bass. The actual performance realization is up to the interpreters, the performance circumstances, and most importantly, what instrument(s) accompany the voice.

Ornamentation

Strozzi's works contain examples of written-out *trilli, gruppi, passaggi,* and other customary ornaments. Frequently the sign *t,* indicating either a *trillo* or *gruppo,* appears. Given the high degree of composed ornamentation, much more decoration would seem excessive.

There are two situations in which additional ornamentation is appropriate. The first is when cadences call for ornamental cadential formulas. Strozzi writes many cadences out, but even more are left unadorned, especially those concluding triple-metered *arie* and *ariosi.* The second situation involves repeated musical segments. An example of Strozzi's own ornamentation occurs in *Aure giacche non posso,* op. 8, no. 5; the *aria,* beginning at measure 37, recurs at measure 47 in a highly decorated version.

Dynamics

Strozzi includes *piano* and *forte* markings in her work; however, these are invariably connected with small-scale repetitions and echo effects. Dynamic markings applying to larger sections are nonexistent. This leaves the choice of dynamics up to performers; the only possible way of applying them is in conjunction with the text. A sensitivity to the nuances of the Italian language is of utmost importance.

Tempo

The overriding factor determining tempo should be the text itself. Other considerations are the implied relation between tempo and meter/proportion, and Strozzi's frequent and explicit verbal tempo indications, which support the *tactus* implied by the metric proportions. Strozzi's *presto-presto* marking would be pointless if the text is unintelligible. In the *recitativo cantando* sections, the poetry and its intended affect would determine the range of possible tempi. Fortunately, Strozzi rarely, if ever, indicates or implies by choice of metric proportion a tempo contradictory to the sense of her poetry.

Notes

1. Cited in the most complete biography currently available: Ellen Rosand's "Barbara Strozzi, *virtuosissima cantatrice:* The Composer's Voice." *Journal of the American Musicological Society* 31(Summer 1978), pp. 241–81. Reprinted in slightly revised form in Jane Bowers and Judith Tick, ed., *Women Making Music: The Western Art Tradition, 1150–1950* (Urbana: University of Illinois Press, 1986).

2. Margaret Murata, *Operas for the Papal Court, 1631–1668* (Ann Arbor: UMI Research Press, 1981), 162.

3. Style of poetry named after Giambattista Marini (1569–1625). It is a Baroque and Mannerist poetic style of luxuriant imagery, obscure syntax, and extravagant metaphors.

4. Italian poetry syllabification is numerative. Endings on the *piano* (penultimate), *sdrucciolo* (antepenultimate), and *tronco* (ultimate) syllables are considered equal in terms of syllable count.

5. There is apparently no normal Italian term for a three-syllabled poetic line (such as *ottonario* [8] or *endecasillabo* [11]); this is highly irregular.

6. The exceptions being the two occasional cantatas of op. 2 composed for Adamo Franchi which ascend to high C and high D.

7. The exception being op. 2 which was meant for the castrato, Adamo Franchi ("Queste mie noiose Cantilene dall divina voce del Sig. Adamo Franchi gentilmente portate alle benigne orecchie di V. M . . .").

8. Tharald Borgir, *The Performance of the Basso Continuo in Italian Baroque Music* (Ann Arbor: UMI Research Press, 1987), 37.

9. The reoccurring diminished 7th chord on C♯ functions as a surrogate dominant within this D G tonal context.

10. The one exception is "È pazzo il mio core," (no. 9) in which the 3 inexplicably indicates a meter of 6/8.

Bibliography
Works of Barbara Strozzi

Strozzi, Barbara. *I primo libro di madrigali a due, tre, guattro e cinque voci,* op. 1. Venice: Vincenti, 1644. Microfilm, Bologna: Civico Museo Bibliografico Musicale, BB 366.

Cantate, ariette e duetti, op. 2. Venice: Gardano, 1651. Microfilm; London: British Museum, K.7.g.4.(2).

Cantate ariete a una, due e tre voci, op. 3. Venice: Gardano, 1654. Microfilm; London: British Museum K.7.g.4.(1).

I sacri musicali affetti, op. 5. Venice: Gardano, 1655 [facsimile reprint; New York: Da Capo Press, 1988. Microfilm of separate vocal part; Wroclaw, Poland: Biblioteka Uniwerstyecka, 50835 Muz].

Ariette a voce sola, op. 6. Venice: Magni, 1657. Microfilm; Bologna: Civico Museo Bibliografico Musicale, BB 367.

Diporte di Euterpe overo cantate e ariette a voce sola, op. 7. Venice: Magni, 1659. Facs. rpt.; Florence: Studio per Edizione Scelte, 1980.

Arie, op. 8. Venice: Magni [detto Gardano], 1664. Facs. rpt.; Bologna: Antiquae Musicae Italicae Studiosi, 1970.

"Aure giacchè non posso." Microfilm of manuscript, n.d.; Modena: Biblioteca Estense MS P.

Cantatas, selected. Ellen Rosand. New York: Garland Publishing, 1986. Fac. rpt. selected cantatas.

Works Cited

Borgir, Tharald. *The Performance of the Basso Continuo in Italian Baroque Music.* Ann Arbor: UMI Research Press, 1987.

Bowers, Jane and Judith Tick. *Women Making Music: The Western Art Tradition, 1150–1950.* Urbana: University of Illinois Press, 1986.

Fontei, Nicolò. *Bizzarrie poetiche.* Venice: Magni, 1635. Microfilm, Oxford: Christ Church Library, 448 (1).

Bizzarrie poetiche, libro secondo. Venice: Magni, 1636. Microfilm, Oxford: Christ Church Library, 795 (2).

Murata, Margaret. *Operas for the Papal Court, 1631–1668.* Ann Arbor: UMI Research Press, 1981.

Rosand, Ellen. "Barbara Strozzi, *virtuosissima cantatrice:* The Composer's Voice." *Journal of the American Musicological Society* 31 (Summer 1978): 241–81.

Selected Discography

Barbara Strozzi-Alessandro Stradella. Isabelle Poulenard, soprano. ADDA 581 173.

Barbara Strozzi: Cantates. Judith Nelson, soprano. Harmonia Mundi France. HM 1114.

"Barbara Strozzi und ihre Zeit." Record 2 of *Tage alter Musik in Herne 1986.* Judith Nelson and Randall Wong, sopranos. Stadt Herne/Westdeutscher Rundfunk 66.30091.

Kurtisane und Nonne. Rosina Sonnenschmidt, soprano. Bayer Records 100 078/79.

Editorial Procedures

The Text

< > signs set around text appear in the original as *ij*, which indicate exact repetitions of textual phrases. Square brackets indicate editorial additions where text is lacking in the original. Brackets are also used to indicate suggestions for underlay of subsequent verses. In general, original and archaic spellings have been retained. Major exceptions are:

1. Diacritical marks as shorthand for an *m* or *n* (for example, *séza = senza*).

2. Ambiguities between *u* and *v* (*haurò = havrò*).

3. sij = sì.

4. Ambiguities between *s* and *f* (*fine = sine*).

5. Adaggio has been replaced by the modern *adagio*.

The infrequent punctuation has been retained; editorial additions have been tacitly introduced. Syllabification has been clarified by the use of modern note beamings. In the original, slurs inconsistently denote syllable underlay. These slurs have been retained except in cases where the beaming makes them redundant. Under no circumstances do slurs indicate legato phrasing.

Music

Accidentals have been standardized in accord with modern principles. Accidentals apply to a complete measure; in the original, accidentals only apply to the note immediately following or repeated notes of the same pitch. Strozzi's cautionary accidentals have been retained. Editorial accidentals have been placed over the notehead above the staff.

All the vocal lines have been changed from the original soprano clef to treble. Continuo passages in tenor clef have been modernized as treble or bass clefs.

All original time signatures and note values have been retained (except for colorations, which have been modernized). 3 equals 3/2 or a compound meter built of units of the 3/2 (e.g., 6/2, 9/2, 12/2).[10]

Solid barlines are in the original. Double barlines are either in the original or have been added to denote separate sections. Dotted barlines have occasionally been added to clarify and subdivide large measures (e.g., 12/2) or where, in the original, the end of a line lacks a barline. The inconsistencies of Strozzi's original barring have been preserved throughout.

Original bass figures are retained. Editorial bass figures are bracketed. Brackets also indicate other editorial additions, which may be inferred by analogy, for example, [t] for a *trillo* or *gruppo* or tempo indications, dynamics, and designations of *aria*.

L'Astratto

Voglio sì, vò cantar,	I wish, yes, I want to sing!
forse cantando trovar	Perhaps in singing I will find
pace potessi al mio tormento;	relief from my torment; music
h'à d'opprimere il duol forza il concento.	has the power to conquer sorrow.
Sì, sì, pensiero aspetta;	Yes, wait, my thoughts;
a sonar comintiamo	let us begin to play
e a nostro senso una canzon troviamo.	and find a song to fit our mood.
"Hebbe il core legato un di d'un bel crin . . ."	*"If one day, my heart is bound to some beautiful tresses . . ."*
La stracerei! Subito ch'apro un foglio	I'd tear it away. As soon as I turn
sento che mi raccorda il mio cordoglio.	a page I feel the memory of my grief.
"Fuggia la notte e sol spiegava intorno . . ."	*"The night fled and the sun began to spread his light . . ."*
Eh! Si confondon qui la nott'e'l giorno.	Ah! Now we are confusing night and day.
"Volate ò furie e conducete	*"Fly, oh Furies, carry this poor*
un miserabile al foco eterno . . ."	*wretch to the eternal fires . . ."*
à che fò nel inferno.	But I am already in Hell.
"Al tuo ciel vago desio	*"To your heaven, my heart's*
spiega l'ale e vanne . . ."	*desire, spread your wings and take flight . . ."*
à fè che quel che ti compose	but whoever composed this
poco sapea del amoroso strale;	knew little of Love's darts;
desiderio d'amante in ciel non sale.	a lover's desire does not rise to heaven.

"Goderò sotto la luna . . ."
hor questa si ch'è peggio,
sà il destin de gl'amanti e vuol fortuna.

Misero i guai m'han da me stesso astratto,
e cercando un soggetto
per volerlo dir sol cento n'ho detto.

"Chi nel carcere d'un crine
i desiri hà prigionieri,
per sue crude aspre ruine
ne men suoi sono i pensieri.

Chi ad'un vago alto splendore
diè fedel la libertà
schiavo alfin tutto d'amore
ne men sua la mente havra."

Quind'io misero è stolto
non volendo cantar, cantato hò molto.

"I will rejoice by moonlight . . ."
Now this is even worse!
He knows the fate of lovers, yet still expects good fortune.

Miserable, these woes have made
me distraught, and in seeking a
subject about which to speak, I have found a hundred.

"He who has his desires
imprisoned by golden tresses
discovers, to his cruel and bitter
ruin, that his thoughts are no longer his own.

He who, in good faith, gives up his
freedom to a fair and unreachable
beauty, at last becomes a slave to
love, without even a mind to call his own."

Therefore I, miserable and stupid,
not wishing to sing have already sung too much.

Hor che Apollo

Hor che Apollo è à Theti in seno
e il mio sol stà in grembo al sonno
hor ch' à lui pensand'io peno
ne posar gl'occhi miei ponno.
À questo albergo per sfogar il duolo
vengo piangente innamorato e solo.

Si, si Filli questo core
che per Amor si more
à te vien supplicante
de tuoi bei lumi amante.

Mira al pie tante catene
lucidissima mia stella
e se duolti ch'io stia in pene
sì men cruda ò pur men bella.

Se men cruda pietade havrò
del mio servir saprò
che m'ami
e se men bella io frangerò
i legami.

Vedi al core quante spine
tu mi dai vermiglia rosa
e se sdegni mie rouine
si men fiera ò men vezzosa.

Mà isfogatevi,
spriggionatevi,

miei sospir, s'io già comprendo
che di me ride Filli, anco dormendo.

Ride de miei lamenti certo, questa crudele,
e sprezza i preghi miei le mie querele.

Deggio per ciò partir senza conforto
se vivo non mi vuoi, mi vedrai morto.

Mentre altrove il piè s'invia
io ti lascio in dolce oblio
parto, Filli, parto anima mia
questo sia l'ultimo à Dio.

Now that Apollo rests in the arms of
Thetis and my sun rests in the bosom
of sleep, now, thinking of my love
I suffer, nor can my eyes rest.
To this place, for to vent my grief
I come weeping, enamoured, and alone.

Yes, yes Phyllis, this my heart of mine
which is dying for love,
comes to beg of you,
so in love with your beautiful eyes.

See at my feet these many chains
oh, my brightest star,
and if you are sorry that I am in pain
be less cruel or be less beautiful.

If you are less cruel, and show mercy if
you accept my devotions, I will know
that you love me;
If instead I find rejection, I will cut
loose my bonds.

Look at my heart and see how many thorns
you have given me, oh, my reddest of roses,
and if you would not see me utterly ruined
be less fierce, or be less charming.

But give vent,
burst from my body

oh my sighs, if I come to understand
that Phyllis laughs at me, even as she sleeps.

She derides my laments, this cruel one
and despises my prayers and complaints.

I must therefore go without comfort;
if you do not want me while alive, you will see me dead.

As I begi to depart
I leave you in sweet oblivion,
I go, Phyllis, I go, my own soul,
Let this be the last farewell.

L'Astratto
IV

Barbara Strozzi
Randall Wong, editor

Vo-glio sì, vò can-tar, _____ for - se can-

tan - - do tro - var pa - ce po-tes - si al mio tor-men - -

- - - - - - - - - - -

to; h'à d'op-pri - me - re il duol for - -

Note: The bass realizations of this edition are in no way meant for actual performance; they are merely one possible and plausible way of interpreting the largely unfigured bass. The actual performance realization is up to the interpreters, the performance circumstances, and most importantly, what instrument(s) are accompanying the voice and their idiomatic realization.

ne men suoi so - no i pen - sie - ri, i___ pen - sie - ri.
ne men sua la - men te hav - ra, ___ la - men - te hav - ra."

Quin-d'i - o, mi - - - - se-ro è

stol - to, mi - - - - - - - -

- se-ro è stol - to, non vo - len - do can - tar,___

Hor che Apollo

Barbara Strozzi
Randall Wong, editor

Note: The bass realizations of this edition are in no way meant for actual performance; they are merely one possible and plausible way of interpreting the largely unfigured bass. The actual performance realization is up to the interpreters, the performance circumstances, and most importantly, what instrument(s) are accompanying the voice and their idiomatic realization.

te _____ vien sup - - pli - can - te, à ___

te _____ vien sup - - pli - can - te, de tuoi bei lu - mi,

<de tuoi bei lu - mi>, a - man - te. ___

79 Ritornello allegro

Vln. 1

Vln. 2

[7 - 8]

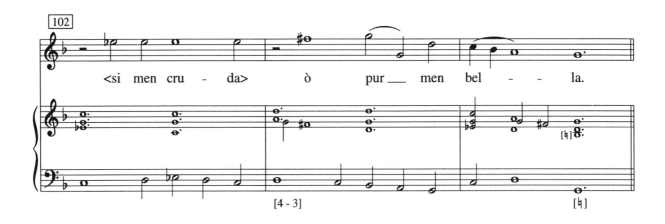

<si men cru — da> ò pur __ men bel - - la.

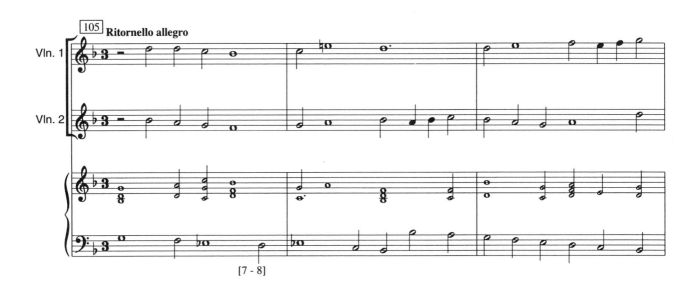

mor - - to. _____

Men - tre al - tro - ve il piè s'in - vi - - - - - - - a, io ti la - scio, ti

la - scio, io ti la - scio in dol - ce o - bli - - -

Chiara Margarita Cozzolani

(1602–ca. 1677)

ROBERT L. KENDRICK

Among the nuns who composed music in seventeenth-century Milan, Chiara Margarita Cozzolani left both the largest and most varied output. She was born in 1602, into a well-off family that would send most of its daughters to the Benedictine house of Santa Radegonda; Cozzolani herself professed her final vows in 1620. Several of her nieces, at least, were singers in one of the monastery's two choirs. Cozzolani published four collections between 1640 and 1650. Later in the 1660s and 1670s, she served as abbess and prioress. This was during a time of great troubles for the house, when the strict Archbishop Alfonso Litta attempted to restrict the sisters' music making in the wake of a disciplinary scandal. Her name is absent from the lists of nuns who signed off on documents between 1676 and 1678.

Cozzolani's collections are the following: *Primavera de fiori-musicali* (Milan: probably Rolla, 1640; this print is now lost); *Concerti-sacri,* op. 2 (Venice: Vincenti, 1642); *Scherzi di sacra melodia,* op. 3, a solo motet book (Venice: Vincenti, 1648; only the voice partbook survives, without the continuo) and *Salmi a otto . . . con concerti, dialoghi,* also published as op. 3 (Venice: Vincenti, 1650). *Concerti sacri* consists of motets for two to four voices, while the *Salmi a otto* represent the largest-scale application of *concertato* Vespers music—cast in the relatively new form of the *salmo arioso*—to be found in Milan. The latter print also includes several concertos for two to five voices; two psalm settings also include parts for violin, instruments which were theoretically forbidden in the liturgy of nuns, another mark of the wide gap between formal orders and daily practice in the daily musical life of the female houses.

The two motets presented here reflect some of the varied characteristics of these two collections. *O dulcis Jesu* (1642) includes some of the most central characteristics of the "new Lombard style" of the 1640s, which are found in the works of Gasparo Casati (Isabella Leonarda's teacher), Cozzolani herself, and Francisco della Porta. These include highly personalized and emotive texts, focusing on the individual

Christian's relationship to Christ and on the specifically bodily (Passion, Eucharistic) aspects of His presence; quick, almost mercurial, declamation and meter changes; longer, sectionalized structures for individual motets; and a sense of local climax afforded primarily by texture and harmonic piquancy. Although no specific source has been identified for the literary text, its vocabulary and emphasis on individual enlightenment through Christ are typical of the late medieval pseudo-Bonaventuran tradition. Somewhat unusually for the midcentury Lombard motet, *O dulcis Jesu* features a complete *da capo* of its opening section, and this feature, along with strongly contrasted internal sections, which move away from and then return to a G *finalis* in the system of *cantus mollis* (mm. 86 and 105), contributes to a certain kind of classic balance not always found in the repertory. That the piece was included by the tireless Breslau anthologizer Ambrosius Profe (Profius) in his 1649 *Corollaneum geistlicher Collecteaneorum* (RISM 1649/6) as the only Milanese motet in the transalpine collection testifies to contemporary views of *O dulcis Jesu* as typical of the new style.

The somewhat large-scale *O caeli cives,* scored for three canti, two tenors, and continuo, is the last item in the 1650 *Salmi a otto,* a collection that contains a complete set of Vespers psalms in Benedictine Use and a number of motets, or concertos. The work reflects some trends in that collection's larger-scale concertos. First is its employment of the dialogue, an enormously popular genre both in Milan as a whole and in Cozzolani's books. This piece is set out as a sort of acclamatory exchange between unnamed characters, of which the two tenors represent earthly inhabitants and the three sopranos heavenly ones; the scoring may well have been designed to show off the vocal extremes of Santa Radegonda's two choirs of nuns.[1] The procedures of the concerto determine the writing; especially noteworthy is the "celestial" high *falsobordone*-like writing, harmonically static, for the three canti. Indeed, the "angelic" singing of female monastic musicians is a commonplace in contemporary urban panegyric literature. As the tenors' questions become more elaborate in the course of the dialogue, so too does the writing for the soprano parts progress from strict homophony to imitation, designed to show off Santa Radegonda's singers. Like most of Cozzolani's large-scale concerti, this dialogue contrasts blocks of tonally stable material.

One apparent anomaly is reflected in the text. The numerous references to the queenly status of the saint (who "rules" and "reigns") fit the hagiographic tradition of St. Catherine of Alexandria better than the more plebeian eponymous figures from Genoa or Siena. The printed version of the motet may possibly be a change from an original version that honored the patroness of Cozzolani's monastery, St. Radegund, a sixth-century Frankish queen and nun (the Latin forms *Catharina* and *Radegunda* scan similarly). Simone Peterzano's late sixteenth-century altarpiece for the external church of Santa Radegonda portrayed the Mystic Marriage of St. Catherine of Alexandria, along with St. Radegund and St. Justina, the patroness of the Cassinese Benedictine congregation to which Cozzolani's monastery belonged (today the painting hangs in the church of S. Maria della Passione in Milan). Radegund's cult in Italy was largely confined to Milan, and hence the printed text of *O caeli cives,* which honors Catherine, may represent a version of this motet aimed at a wider audience than simply that of the Milanese patricians who flocked to hear the music at Santa Radegonda.

Notes

1. See Frits Noske's sympathetic discussion of this piece in *Saints and Sinners: The Latin Musical Dialogue in the Seventeenth Century* (Oxford: Clarendon Press, 1993), p. 15. The characters in this dialogue are not specifically named as Homines and Angeli.

Bibliography

Sources

O dulcis Jesu. In *Concerti sacri,* op. 2. Venice: Vincenti, 1642. Textual source/liturgical use: Unknown/none.

O caeli cives: Dialogo. Salmi a otto concertati . . . motetti, dialoghi, op. 3 [sic]. Venice: Vincenti, 1650. Textual source/liturgical use: Free/St. Catherine of Alexandria's feast-day, November 25.

Books

Kendrick, Robert L. "The Traditions of Milanese Convent Music and the Sacred Dialogues of Chiara Margarita Cozzolani." In *The Crannied Wall: Women, Religion and the Arts in Early Modern Europe,* edited by Craig A. Monson. Ann Arbor: University of Michigan Press, 1992, 211–33.

———. *Celestial Sirens: Nuns and their Music in Early Modern Milan* (Oxford: Clarendon Press, 1996).

Meyer[-Baer], Kathi. *Der chorische Gesanq der Frauen, mit besonderer Bezugnahme seiner Betätigung auf geistlichem Gebiet.* Leipzig: Breitkopf und Härtel, 1917, p. 33 and app. III.

Noske, Frits. *Saints and Sinners: The Latin Musical Dialogue in the Seventeenth Century.* Oxford: Clarendon Press, 1993, pp. 15–16, 45–46, 110–11.

Editorial Procedures

1. Time values and time signatures have been left unaltered. All variants in rhythm or pitch found in the source are noted using the following shorthand: [measure number].[part-name, abbreviated].[note number (rests are prefixed with the letter r)]: [original reading]. Hence a given variant might be designated as: 34.CII.3–4: c#″-b′, meaning m. 34, Canto II, notes 3–4 were originally c#″ and b′.

2. Barlines have been supplied when missing.

3. Clefs have been modernized; key signatures (actually indications of *cantus*) are as in the source.

4. Accidentals apply to the entire measure plus any notes tied into the next measure, as in normal modern notation. Editorial *musica ficta* are given above the staff; such *ficta* apply only to the note over which they are placed.

5. Text underlay is as in the original prints or manuscript; repetitions indicated by the abbreviation *ij* have been expanded and placed inside brackets < >. Punctuation is editorial and has been kept to a minimum.

6. All slurs are original.

7. Ligatures have been indicated by whole brackets; *minor color* is set off by half brackets.

8. Continuo figures have been moved from above the staff to below; dashes have been added to suspensions: 4–3. The continuo realization is only a guide and should be adopted to the actual chordal instrument used—organ, theorbo or chitarrone, or harpsichord, all of which were played by Milanese nuns in this period. The use of a string bass (violoncello or bass violin) to double the continuo line is generally anachronistic, at least before the generation of Badalla and Meda.

Abbreviations: C = Canto or Cantus; A = Alto; T = Tenor; Bc = Basso continuo; Vln = Violin; pitch designations employ the Helsholtz system (e.g., 440 Hz = a′). Sigla for music libraries are those found in *RISM Einzeldrucke.*

Variants

O dulcis Jesu. Variants: In the 1642 edition, the tail is missing on the *cum opposita proprietate* ligature at the following locations: 5.CI.1–2; 10.CII.1–2; 17.CI.1–2; 33.CI and CII.1–2; 37.CI and CII.1–2; 107.CI.1–2; 108.CI and CII.1–2; 109.CI and CII.1–2; 136.CI.1–2; 141.CII.1–2; 148.CI.1–2; 156.CI and CII.1–2; 160.CI and CII.1–2.

O caeli cives: Dialogo. Variants: 164–166.TI and TII: text reads *quiescio.*

O dulcis Jesu

O dulcis Jesu,
Tu es fons pietatis
tu es fons bonitatis
fonsque amoris,
et apud te est fons vitae,
o dulcis Jesu.

Bibat ergo in te solo anima mea
ad te solum confugiat
ad te die nocteque clamet;
Quia in te solo vera est quies,
vera dulcedo,
veraque pax et vita.
Praebe mihi, amantissime Jesu,
tuum dulcissisimum lumen,
infunde, suavissime Domine,
in animam meam amabilissime
tuae lucis scintillam,
ut sic illustrata
irradiataque valeat
te videre, te amare,
amando te frui,
fruendo te possidere,
cum sanctis tuis in aeternum.
O dulcis Jesu . . .

O sweet Jesus,
you are the source of devotion
you are the source of goodness,
and the source of love
and in you is the source of life,
o sweet Jesus.

So let my soul drink only from you
let it seek refuge only with you
let it cry to you day and night;
For in you only is true rest
true sweetness
true peace and life.
Grant me, most beloved Jesus,
your sweetest light,
most pleasant Lord
lovingly infuse your light's ray
into my soul,
so that thus illuminated
and radiant, it may be worthy
to see you, to love you,
in loving you to enjoy you,
in enjoying you to possess you,
with your saints for eternity.
O sweet Jesus . . .

O caeli cives: Dialogo

[2 Tenors:] O caeli cives,
o angeli pacis, audite,
volate, venite, narrate:
ubi pascat, ubi cubet
Christi sponsa Catharina?

[3 Canti]: In caelo quiescit
et inter sanctos pax illius est.

T: O felix requies, beata sors!
Dicite nobis:
ubi regnat exaltata coronata
Christi sponsa Catharina?

C: In caelo nunc regnat
et inter sanctos regnum eius est.

T: O felix regnum, aeternum regnum,
beata sors!
Dicite nobis, angeli Dei:
ubi regina gloriosa triumphat?

C: In caelo triumphat,
et inter sanctos palma illius est.

T: O felix triumphus,
O palma beata,
beata sors!
Dicite nobis:
ubi jubilans gaudet,
exultat, laetatur
jocunda Catharina?

O citizens of heaven,
o angels of peace, listen,
hurry, come, tell us:
where might she dine, where rest,
Catherine, Christ's bride?

In heaven she rests
and among the saints is her peace.

O happy rest, blessed fate!
Tell us: where does she rule, exalted, crowned,
Catherine, Christ's bride?

In heaven she reigns now
and among the saints is her realm.

O happy and eternal realm,
blessed fate
Tell us, angels of God:
where does the glorious queen triumph?

In heaven she triumphs,
and her victory is among the saints.

O happy triumph
O blessed victory,
blessed fate!
Tell us:
where does she cry out in delight
where does she rejoice, exult,
happy Catherine?

C: In caelo congaudet,
exultat, laetatur
et gaudium eius plenum est.

T: O dulcis risus, o felix gaudium,
o beata sors!
Ergo casta Christi sponsa Catharina
in caelo quiescit?

C: In aeternum

T: In caelo nunc regnat?

C: In aeternum

T: In caelo triumphat?

C: In aeternum

T: In caelo laetatur?

C: In aeternum.

Tutti: In aeternum, in caelo
nunc regnat, quiescit,
triumphat, exultat, laetatur
in aeternum cantabit; "alleluia."

In heaven she delights,
rejoices and exalts
and her joy is complete.

O happy laughter,
blessed joy, blessed fate
So does Catherine, Christ's chaste
bride, rest now in heaven?

C: Forever

T: Does she reign now in heaven?

C: Forever

T: Does she triumph in heaven?

C: Forever

T: Is she joyous in heaven?

C: Forever.

Forever in heaven
now she reigns, rests,
triumphs, rejoices, is glad
forever she will sing "alleluia".

I thank my colleague Christine Thomas for her suggestions on the translation.

O dulcis Jesu

Chiara Margarita Cozzolani
Robert Kendrick, editor

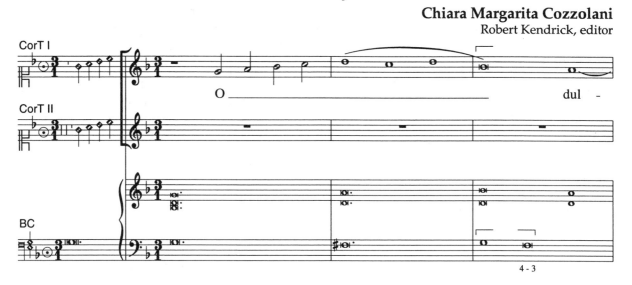

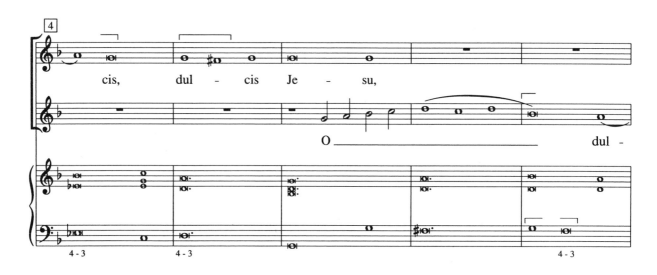

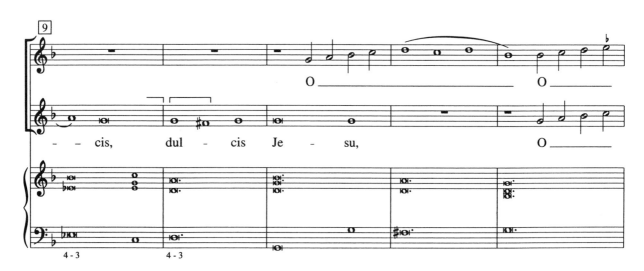

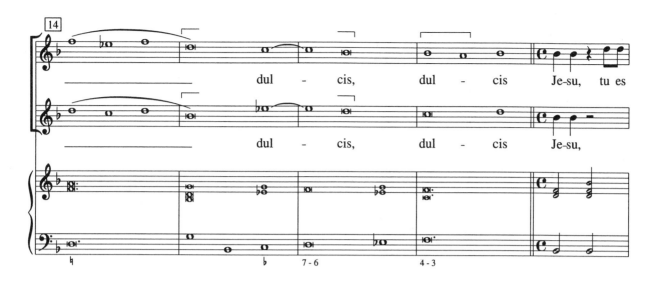

dul - cis, dul - cis Je-su, tu es

dul - cis, dul - cis Je-su,

fons _ pi - e - ta - tis, fons - que a - mo - ris, ‹fons -

tu es fons _ bo - ni - ta - tis, fons - que a - mo - ris, fons -

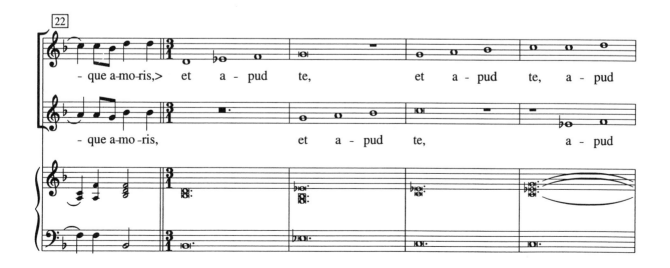

- que a-mo-ris,› et a - pud te, et a - pud te, a - pud

- que a-mo -ris, et a - pud te, a - pud

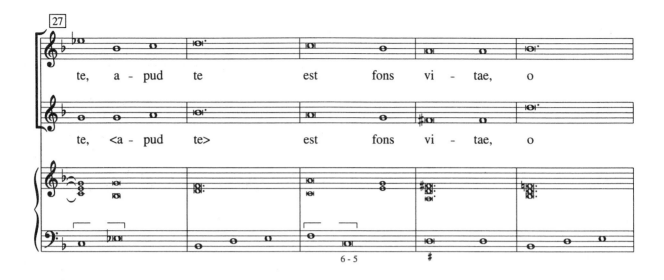

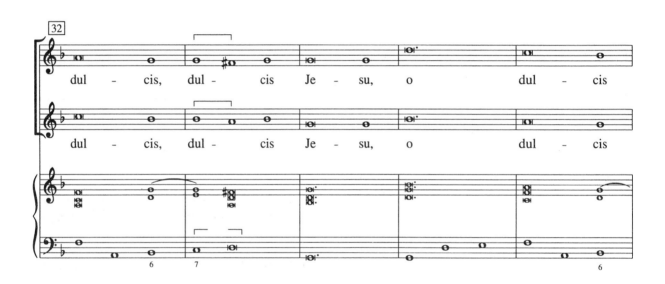

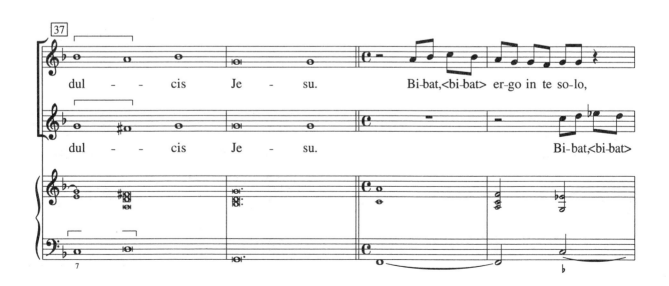

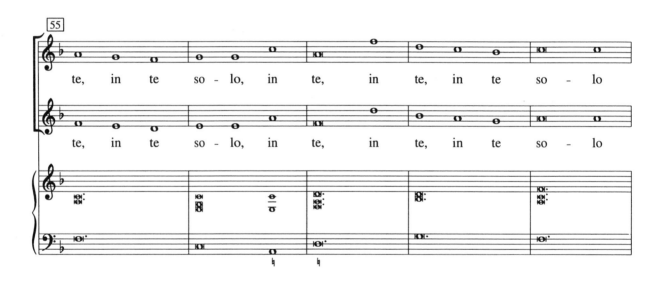

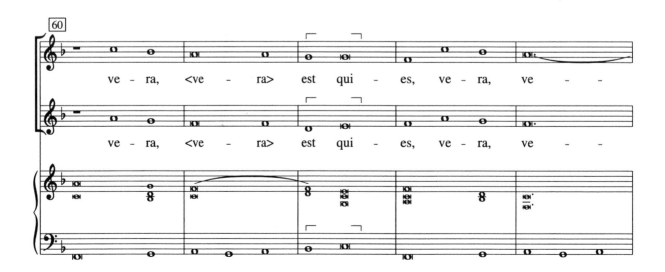

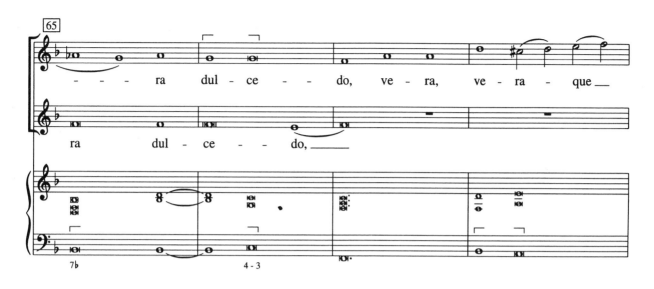

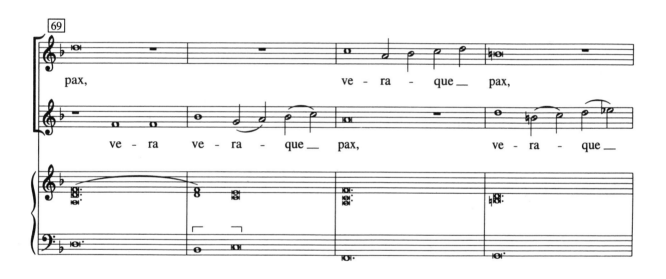

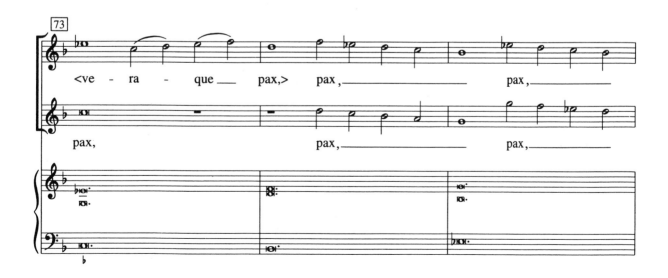

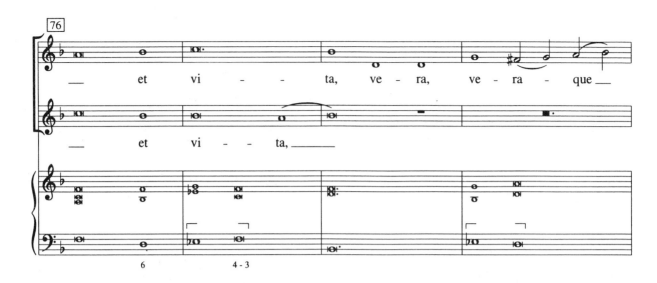

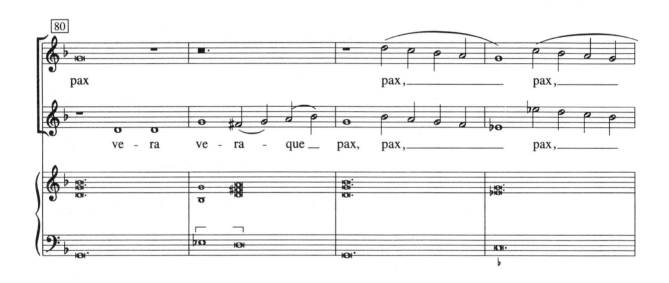

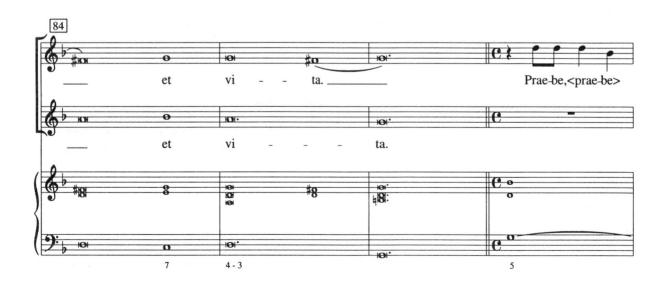

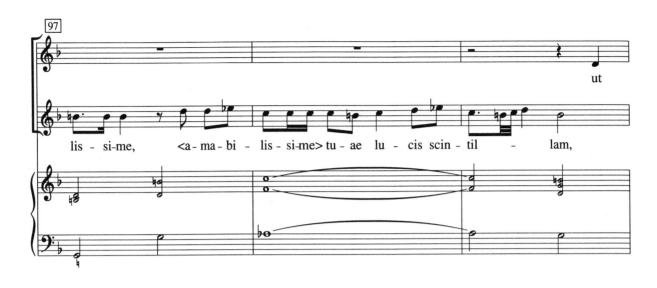

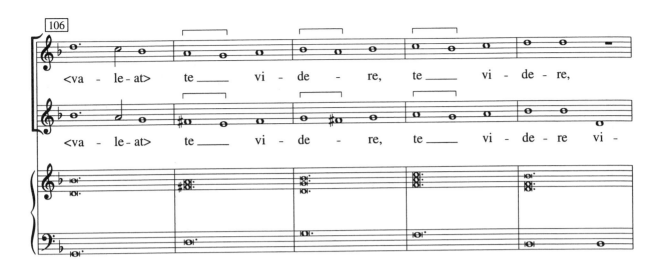

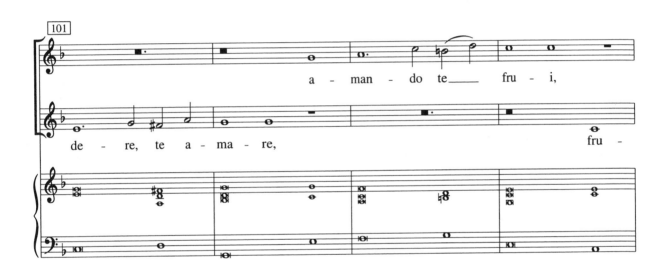

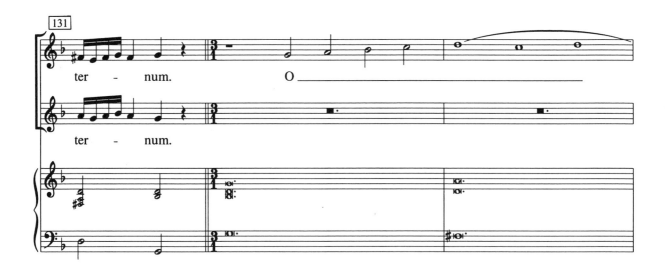

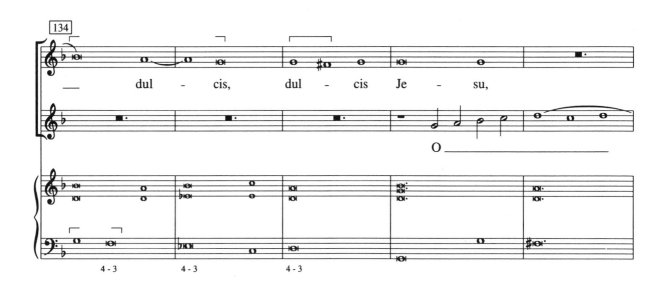

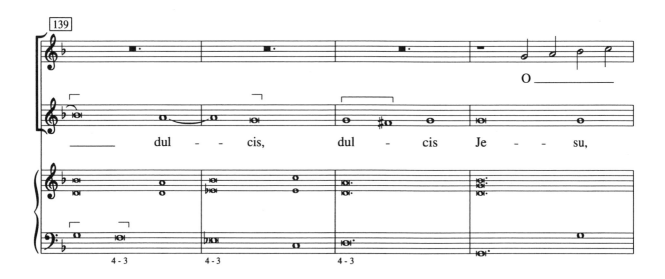

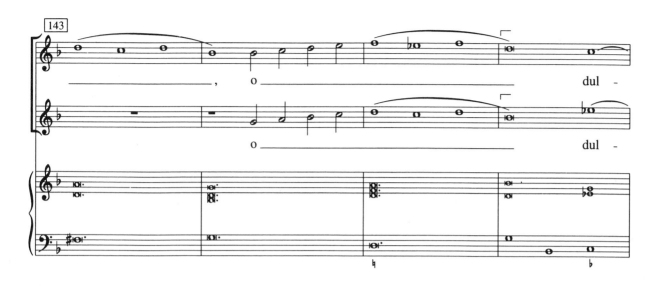

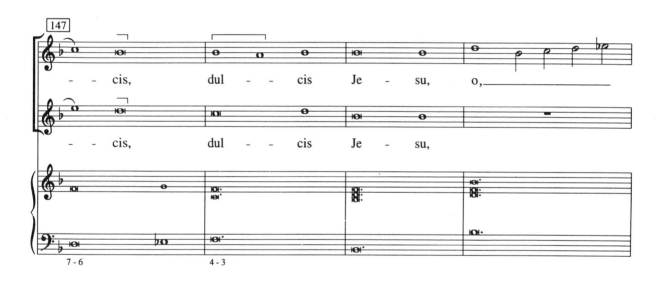

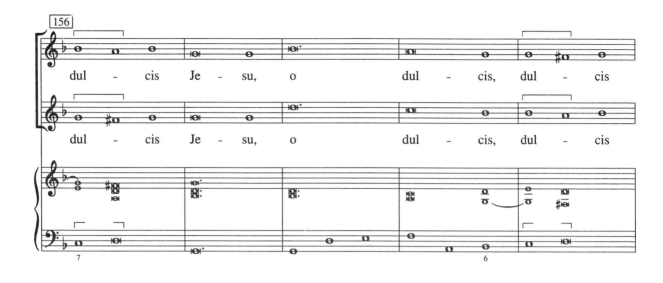

O caeli cives

Chiara Margarita Cozzolani
Robert Kendrick, editor

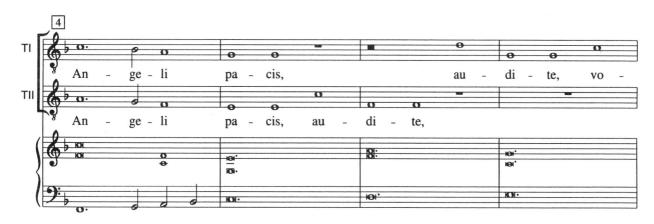

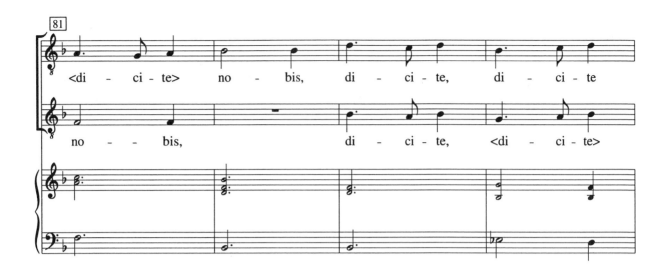

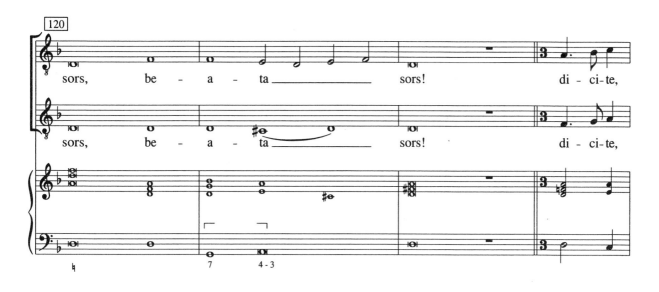

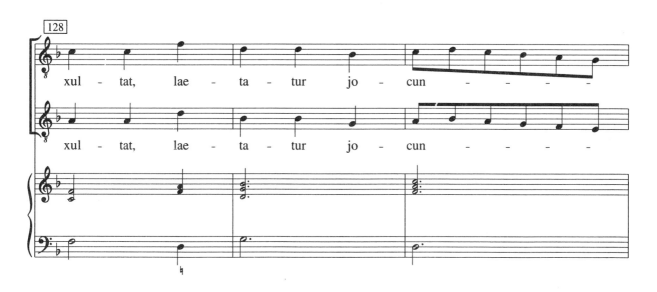

Isabella Leonarda

(1620–1704)

STEWART CARTER

There was a sudden flowering of compositional activity among women in the seventeenth century. Not surprisingly, it was centered in Italy, the fountain of Baroque music: at least twenty-four Italian women published music in the seventeenth century, far more than in all other European countries combined.[1] Isabella Leonarda (1620–1704) occupies a place of special importance among these women, if only because of the sheer volume of music she produced: nearly two hundred individual compositions survive, many of them of substantial length. Moreover, she was the first woman of any nation to publish sonatas.

She was born Anna Isabella Leonarda, in the city of Novara, west of Milan, on September 6, 1620, and was baptized the same day.[2] Her parents were Giannantonio Leonardi and his wife Apollonia (née Sala).[3] The Leonardi were a venerable and prominent Novarese family whose members included leading civic and church officials and knights palatine.[4] Giannantonio (1584–1640) held the title of count and, according to a family tradition, took a degree in canon and civil law at the University of Pavia. He was admitted to the College of Doctors in Novara in 1603.[5]

At least six children were born to Giannantonio and Apollonia Leonardi. These include, in addition to Isabella: Gianpietro (1613–36), who became *canonico coadiutore* at Novara cathedral;[6] Gianfrancesco II (b. 1622), who inherited his father's title and became *decurione* of the city of Novara; Gianbattista (b. 1625),[7] who became canon at the cathedral in Novara; and Orsola Margherita (1626–99), who, like Isabella, entered the Collegio di Sant'Orsola.[8] There seems also to have been a third sister, Anna. A document dated 1665 in the possession of the Leonardi family identifies her as *madre* of the congregation of S. Orsola and refers to Orsola Margherita and Isabella as her sisters.[9]

In 1636 Isabella entered the Collegio di Santa Orsola, an Ursuline convent located in Novara. Ecclesiastical authorities made periodic visits to convents and prepared reports. A document of 1638, relating to such an inspection, describes

Isabella Leonarda as able to sing, write, compute, and compose music.[10] She professed vows in 1639, upon examination by the Bishop of Novara,[11] and she remained in this convent until her death in 1704.[12]

The family maintained close ties with the convent: they established a benefice in its favor, and a nephew of Isabella, Nicolo Leonardi (son of Gianfrancesco II), served as "protector" of the congregation.[13] Nicolo also wrote a sonnet in praise of Emperor Leopold I for his victory over the Turks that appears in the preface to Isabella's *Motetti a voce sola* (opus 12, 1686, dedicated to the Emperor). A cousin, Lorenzo Leonardi, is mentioned in the dedication of her first book of solo motets (opus 6, 1676), where he is referred to as ". . . canonico archidiacono nella Cattedrale di Novara."[14] Lorenzo, without a trace of false modesty, writes that Isabella calls to mind the glories of her family "from whom have issued forth so many heroes, immortal for the splendor of their robes, notable for their courage in arms, eminent for the glory of their saintliness."[15]

The financial support that Isabella's family provided for the Collegio di S. Orsola may have enhanced her position within her religious community, for she occupied various positions of authority. A document of 1658 identifies her as *mater et cancelleria* ("mother and clerk") and also *magistra musicae* ("music teacher").[16] Title pages of her musical publications recount the further progress of her religious career. She calls herself *madre* in opera 6 (1676) through 11 (1684), *superiora* in opera 12 (1686) through 15 (1690), and *madre vicaria* in opus 16 (1693). She is once again *superiora* in opus 17 (1695), but she reverts to *madre vicaria* in opus 18 (1696). In opus 19 (1698), she is identified as Donna Isabella Leonarda, an odd reversion to her title of nobility and perhaps an indication that at the advanced age of seventy-eight she was no longer active in the administration of her congregation. The title page of her last publication, opus 20 (1700), identifies her as *consigliera*. The exact significance of these titles is not clear, but *superiora* was probably the highest office in the convent. *Consigliera* (counselor) may have been an honorary title, conferred in her old age in acknowledgment of decades of faithful service.

As convents go, the Collegio di Sant'Orsola was a comfortable and prestigious institution. It occupied an imposing building (long since demolished[17]) in the parish of S. Eufemia. The Ursulines were (and still are) a teaching order, and the school attached to the convent attracted students from the families of the local aristocracy. In the church attached to the convent, the nuns celebrated certain feasts quite lavishly, notably those of St. Urusla, St. Philip Neri, the Annunciation, and the Dedication of the Church (December 10).[18]

Music probably figured prominently in these services and indeed seems to have been an important feature of convent life. The aforementioned document of 1658 identifies fifteen nuns at S. Orsola and comments that in the singing of polyphonic music eleven were considered "excellent" (*optime*), one "laudable" (*laudabilis*), and two "tolerable" (*tolerabiliter*); it also reports that Leonarda herself was skilled in "plain or figured song" (*cantum firmum seu figuratum*).[19] The same document identifies one Elisabeth Casata (1598–after 1658) as mistress of the novices. Casata came from a family of Novarese musicians; she was known to be an organist and was accepted into the convent in 1616 with a dowry smaller than was customary, on the condition that she play the organ and teach music.[20] Other documents attest to the presence of an organ in the convent.[21] A further indication of the musical skills of the nuns of S. Orsola is evident in inscriptions for two motets, *Paremus nos, fideles* and *Cor humanum* (both from opus 13, 1687),[22] dedicated to two colleagues from S. Orsola, Flaminia Morbida and Chiara Margarita Gattica respectively, each of whom Leonarda calls *musica virutosissima*.[23] Though we cannot know for certain, it seems likely that Leonarda wrote many of her compositions for convent performances. Her solo motets for canto voice, such as *Spes mondane* (included in this edition), would of course be most suitable for convents, as would duets for two high voices, such as *Ad arma, o spiritus*.[24] However, the presence of parts for tenor and bass voices may not have precluded convent performances. Ignazio Donati, who worked in Novara in the early part of the seventeenth century, states in the preface to his *Salmi boscarecci* (1623):

> First, then, the first six partbooks may be sung by six solo
> voices. Parts may be omitted; but if there are not enough
> sopranos, the first soprano may be sung by a tenor, placed some
> distance from the principal tenor. *Nuns wishing to use them may
> sing the bass an octave higher, thereby making a contralto part* [italics
> mine].[25]

Nuns may also have transposed the tenor parts up an octave, but female singers with unusually low voices—even extending to the bass range—were not unknown in the convents. In 1625 at least two convents in Novara could boast nuns who regularly sang tenor.[26] As many of Leonarda's works

include parts for instruments—violins, violone, theorbo, and *bassetto,* in addition to the obligatory organ—we may surmise that some of her colleagues at Santa Orsola also played these instruments.[27] Though perhaps technically forbidden, male musicians might have been brought into the convent for musical performances; or conversely, the nuns of Orsola, who certainly were not cloistered, may occasionally have performed Leonarda's compositions for religious services elsewhere in the city.

Dedications of Leonarda's publications yield scant information about her life. Several of her publications are dedicated to the Virgin Mary, a reflection of her intense religious devotion; and many have a second dedication, to a living person. Leonarda's dedicatees include such luminaries as the Bishop of Novara, the Archbishop of Milan, and Emperor Leopold I.[28] Financial support for the convent may have been the aim of many of these dedications. A case in point is opus 20 (1700), dedicated to Filippo Avogadro, canon of Novara cathedral, whom Leonarda addresses as "Worthy Conservator of this our Most Noble Collegio."[29]

Regarding Leonarda's musical education, we know very little. She undoubtedly received some instruction from Elisabeth Casata, organist and teacher of music at S. Orsola. It has further been suggested that she studied with Gasparo Casati (d. 1641), who probably was a kinsman of Elisabeth. Casati, a talented but little-known composer, was *maestro di cappella* at Novara cathedral from 1635 until his death.[30] In 1640 he published *Terzo libro di sacri concerti,* which includes, in addition to his own works, two dialogues by Isabella Leonarda, *Ah Domine Jesu* and *Sic ergo anima,* her earliest known compositions. This is the only direct evidence linking Casati and Leonarda, but in seventeenth-century Italy it was not uncommon for masters to include one or two compositions by their students in their own publications.

Leonarda had a long and fruitful career as a composer. Her published works span a period of sixty years, beginning with the dialogues of 1640 and concluding with the *Motetti a voci sola* of 1700. Her last print is identified as opus 20, but four publications, opera 1, 2, 5, and 9, no longer survive.[31] Most of her compositions, in fact all her extant works save the two dialogues of the Casati print, appeared after she reached the age of fifty. Her music is almost exclusively sacred; even her few vocal works with Italian texts have religious subjects, and her lone instumental publication (opus 16, 1693) is devoted to works that may be called *sonate da chiesa,* although they are not so designated. Leonarda was highly regarded in her own city. A directory of the prominent citizens of Novara, Lazaro Agostino Cotta's *Museo novarese,* praises her lavishly:

> Just as Novara has had illustrious men in all the professions, as
> everyone can see in this *Museo,* she also has not lacked virtuous
> women who make her famous. Among these there shines with
> glorious fame the name of Isabella Leonarda, who because of

the singular esteem in which she is held in the art of music could rightly call herself the Novarese Muse *par excellence*. For in her are combined rare invention, universal genius, felicity in the expression of the affections, fecundity of ideas, adornment of fundamental theories, and finally all that which one desires in the perfection of this art.[32]

Cotta relates Isabella's entry into the Ursuline order and her selection as leader of her congregation. He records that she published sixteen volumes of music between 1642 and 1693.[33]

Opus 12 is dedicated to Emperor Leopold I, who, according to Cotta, was presented with the following sonnet by Amedeo Saminiati Lucchese after his victory over the Turks at Buda:

Leopoldo in guerra, e Leonarda in pace
Son portento; ei di Marte, ella d'Apollo
Col brando in mano, e con la cetra al colla
Questa abbatte l'invidia, e quello il Trace.

Degli empi Musulman l'odio pugnace
Cesar doma in dar lor l'ultimo corollo:
Con genio ella d'onor non mai satollo
In un canta celeste i cuor disface.

Spiega d'ambi le glorie un'aurea tromba
Che mieton tutte in vario stil le palme
Aquila armata e musica Colomba.

Un al Regno, una ai cor nutre le calme:
Una col canto, uno col tuon rimbomba:
Ei trionfa dell'Armi, ella dell'Alme.[34]

(Leopold in war and Leonarda in peace
Are wondrous: he like Mars, she like Apollo:
With sword in hand and with the lyre on the shoulder
One vanquishes envy, the other, Thrace.

The impious Moslem, the hateful pugnacious one,
Caesar subdues by giving them the last blow;
She, though talented, is never satiated with honor.
In a celestial song, hearts are melted.

A golden trumpet spreads the glories of both,
And all reap the laurels in various ways;
The armed eagle and the dove of music.

One to reign, the other to nurture calm in the heart;
One with song, the other with resounding thunder:
He triumphs with arms, she with kindnesses.)

Interestingly, Cotta's article on Leonarda is the longest entry in the *Museo* that is devoted to a musician. It is doubtful, though, that Cotta is correct in his assertion that the sonnet above was presented to the Holy Roman Emperor, who probably would not have been flattered by a comparison with a virtually unknown Italian nun.[35]

Leonarda seems to have been little known as a composer in other parts of Italy. None of her publications were reprinted, and none of her individual compositions appeared

in anthologies. Some of her music found its way to France, however, for copies of her opera 7, 13, and 19 were included in the material that Sébastian de Brossard (1655–1730) donated to the Bibliothèque Royale (later the Bibliothèque Nationale). Brossard's high regard for Leonarda's music is revealed in the following entry in the manuscript catalog of his music collection: "All the works of this illustrious and incomparable Isabelle Leonard [*sic*] are so beautiful, so gracious, and at the same time so learned and wise that my great regret is not having all of them."[36]

Musical Style

Leonarda wrote music in virtually every sacred genre: motets and concertos for one to four voices, Latin dialogs, psalm settings, responsories, Magnificats, litanies, masses, and *sonate da chiesa*. She also wrote a few sacred solo songs with vernacular texts.[37]

A notable feature of her works as a whole is flexibility. She seems to have been ever cognizant of the varying resources and needs of contemporary religious establishments. In many of her vocal works, certain vocal and/or instrumental parts may be omitted, refrains are optional, parts for sopranos may be performed by tenors an octave lower, and for some compositions, alternative texts are supplied.

Leonarda composed several works in *stile antico,* but most of her vocal compositions, and her instrumental works as well, employ a composite, sectional structure. In describing the internal divisions of her works, the term *section* seems more appropriate than *movement,* since these units are, for the most part, relatively brief. Contrast among sections is obtained through changes in meter, tempo, texture, and melodic style. In particular, metric contrasts serve as an important formal device: sections in duple meter frequently alternate with sections in triple or compound meter. While a few works follow a completely regular scheme of alternation, irregular patterns are more characteristic. The metrical plan for *Spes mondane* may be considered representative: C3–C–C3/2–C3.[38]

Occasionally, a section returns. The return may be indicated verbally, as in *Surge virgo* in this edition, or it may be written out in full, occasionally with minor alterations.[39] Refrain structures are particularly common in four-voice compositions with nonliturgical texts. Full-scale rondo structures, with several regularly disposed repetitions of a refrain, are rare in her works, though *In caelis gloria,* a Christmas motet from opus 13 (1678), has the form ABACADAEAFAGA (with A involving repetition of text as well as music).[40] This motet might well be described as a vocal concerto, in the sense of Vivaldi rather than Gabrieli, for its structure resembles the *ritornello* form of a late-Baroque solo concerto. The A sections are for the entire ensemble (SATB), while the couplets (B, C, D, and so forth) are solos.

Refrain, or *ritornello,* structures seem to be common in Leonarda's Christmas motets.

Leonarda's harmonic techniques are generally typical of the middle Baroque. In terms of tonal organization, her music reflects the transition from modality to tonality: in many sections the tonal, or modal, center is either ambiguous or unstable and chromatic inflections are inconsistent. The latter is evident in the opening section of *Surge Virgo* (mm. 1–38), which is clearly centered on G, but with the F's sometimes sharped, sometimes not; from a modern historical persepective, G mixolydian is on the verge of becoming G major, even though Leonarda herself would probably not have acknowledged the latter concept. Modality/tonality is always an important unifying force for an entire composition, but individual sections may begin and end in different keys: witness, for example, *Et tamen,* mm. 90–120 of *Spes mondane.*

Vertical structures are principally root-position and first-inversion triads. Sevenths are treated as dissonances, although sometimes they are resolved freely, and suspensions appear often, particularly at cadences. Diminished-seventh chords, Neapolitan chords, diminished triads in root position, and augmented-sixth chords are all part of her harmonic vocabulary, although they are used sparingly. Some of the most advanced harmonic writing is found in her only solo violin sonata, *Sonata duodecima*[41] (especially in mm. 1–15 and 126–50).

A rhythmic device at many cadences is the *anticipatione della sillaba,* which Christoph Bernhard describes as "a type of artifice in which the syllable belonging to the following note is also allotted to the previous one."[42] In other words, a syllable that normally would coincide with a note on a strong beat begins instead on a note on the preceding weak beat (or weak part of a beat) and continues through the strong beat. This device, which is characteristic of Italian vocal music of the mid-seventeenth century, occurs most frequently at cadences (see *Spes mondane,* mm. 88–89); but it also appears occasionally within a phrase.

Leonarda uses word painting extensively. This can be seen in the martial style of *Surge virgo,* mentioned above, and also in several instances in *Spes mondane.* In mm. 92–93 of the latter work, for example, Leonarda shifts to the minor mode and writes *adagio* to underscore musically the word *amarum* (bitter). In the opening section of the same work, running figures underscore the words *volate* (fly) and *veloce* (swift).

Leonarda specifies organ continuo as the only accompaniment for the majority of her vocal works, though in opera 18 and 19 a part for theorbo or violone reinforces the continuo line, and in opus 20, a part for *bassetto* serves the same function. Some of her compositions have parts for two violins as well. In the large-scale works, instrumental writing is essentially vocal in style. Passages for violins alone are usually based on preceding vocal sections. Violins are treated more integrally (though not necessarily more idiomatically) in small-scale compositions.

Sacred Vocal Works with Liturgical Texts

This category, though it comprises only about one-fourth of her total output, includes some of Leonarda's most elaborate compositions. They may be roughly divided into four principal categories: (1) masses; (2) works for Vespers, including responsories, psalm settings, and Magnificats; (3) litanies; and (4) a miscellaneous group, consisting of Marian antiphons, a hymn, and a sequence. Most are in *concertato* style, but a few—including the complete Vespers setting of opus 8—are in *stile antico.*

Incomplete settings of the Mass Ordinary were the rule rather than the exception in Italy in the late seventeenth century. In the four masses she composed—one in opus 4, three in opus 18—Leonarda set only the first three movements, Kyrie, Gloria, and Credo.[43] All of Leonarda's masses are set for four voices, two violins, and organ continuo (though in the opus 4 mass, violins are optional); the opus 18 masses also have a part for violone or theorbo, which largely reinforces the continuo line. In these works, and in other compositions for four voices, Leonarda often juxtaposes familiar style with fugal style, and further varies the texture by interposing vocal solos and duets, as well as instrumental sinfonias.[44]

In masses and in *concertato*-style psalm settings, Leonarda employs a loosely organized sectional form, with musical sections corresponding to important divisions in the text. In psalm settings, customarily each verse of the psalm is set to a new section of music, offering some form of musical contrast to the preceding section, whether in texture, key/mode, meter, rhythm, or a combination of these elements. In psalm settings, the concluding doxology and *amen* often receive extended treatment.

Sacred Vocal Works with Extraliturgical Texts

Sacred vocal compositions with extraliturgical texts constitute approximately three-fourths of Leonarda's vocal works. They are on the whole more modest in dimension than the liturgical compositions, for although most of the latter are choral works, the majority of the extraliturgical works—at least those for one to three voices—are intended to be performed with one singer to a part. The category includes compositions for as many as four voice parts, but solo motets predominate; in fact, seven of her extant collections, opera 6, 11, 12, 14, 15, 17, and 20 are devoted exclusively to this genre. So great was Leonarda's preoccupation with the solo voice that only one of her publications of vocal music, opus 10, contains no solo works at all. *Surge virgo,* for four voices, and *Spes mondane,* a solo motet, both fall into this category. Both works are discussed in greater detail below.

As a genre, sacred vocal compositions with extraliturgical texts constitute well over half of Leonarda's total compositional output. The poets are never identified, and to the best of my knowledge, none of these texts is found in any other source. Evidence of Leonarda's own poetic skill can be seen in the form of two sonnets in praise of Emperor Leopold I in the preface to her opus 12 collection of solo motets (1686). It seems reasonable to speculate, then, that Leonarda herself wrote some or all of the texts she set to music.

Perhaps the most affective texts are found in her numerous solo motets. Many of these are evocative of the religious mysticism prevalent in *seicento* Italy, while some are so sensuous in tone that they may be compared to the secular love poetry of the time. The Latin grammar of the poetry tends to be rather corrupt.

Instrumental Compositions

The twelve compositions that constitute Leonarda's *Sonate a 1.2.3. e 4. Istromenti* (opus 16) are her only instrumental works, and they are apparently the only sonatas by a woman published during the seventeenth century.[45] Eleven of these works are ensemble sonatas for two violins, violone, and organ. The last, *Sonata duodecima,* is for solo violin with organ.[46] Though not so designated, they appear to be *sonate da chiesa,* as none of the sections have dance titles, though most have tempo, character, markings. An interesting aspect of these sonatas is that they are similar in so many ways to Leonarda's motets—in large-scale formal structure, harmonic treatment, occasional use of refrains, and even, to a certain extent, melodic style.

Leonarda's sonatas appeared in 1693, after the appearance of opera 1–3 of Arcangelo Corelli. Yet her sonatas are considerably more conservative, reflecting the style and technique of the generation of composers before Corelli—(Don) Marco Uccellini, and Mauricio Cazzati, for example. None of Leonarda's sonatas follow the slow-fast-slow-fast four-movement form supposedly standardized by Corelli; in fact, only two of the sonatas have as few as four movements; one has eleven. *Sonata duodecima* is a most expressive work. Its two rhapsodic, toccata-like sections are balanced against dancelike sections in triple or compound meter and canzona-like sections in common time.

Sonata prima displays similar sectional contrasts. Its fifth section, marked adagio, consists of three brief improvisatory solo passages, one for each of the violins and one also for the violone. It is thus an example of the *concerted* sonata, a subgenre more representative of the mid-seventeenth century.[47]

Spes Mondane

The text of this solo motet speaks of the temptations of earthly pleasures and the need to remain steadfast with the Lord (see text translations below)—a common theme in Italian sacred music of this time and one that was frequently treated in sacred dramatic dialogues. In spite of its religious intent, the tone of the poetry is not far removed from that of secular love poetry.[48] In fact, Leonarda's solo motets in general and *Spes mondane* in particular are quite similar to contemporary secular cantatas, which consist of a succession of arias and recitatives. But secular cantatas most often alternate in regular fashion—recitative-aria-recitative-aria—whereas Leonarda's solo motets are more irregular in form. *Spes mondane* has four sections, in the pattern aria-recitative/arioso-aria-aria.

The initial aria of *Spes mondane* is in ABA′ form, but it scarcely resembles the full-fledged da capo form of the late Baroque. The return of A (m. 55ff.) is considerably varied and in fact recognizable only because of the (transposed) head motif. Like many of her contemporaries, Leonarda preferred small-scale aria forms with some sort of varied repetition and without strong points of internal division. The continuo is well integrated with the voice, engaging in foreimitation (mm. 1–7) and providing brief cadential "tags" at the ends of phrases. In the concluding aria of this motet, the continuo is exceptionally active.

Surge Virgo

This motet bears the superscription *Motetto á 4. voci per un' Anima, che lascia il Mondo* (Motet for four voices for a soul who is leaving the world). It seems reasonable to assume that it was written on the occasion of the funeral of one of Leonarda's compatriots at S. Orsola. The text urges a virgin figuratively to take arms in the struggle over death. Clearly the one so exhorted is not the Virgin Mary, because in the third section (*Pugna virgo*), the poet says, "Fight, virgin, do not hesitate. Take up arms, piously under the Virgin Mary." We have no hint as to the identity of Leonarda's deceased colleague.

The virgin's struggle to be victorious over death is appropriately represented by martial effects in the music, particularly in the trumpetlike *Pugna virgo, Arma dulcissima,* and *Cesset pugna* sections. The irregularly appearing refrain *Surge virgo* helps to unify the motet. Though written out only at the beginning, its subsequent appearances are indicated in verbal directions in the middle of the piece and again at the end. The second appearance of this refrain is indicated by the words *Surge da capo si placet,* another indication of Leonarda's concern for flexibility in performance. Its structural plan is below:

Structural Plan of *Surge Virgo*

Verse	Measure	Meter	Key/Mode	Voices	Material	Remarks
Surge virgo	1	03/1	G	CATB	A	largo, fugal, ostinato, echo
En Jesus capiti	39	03/1	G/D	CA—CATB CT—AB	B	presto, fugal, ostinato, echo
Pugna virgo	95	C	D-G	CATB	C	fugal, martial
Arma dulcissima	113	03/1	D-G	CATB	D	presto, fugal beginning, homophonic ending, echo
Iam legitime	139	C	G-e	C	E	arioso style
Surge virgo	★	03/1	G	CATB	A	optional
Inter lilia	149	C	G	CATB	F	fugal, many repeated notes in subject
Cesset pugna	160	03/1	G	CATB	G	presto, fugal beginning, martial
Iam ad armis	170	C	G	CATB	H	allegro, fugal
Cesset pugna	178	03/1	G	CATB	G	presto
Clarissima	188	C	G	CATB	I	fugal beginning, homophonic ending
Surge virgo	★	03/1	G	CATB	A	

★The second and third statements of the refrain are not written out.

Throughout this motet, martial images in the text are underscored by martial figures in the music—simple harmonies, static bass lines, and repeated notes.

Conclusion

Leonarda emerges as a talented composer who writes expressively for voices and instruments and shows a keen sense for the practical needs of modestly endowed religious institutions of her day. Her compositions are in many respects more characteristic of the middle of the seventeenth century than the end (when almost all were published), but this may reflect the fact that by 1670, when she began to publish music regularly, she was already fifty years old and her compositional style had matured.

Notes

1. See Jane Bowers, "The Emergence of Women Composers in Italy, 1566–1700," in *Women Making Music: The Western Art Tradition, 1150–1950,* ed. Jane Bowers and Judith Tick (Urbana: University of Illinois Press, 1986), pp. 116–67; and especially appendix, pp. 162–67.

2. Leonarda's baptism is recorded in Novara, Archivio Storico Diocesano, Fondo duomo, Atti di battesimo, Libro 7, fol. 262v; cited in Emilia Dahnk Baroffio, "La compositrice Isabella Leonarda,"

Novarien 13 (1983): 76. I am indebted to Prof. Jane Bowers for providing me with a transcript of this document. Sister Isabella's surname is customarily given as *Leonarda,* although male members of the family used the masculine form, *Leonardi,* or sometimes *Lionardi.* Of Leonarda's prints, those published in distant Bologna invariably give her name as *Leonarda,* while those published in nearby Milan, where Sister Isabella's family was well known, use *Leonarda* for title pages and dedications, but *Leonardi* in the sheet signatures.

3. According to Emilia Dahnk Baroffio ("La compositrice Isabella Leonarda," *Novarien* 13 [1983]: 75), Isabella Leonarda's mother was a Milanese.

4. The family still maintains a villa in Gattico, near Novara, where they keep a small family archive.

5. Baroffio, "La compositrice," p. 75.

6. Ibid., p. 76 n. 6.

7. Ibid., n. 8.

8. Novara, Archivio, Libro 8, fol. 247.

9. Gattico (Novara), Archivio Famiglia Leonardi, I, no. 205, 1665. li 9. aprile. Anna does not appear in the Leonardi family tree, nor does her name appear in the baptismal records of the cathedral. But according to a document in Novara, Archivio Storico Diocesano (AV 286, f. 59; cited in Baroffio, "La compositrice," p. 76 n. 5), she was in 1625 a novice in the Collegio di Sant'Orsola. If, like Isabella, entered the Collegio di Sant'Orsola at approximately the age of 16, she must have been born around the year 1609. Probably she

was an older sister of Isabella's. Most likely she died prior to 1674, for in that year Isabella Leonarda identifies herself as *madre* of Sant' Orsola on the title page of her *Motetti a voce sola* (opus 6).

10. "Scit canere, scribere et computa facit et cantum componit." Novara, Archivio Storico Diocesano, Atti di Visita Pastorale 286 f. 318v. Cited in Baroffio, "La compositrice," p. 80.

11. Baroffio, "La compositrice," p. 76.

12. Leonarda's death, which occurred February 25, 1704, is recorded in Gattico (Novara), Archivio di Famiglia Leonardi, I, no. 252A. The document itself is dated December 20, 1713.

13. Baroffio, "La compositrice," p. 78.

14. Baroffio (ibid., p. 75) identifies Lorenzo Leonardi as Isabella's cousin.

15. Dedication of Isabella Leonarda's opus 6 (1676); cited in Baroffio, "La compositrice," p. 75: "Da cui uscirono tanti eroi, immortali per lo splendor delle toghe, riguardevoli per il valor dell'armi, eminenti per il lustro della santita."

16. Novara, Archivio Storico Diocesano: Atti di visita pastorale, 266, fols. 467–95. Cited in Baroffio, "La compositrice," pp. 78–79. Baroffio (p. 80) states that Leonarda in 1658 was also identified as *madre discreta,* a title which he equates with *madre.* Baroffio further states that four sisters in the convent held this title.

17. It is difficult to determine when the building was demolished, but the convent itself was closed September 4, 1811, during the general suppression of such religious institutions instigated by Napoleon. The closure of the convent and an inventory of its property is recorded in Milan, Archivio di Stato, Amministrazione del fondo de religione, busta 2486. Notably, one of the most valuable items listed in the inventory is an organ. Conveyed in a letter to the author from Jane Bowers, March 1, 1979.

18. Sac. Angelo Stoppa to Jane Bowers, April 7, 1981.

19. Baroffio,"La compositrice," p. 78.

20. See Baroffio, "La compositrice," p.79. Baroffio says that Elisabeth was the youngest daughter of Hieronymo Casato, a Novarese organist. Probably her father was not the Girolamo Casati (ca. 1590–after 1657; called *Il Filago*) who was employed at the Novara cathedral in 1609 but is more likely an earlier organist of the same name, identified by Jerome Roche as the composer of two madrigals in *RISM* 1605 (*The New Grove Dictionary of Music and Musicians,* s.v. "Casati, Girolamo," by Jerome Roche). It is reasonable to assume that Elisabeth was also related to Gasparo Casati, who in 1640 published two of Leonarda's sacred compositions in a collection otherwise devoted to his own works (see main text below).

21. Baroffio, "La compositrice," p. 79.

22. For a modern edition of *Paremus nos, fideles,* see Isabella Leonarda, *Selected Compositions,* ed. Stewart Carter (Madison, WI: 1988), Recent Researches in the Music of the Baroque Era, no. 59, pp. 70–82.

23. For the complete inscriptions for *Paremus nos, fideles,* see Leonarda, *Selected Compositions,* p. xv.

24. In Leonarda, *Selected Compositions,* pp. 70–82.

25. Translated by the present writer. "Prima dunque si potrá cantare a sei voci sole con li primi sei libri; ne si puó tralasciare alcuna di queste sei parti, ma per penuria di Soprani si puó cantare il primo Soprano in Tenore, discosto peró alquanto dal Tenor principale. Et volendo servirsene le Monache portranno cantare il Basso all'Ottava alto, che riuscira un Contralto." Quoted in Gaetano Gaspari, *Catalago della Biblioteca Musicale G. B. Martini di Bologna* (1892; reprint, Bologna, 1961), 2: 216.

26. Baroffio ("La compositrice," p. 83 n. 43) says that the convent of Sant'Agnese in Novara had two tenors among its singers, while another, Sant'Agostino, had one. Jane Bowers ("Emergence," p. 126) mentions a bass singer at the convent of San Vito in Ferrara.

27. Regarding women instrumentalists at another convent, San Vito in Ferrara, see Bowers, "Emergence," pp. 125–26. It is possible that Isabella Leonarda herself played the violin. Most Italian composers of her day who wrote solos for violin were also performers on the instrument.

28. See Stewart Carter, "The Music of Isabella Leonarda (1620–1704)" (Ph.D. diss., Stanford University, 1982), Appendix I; and Baroffio, "La compositrice," pp. 89–91 nn. 63–78.

29. "Degno Conservatore di questo nostro Nobilissimo Collegio."

30. Claudio Sartori, ed., *Dizionario Ricordi della musica e dei musicisti* (Milan, 1959), s.v. "Casati, Gasparo." See Jerome Roche, *North Italian Church Music in the Age of Monteverdi* (Oxford, 1984), pp. 75, 77, 80, 103–4.

31. François-Joseph Fétis, *Biographie universelle des musiciens et bibliographie générale de la musique.* 8 vols. (Paris, 1878–80), s.v. "Leonarda, Isabelle," mentions a publication by Leonarda that apparently does not survive—*Motetti a tre voci, libro primo* (Milan, 1665). Fétis says that in the preface to this publication Leonarda gives her age as twenty-four. This led him to conclude that she was born in 1641—an error repeated by several subsequent writers. This elusive publication may be a reprint of a work originally published in 1644, perhaps Leonarda's missing Opus 2 (see Bibliography, below). But Fétis might be mistaken on this point, and there are two aspects of his report that strike this writer as suspect. First, it was quite unusual in the seventeenth century—or indeed any era—for a composer to state his or her age in the preface of a publication. Second, while Italian composers at this time did of course write three-voice motets, it was not one of the more popular combinations and it was rare for a composer to devote an entire volume to this combination. Leonarda never did again.

32. Milan, 1701, p. 169. "Siccome Novara ha avuto uomini illustri in tutte le professioni, come ciascuno puó vedere in questo Museo, cosí ancora non vi sono mancate donne virtuose che la illustrino. Tra queste risplende con fama gloriosa di suo nome Isabella Leonarda, che per il singolar pregio che ella tiene nell'arte della Musica potrebbe con ragione chiamarsi per antonomasia la Musa novarese. Imperocchè in lei concorrono pergrine invenzioni, genio universale, felicità nelle impressioni degli affetti, fecondità d'idee, adornamento di teoriche fondamentali, e finalmente tutto quanto sa desiderare la perfezione di quell'arte."

33. See Leonarda, *Selected Compositions,* p. xvii, n. 19.

34. Quoted in Cotta, *Museo*, p. 270. Translated by the present writer. The eagle mentioned in stanza 3 is on the Habsburg family crest.

35. See Leonarda, *Selected Compositions*, pp. xvii–xviii, n. 22.

36. Sébastien de Brossard, "Catalogue des livres du musique . . . Fait et escrit en l'année 1724" (Paris, Bibliothèque Nationale, Res. Vm 20), p. 137. "Tous les ouvrages de cette illustre et incomparable *Isabelle Leonard* [*sic*] sont si beaux si gracieux, si brillans, et en même tems si sçavans [*sic*] et si sages; que mon grand regret est de ne les avoir pas tous."

37. For a complete catalog of her works, see Carter, "Leonarda," Appendix I, pp. 290–310.

38. The concluding section in C3 is effectively in 3/8 time.

39. See *Volo Jesum*, in Leonarda, "Selected Compositions," pp. 36–48.

40. See Carter, "Leonarda," pp. 30–32, 245.

41. Modern ed. in Leonarda, *Selected Compositions*, pp. 96–104.

42. Christoph Bernhard, *Von der Singe-Kunst oder Manier* (ca. 1650), in Joseph Müller-Blattau, *Die Kompositionslehre Heinrich Schützens in der Fassung seines Schülers Christoph Bernhard*, 2nd ed. (Kassel, 1963), p. 34. "Ein solch Kunststück, welches die zu der folgenden Note gehörende syllabe auch der Vorhergehenden in etwas zutheilet. . . ."

43. The practice of omitting the Sanctus and the Agnus Dei seems to have originated in Venice. Such abbreviated settings of the Mass were sometimes designated *alla veneziana* and their use apparently had been approved by the Church for that city. See Günther Massenkeil, "Die konzertierende Kirchenmusik," in *Geschichte der katholischen Kirchenmusik*, ed. Karl Gustav Fellerer (Kassel, 1976), 2: 99.

Among Bolognese composers, omission of the Credo as well, leaving only two movements, was not uncommon. See Sr. Mary Nicole (Anne) Schnoebelen, "The Concerted Mass at San Petronio in Bologna, ca. 1660–1700: A Documentary and Analytical Study," Ph.D. diss., University of Illinois, 1966, p. 186.

It is important to remember, however, that even though certain portions of the Ordinary of the Mass might not be sung, the missing texts were not actually disregarded but were recited by the priest in a low voice. See Stephen Bonta, "Liturgical Problems in Monteverdi's Marian Vespers," *Journal of the American Musicological Society* 20 (1967): 94.

44. See the Kyrie from the *Messa concertata* of opus 4 in Leonarda, *Selected Compositions*, pp. 1–18.

45. Marieta Prioli is the first woman known to have published independent instrumental music, but her lone collection of music, *Balletti et Correnti a due violini & violone, agionta la spineta*, contains no compositions designated *sonata*.

46. For modern editions of *Sonata prima* and *Sonata duodecima*, see Leonarda, *Selected Compositions*, pp. 83–104.

47. See Eleanor Selfridge-Field, *Venetian Instrumental Music from Gabrieli to Vivaldi* (New York, 1975), pp. 123, 134–38, 176–8.

48. See Carter, "Leonarda," pp. 189–91.

49. Cited in Fétis, *Bibliographie universelle*.

Bibliography
Leonarda's Published Works
(All with part for organ)

Motetti . . . libro primo, 3 voices, [opus 2?] (Milan, 1665), lost.[49]

Sacri concenti, 1–4 voices, opus 3 (Milan, 1670).

Messa e salmi, concertati, & a cappella con istromenti ad libitum, 4 voices, 2 violins, opus 4 (Milan, 1674).

Motetti, 1 voice, 2 violins, opus 6 (Venice, 1676).

Motetti . . . con le litanie della beata vergine, 1–4 voices, 2 violins, opus 7 (Bologna, 1677).

Vespro a della beata vergine e motetti concertati, 1–4 voices, opus 8 (Bologna, 1678).

Motetti con le litanie della beata vergine, 4 voices, opus 10 (Milan, 1684).

Motetti, 1 voice, opus 11 (Bologna, 1684).

Motetti, 1 voice, opus 12 (Bologna, 1686).

Motetti, 1–3 voices, 2 violins, opus 13 (Bologna, 1687).

Motetti, 1 voice, opus 14 (Bologna, 1687).

Motetti, 1 voice, opus 15 (Bologna, 1690).

Sonate, a 1–4, opus 16 (Bologna, 1693).

Motetti, 1 voice, opus 17 (Bologna, 1695).

Messe concertate con strometi, & motetti, 1–4 voices, 2 violines, violone/theorbo, opus 18 (Bologna, 1698).

Salmi concertati, 4 voices, 2 violins, violine/theorbo, opus 19 (Bologna, 1698).

Motetti, 1 voice, 2 violins, *bassetto*, opus 20 (Bologna, 1700).

Two sacred works in Gasparo Casati, *Terzo libro de sacri concenti*, Venice, 1640.

Modern Editions

Briscoe, James, ed. *Historical Anthology of Music by Women.* (Bloomington: Indiana University Press, 1987). Includes excerpts from *Messa prima* of opus 18.

Leonarda, Isabella. *Ave Regina coelorum* [opus 10]. Edited by Stewart Carter. Nine Centuries of Music by Women. New York: Broude Brothers, 1980.

——. *Selected Compositions*. Edited by Stewart Carter. Recent Researches in the Music of the Baroque Era, no. 59. Madison, WI: A-R Editions, 1988.

——. *Messa prima*. Edited by Barbara Garvey Jackson. Fayetteville, Arkansas: ClarNan Editions, 1981.

———. *Quam dulcis es* [opus 13]. Edited by Barbara Garvey Jackson. Fayetteville, Arkansas: ClarNan Editions, 1984.

———. *Sonata duodecima* [opus 16]. Edited by Barbara Garvey Jackson. Ottawa: Dovehouse, 1983.

Solo Motets from the Seventeenth Century. Vols. 4–5: *Novara I–II.* Edited by Anne Schnoebelen. New York: Garland, 1987–88.

Books and Articles

Baroffio, Emilia Dahnk. "La compositrice Isabella Leonarda." *Novarien* 13 (1988), pp. 75–92.

Bowers, Jane. "The Emergence of Women Composers in Italy, 1566–1700." In *Women Making Music: The Western Art Tradition, 1150–1950.* Edited by Jane Bowers and Judith Tick. Urbana and Chicago: University of Illinois Press, 1986, pp. 116–61.

Carter, Stewart. "The Music of Isabella Leonarda (1620–1704)." Ph.D. diss., Stanford University, 1982.

Choron, A., and F. Fayolle. *Dictionnaire historique des musiciens. . . .* 2 vols. 1817. Reprint, Hildesheim: Olms, 1970.

Cotta, Lazaro Agostino. *Museo novarese.* Milan, 1701, pp. 269–70.

Eitner, Robert, ed. *Biographisch-bibliographisches Quellen-Lexikon.* 10 vols. 1898–1904. Reprint, New York, n.d. S.v. "Leonarda, Isabella."

Enciclopedia della musica. Edited by Claudio Sartori. 4 vols. Milan: Ricordi, 1964. S.v. "Isabella Leonarda."

Fedeli, Vito. "Antichi musicisti novaresi." *Bollettino storico per la provincia di Novara* 18 (1924): 308–12.

Fétis, François Joseph. *Biographie universelle des musiciens et bibliographie générale de la musique.* 8 vols. Brussels, 1833–44. 2nd ed. Paris, 1860–65. (2 vols. supplement 1878–80). S.v. "Leonarda, Isabelle."

Frati, Lodovico. "Donne musiciste bolognesi." *Rivista musicale italiana* 37 (1930): 387–400.

Die Musik in Geschichte und Gegenwart. Edited by Friedrich Blume. 16 vols. Kassel: Bärenreiter, 1949–79. S.v. "Isabella Leonarda," by Franz Giegling.

The New Grove Dictionary of Music and Musicians. Edited by Stanley Sadie. 20 vols. London: Macmillan, 1980. S.v. "Isabella Leonarda," by Rosemary Roberts.

Schmidl, Carlo. *Dizionario universale dei musicisti.* 2 vols. Milan: Sonzogno, 1937. S.v. "Leonarda, Isabella."

Schnoebelen, Mary Nicole [Anne Schnoebelen]. "The Concerted Mass at San Petronio in Bologna, ca. 1660–1700: A Documentary and Analytical Study." Ph.D. diss., University of Illinois, 1966, pp. 342–64.

Weissweiler, Eva. *Komponisten aus 500 Jahren.* Frankfurt am Main: Fischer Taschenbuch Verlag, 1981.

Discography

Music for the Mass by Nun Composers. Schola Cantorum of the University of Arkansas, Fayetteville, directed by Jack Groh. Contains Leonarda's *Messa prima,* opus 18. Leonarda Productions, LPI 115.

Sources

Spes Mondane:

MOTETTI / A VOCE SOLA / *Parte con istromenti, e parte senza* / DI / ISABELLA LEONARDA MADRE / *nel Collegio di Santa Orsola in Novara* / *Opera Sesta* / *Consecrata* / ALL' ILL E REV.^mo SIG.^re LORENZO LEONARDI / *Canonico Archidiacono nella Cattedrale di Novara* / IN VENETIA 1676 / *Stampa del Gardano.* In score.

Surge Virgo:

CANTO / MOTETTI A QUATTRO VOCI / CON LE LITTANIE DELLA B.V. / DI / ISABELLA LEONARDA / *Madre nel Collegio di S. Orsola di Novara* / OPERA DECIMA / *Dedicata al merito dell'Illustris.*^ma, *ed Eccell.*^ma *Sig.*^ra / La Signora Donna / GIULIA RANGONI / *Marchesa Ariberta* / *In Milano, Nella stampa de fratelli Camagni alla Rosa* / *Con Licenza de' Superiori.* Five partbooks: C, A, T, B, org.

Editorial Procedures

1. Modern clefs are used instead of C-clefs for canto, alto, and tenor parts.

2. Barlines appear in the sources, but their frequency is somewhat less than half that which modern convention would dictate. In this edition, barlines have been added wherever necessary to conform to modern usage.

3. Meter signs used in the edition follow the original, except as noted below in Critical Notes.

4. Editorial accidentals supplied by the editor are enclosed in parentheses. Accidentals that do not conform to modern usage have been altered accordingly (i.e., a sharp sign used to cancel a flat has been altered to a natural sign), and accidentals redundant by modern convention have been eliminated entirely.

5. Coloration in the sources, used exclusively for hemiola patterns, is identified by dotted brackets in this edition.

6. Capitalization of words in the text has been altered to conform with modern practice.

Critical notes

Spes Mondane: M. 1, meter sign is C3. M. 32, org., note 3, through m. 35, note 1, tenor clef. M. 70, org., through m. 72, tenor clef. M. 76, org., note 1 though m. 80, tenor clef. M. 83, C, word on note 4 is &. M. 89, meter sign is C3/2. M. 107, org., note 2 is F. M. 120, meter sign is C3. M. 151, org., note 2 through

m. 156, note 1, tenor clef. M. 211, org., n. 1, through m. 213, tenor clef. M. 221, org., note 1, through m. 221, tenor clef.

Surge virgo: Mm. 1–2, C, text is *Surge fortunata.* M. 14, C has extra breve rest. M. 28, T, four breves rest missing. M. 36, A, first note is whole note. M. 74, C, *clypeo.* M. 82, A, one breve rest missing. M. 84, org., one breve rest missing. M. 120, T, first word is *que.* M. 154, A, last two notes are eighths. M. 170, C, T, second word is *ab,* M. 172, third word is *arma.* Mm. 184–87, org., A in

source. M. 188, org., through m. 190, note 4, soprano clef. M. 189, C, second complete word is *tú.* M. 191, C, second word is *tú.* M. 198, C, first word is *tú.* M. 198, org., notes 2 through 6, alto clef; note 6 through m. 22, note 1, tenor clef. M. 200, third word is *tú.* M. 202, C, third word is *tú.* M. 203, C, second complete word is *tú.* M. 205, C, idem. M. 206, C, third word is *tú.* M. 209, C, second complete word is *tú.* M. 211, C, second word is *tú;* org., note 6 is sixteenth. M. 212, C, third word is *tú.*

Spes mondane

Spes mondane inside sirenes e volate abite veloces vestros cantus mortales voraces, hoc coesse abite crudeles.

Dulcissima esse dicitis mundi delicias voluptates amabilis, et leta voce desiderabiles canitis honores.

Et tamen nihil magis amarum anime meae dulcedine terrena nihil mages detestabile voluptate nihil honore magis periculosum.

Vos ergo non curo, non volo, non amo, nam vestri amores, nam vestri honores, sunt diri, sunt vani, sunt semper insani. Sine vobis, inside sirenes, tuta leta in Domino sto.

May it be the hope of the world that your swift sirens fly away with your ravenous cries, these cruel cries—Oh, hope of the world . . .

You say you are the sweetest delights in the world, lovable pleasures, and with joyous voice settle down like a plague and sing of your charms.

Yet there is nothing more bitter, nothing more loathsome on the sweet earth than the pleasure you offer, nothing more dangerous than your charm.

So I care not for you. I do not want you, I do not love you. For your charms, your offers of love, are awful, are empty, and are always mad. Without you, sirens, I stand safely and joyfully by the Lord.

Surge virgo

Surge virgo ad arma
Surge fortunata ad certamen.
En Jesus capiti candoris galeam
Porrigit Virginum invicta dux
Constantem animan Maria clipeo
Virtutis instruit triumphat lux.

Pugna virgo ne dubites
Assume arma pia
Sub Virgine Maria.

Arma dulcissima
Maria dat
Quae fortis anima
Sunt vera pax.

Iam legitime certando
Saequaere collige palmas
Fortis sicut leo
Decorate victoris.
(Surge da capo si placet)

Inter lilia Mariae
Inter virgines victrices
Rosa splendens ista dies
Novum lilium novus flos.

Cesset pugna.

Iam ad armis fortunata
Ad triumphos est vocata.

Arise happily, oh Virgin,
arise to arms. Arise happily to the struggle.
Lo, Jesus, wearing a dazzling helmet,
presents the invincible leader of the Virgins,
Mary, shield of the steadfast soul.
Virtue prepares, light triumphs.

Fight, Virgin, do not hesitate.
Take up arms piously under the Virgin Mary.

Mary presents the sweetest armaments.
Such strong souls are true peace.

Now by fighting fairly, give chase,
bring together the palms [of victory].
Strong like the lion, adorn yourself in victory.

Among the lilies, among the victorious virgins,
Mary, let that day shine forth like a rose,
a new lily, a new flower.

Let the battle cease.

Now made prosperous by force of arms,
be called to triumph.

Cesset pugna.

Clarissima victoria
Quae tu coronas te est felix caeli gloria
Quae facit choros virginum
Laetantes inter se.
(Surge da capo)

Let the battle cease.

The brilliant victory with which you crown yourself
is the fruitful glory of heaven,
which has made the chorus of virgins
joyous together.

Translated by James Callahan.

Spes mondane (Op. 6, 1676)

Isabella Leonarda
Stewart Carter, editor

ni - hil__ ho - no - re__ ma -

gis__ pe - ri - cu - lo - - - - -

rum.

sem - per in - sa - - ni ___ sunt di - ri sunt

va - ni sunt sem - pre in - sa - - - -

- - - - - - - - - - - -

ni, Si - ne ___

Surge virgo (op. 10, 1684)

Isabella Leonarda
Stewart Carter, editor

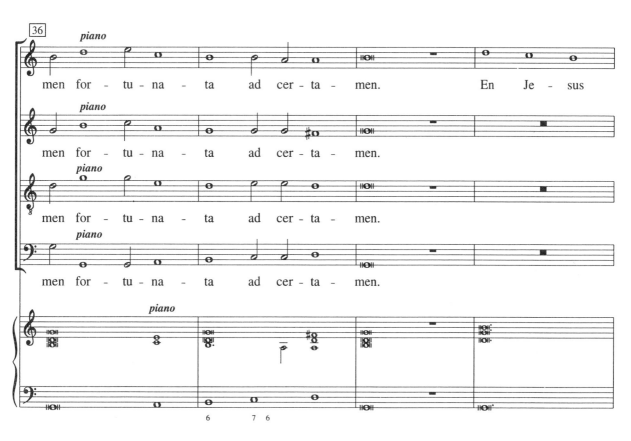

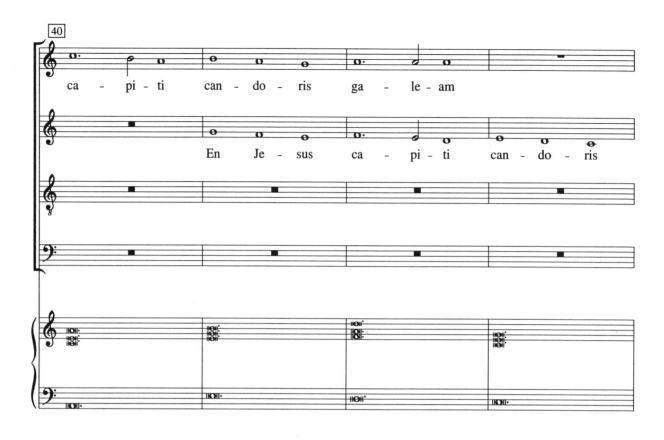

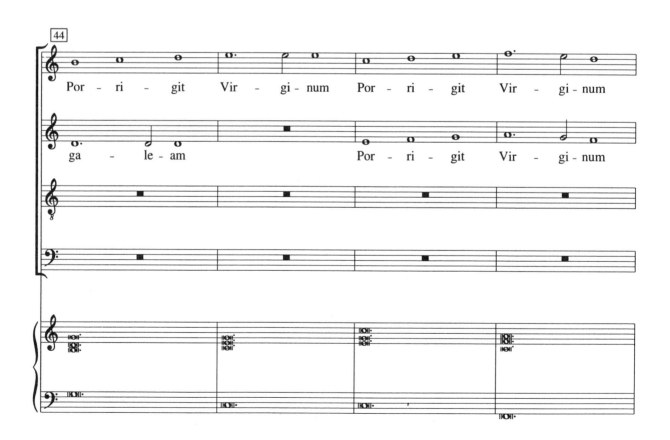

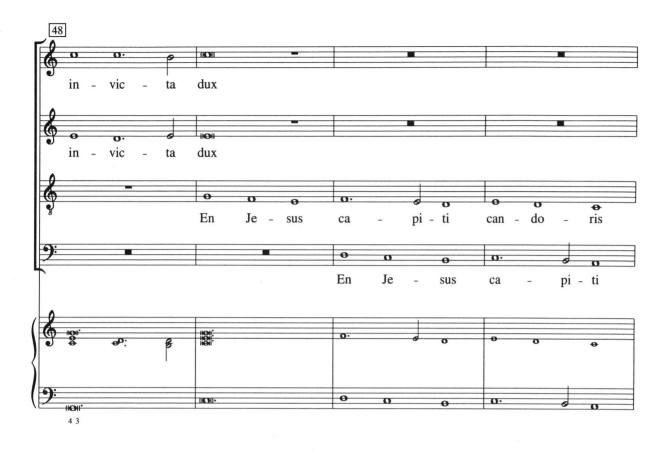

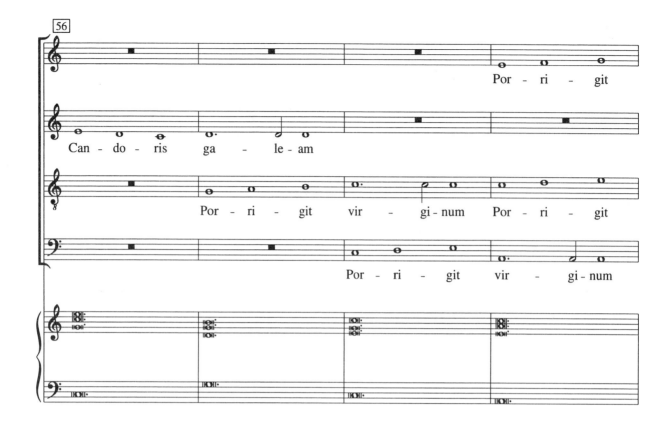

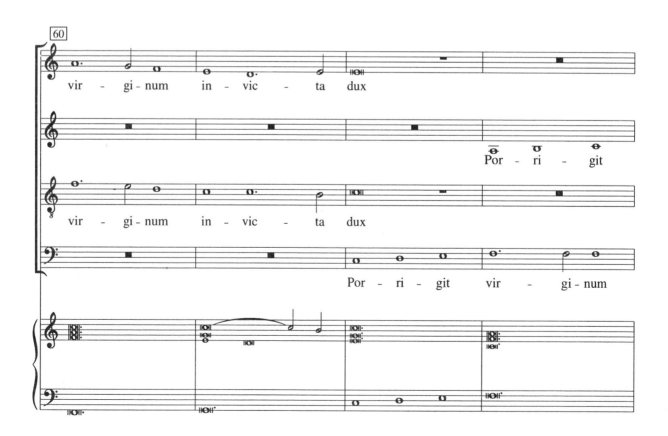

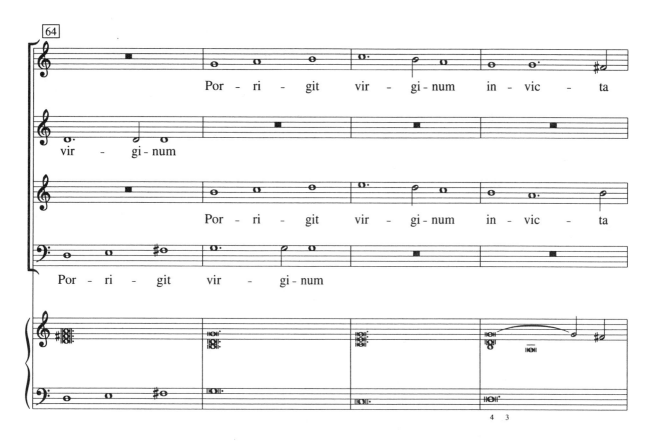

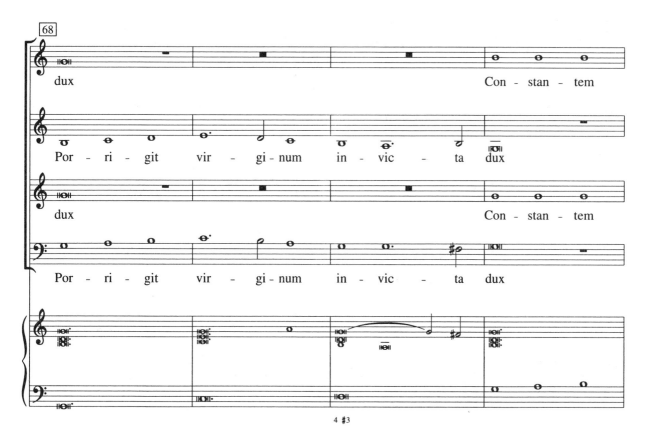

a - ni - man Ma - ri - a cli - pe - o vir - tu - tis

a - ni - man Ma - ri - a cli - pe - o vir - tu - tis

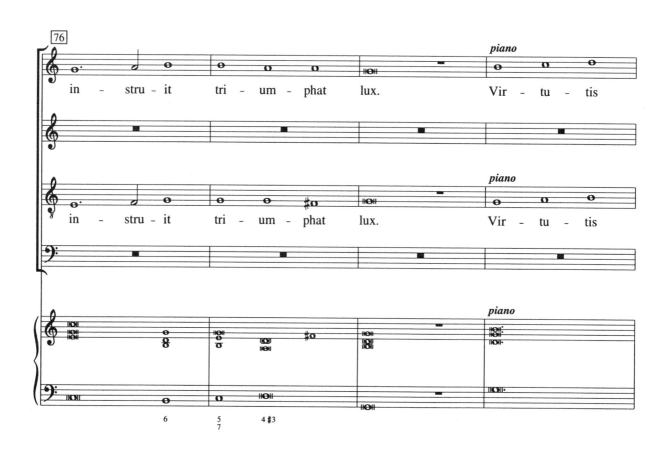

in - stru - it tri - um - phat lux. Vir - tu - tis

in - stru - it tri - um - phat lux. Vir - tu - tis

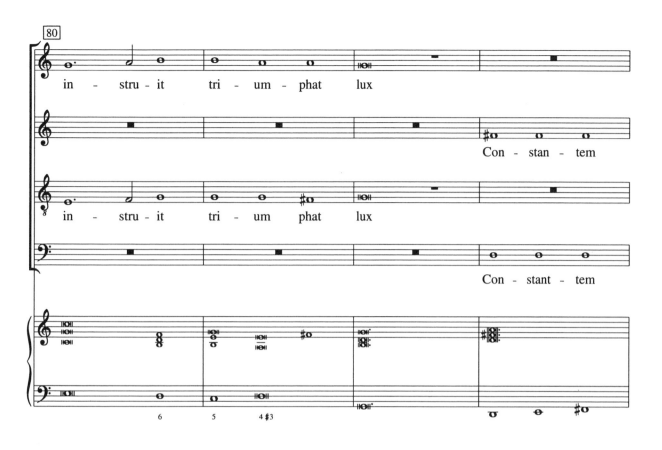

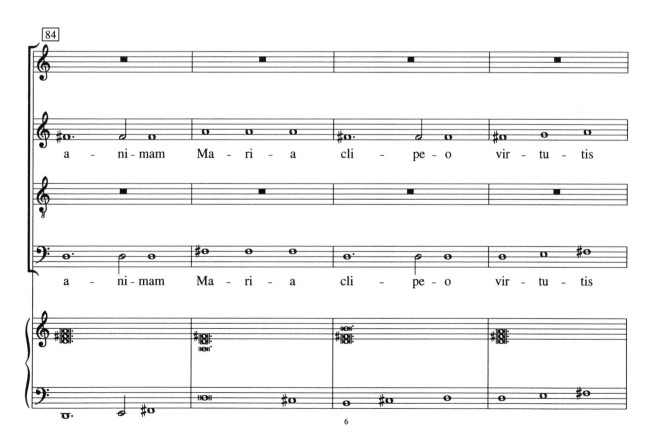

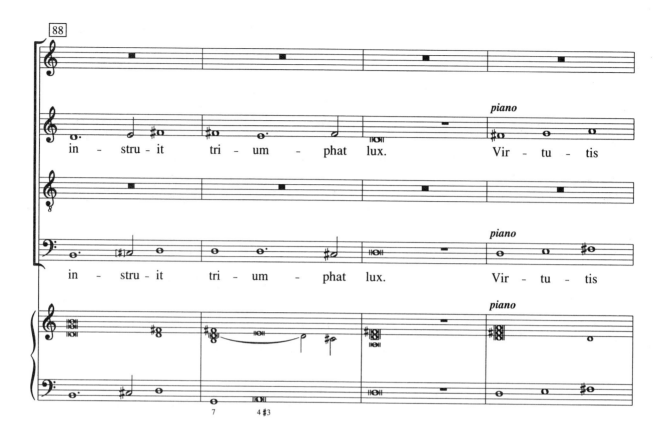

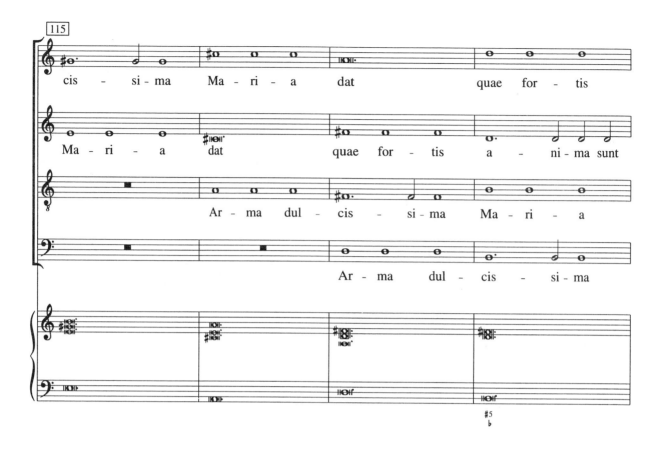

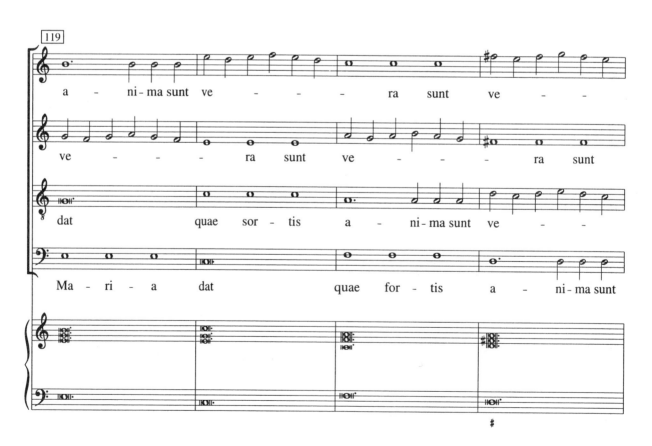

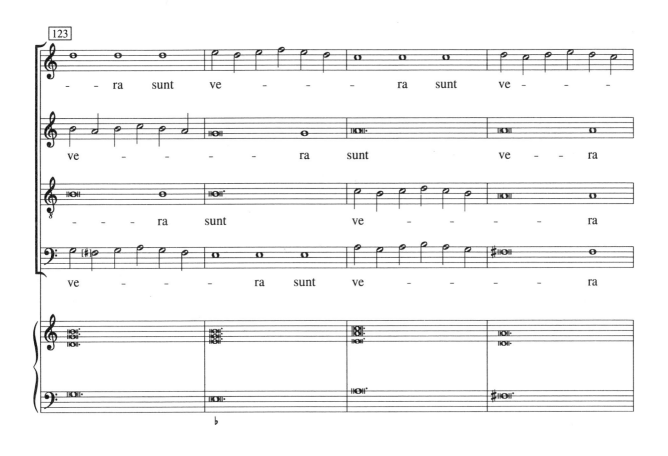

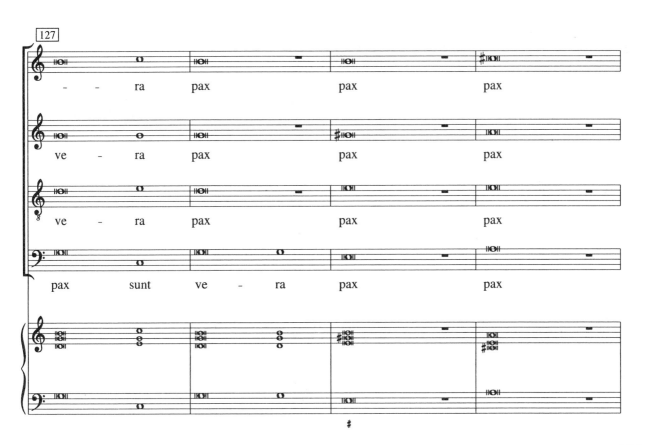

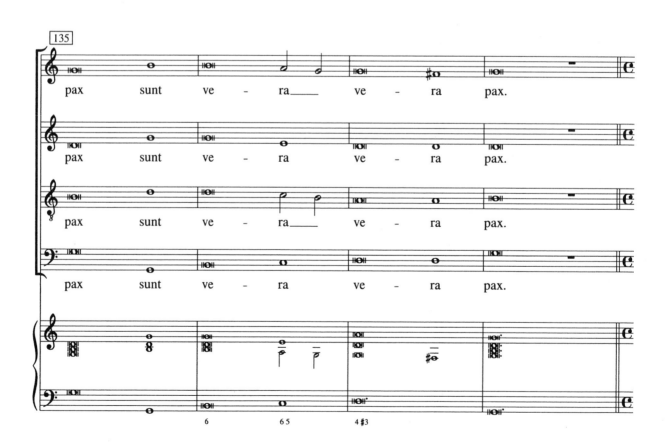

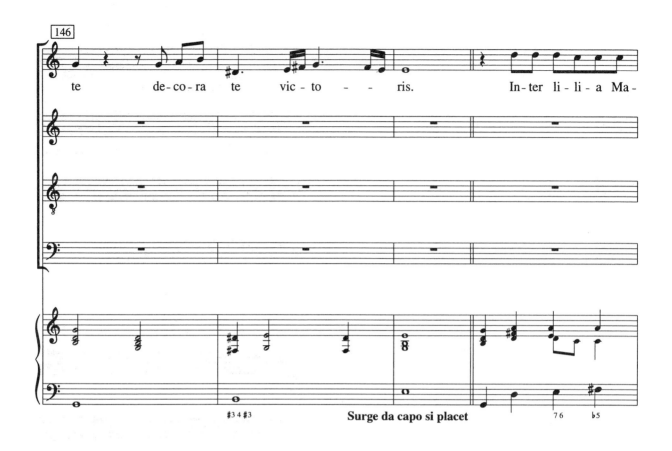

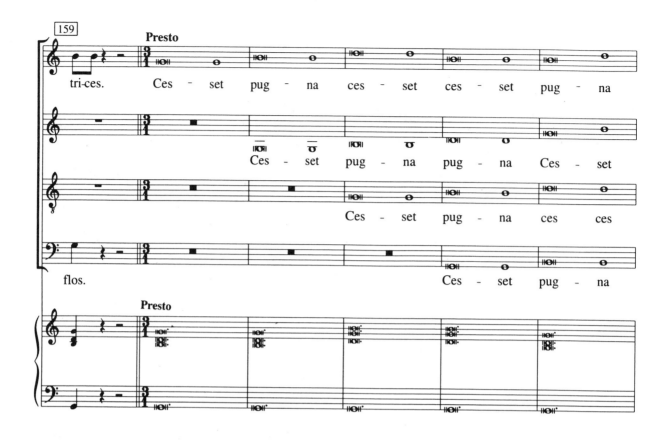

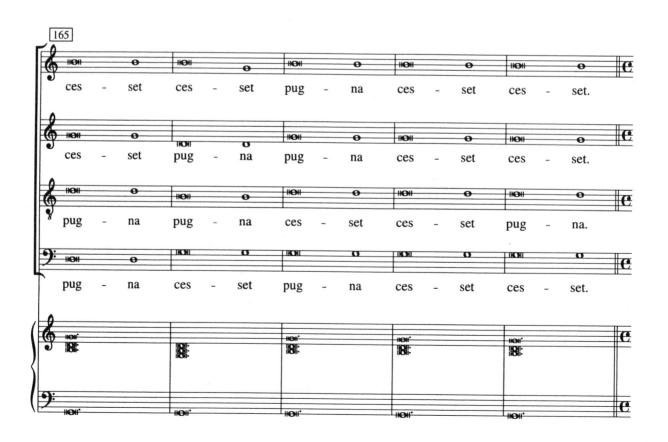

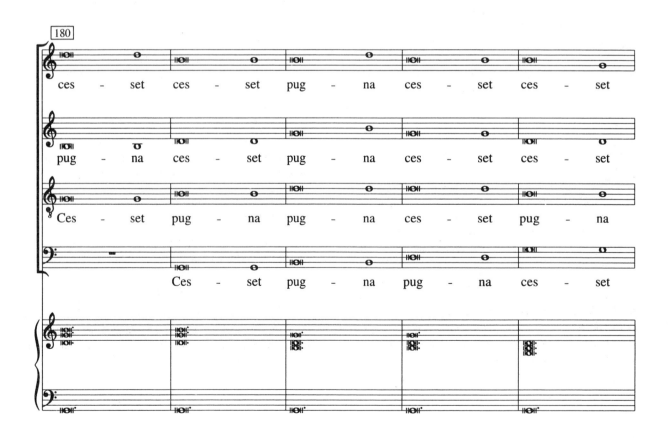

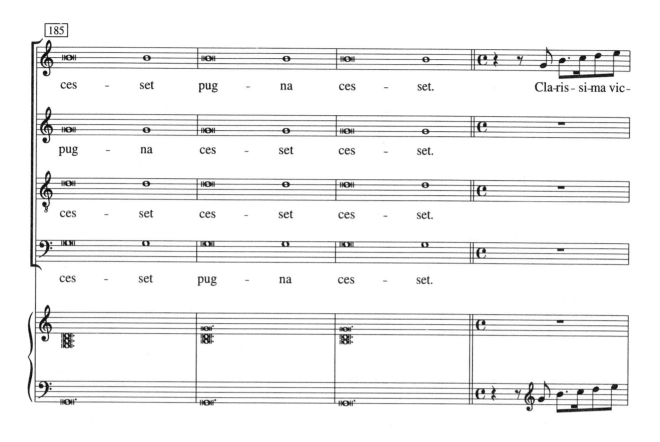

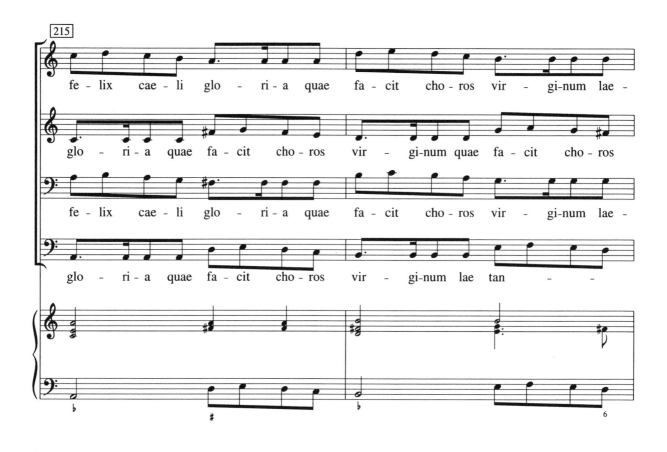

Mary Harvey, the Lady Dering

(1629–1704)

LISA A. URKEVICH

Mary Harvey, the Lady Dering, is the first woman in English history to have had music published under her own name. Her three extant songs, all with lyrics by her husband Edward Dering, the Parliamentary politician, were printed in 1655 in the second book of Henry Lawes's *Ayres and Dialogues*. Harvey studied with Lawes and was apparently one of his most gifted pupils. Hers are the only compositions in the songbook other than his own. Moreover, Lawes dedicates the entire volume to Harvey with the following:

To the Honorable, the Lady Dering,
Wife to Sir Edward Dering of Surenden Dering, Baronet
Madam,

I have considered, but could not find it lay in my power to offer this book to any but your Ladyship. Not only in regard of that honor and esteem you have for music, but because those songs which fill this book have received much luster by your excellent performance of them; and (which I confess I rejoice to speak of) some which I esteem the best of these ayres, were of your own composition, after your noble husband was pleased to give the words. For (although your Ladyship resolved to keep it private) I beg leave to declare, for my own honor, that you are not only excellent for the time you spent in the practice of what I set, but are yourself so good a composer, that few of any sex have arrived to such perfection. So as this book (at least a part of it) is not dedicated, but only brought home to your Ladyship. And here I would say (could I do it without sadness) how precious to my thoughts is the memory of your excellent mother (that great example of prudence and charity) whose pious meditations were often advanced by hearing your voice. I wish all prosperity to your Ladyship, and to him who like yourself is made up of harmony, to say nothing of the rest of his high accomplishments of wisdom and learning. May you both live long happy in each other's, when I am become ashes, who while I am in this world shall be ever found, Madam, Your Ladyship's humble admirer and faithful servant,

Henry Lawes.

Mary Harvey, Henry Lawes, Edward Dering, and most of the contributors of text to the songbook were connected to the well-known literary circle spirited by the English poet Katherine Philips (1631–64), better known as "the Matchless Orinda."[1] Comprising Cavalier writers and musicians, Philips's group was largely concerned with preserving the cultural ideals of the Caroline court that had crumbled under the Civil Wars and Cromwell's Commonwealth (1649–1660). Harvey, a childhood friend of Philips's, was no doubt present at the beginnings of the coterie and probably introduced her husband and Lawes to the poet. Henry Lawes (1596–1662), who had been a favorite court musician of Charles I, was often patronized by such staunch Royalists as the Derings and their associates. The composer grew close to the circle and apparently wanted to honor his accomplished student and other talented friends in print; the second book of *Ayres and Dialogues* is this tribute.[2]

Mary Harvey was born in 1629 into a prestigious middle-class family with decided Royalist sympathies.[3] She was the daughter of Elizabeth Kynnersley[4] and Daniel Harvey (of Folkstone, Kent, and Combe in Surrey), a chief importer of spices and silks with the Levant and East India Company. Mary Harvey's uncle, William Harvey (1578–1657), was the internationally renowned scientist recognized as the first to demonstrate the function of the heart and the complete circulation of blood. The composer had three siblings, two of whom were connected to Philips's coterie. Her brother Daniel, the ambassador to Constantinople, married Elizabeth Montagu whose aunt through marriage was Philips's closest friend, Mary Aubrey. Harvey had a younger sister, Sarah, and an elder sister, Elizabeth, who married Heneage Finch, the first earl of Nottingham and nephew of Francis Finch, the "Palaemon" of Philips's poems and a contributor to Lawes's 1655 publication.

Little is known about Mary Harvey's life. Around 1640, she attended a school in Hackney run by Mrs. Salmon, "a famous schoolmistriss, Presbyterian." Mrs. Salmon's was one of several boarding schools that emerged in the London sub-urbs during the first half of the seventeenth century for daughters of the rising middle class. There, Harvey likely studied modern languages, certainly music, and other "ac-complishments" necessary for young women. Her earliest friends at Mrs. Salmon's included Philips herself (*née* Kather-ine Fowler), who was also a prosperous city merchant's daughter, and Mary Aubrey, the cousin of the antiquary John Aubrey and the "Rosania" of Philips's writings.[5]

At the age of sixteen, it seems that Harvey clandestinely married her father's first cousin, William Hauke. According to Sir Roger Twysden, a friend of Edward Dering:

> [She] was indeede contracted if not married to one William Hauke, her cousin and her father's servant, one who had been his apprentice, but was now free, he in a morning going through Colmans Streete with her got her very young into a church and did with a ring marry her about 1645, and caused it to be registered in the book of marryages of the parish: she was in this to bee excused because hee assured her he had her father's consent, which he never had. . . . after a legal hearing in the Ecclesiastical Courts . . . she was by sentence cleared, and—after to be marryed to Sir Edward Dering . . . Her friends and she told him all the fact and showed him her sentence for being free under the seal of the Court, and they have lived very lovingly ever since. (She [was] a good wife and means of advancing the family).[6]

On April 5, 1648, Harvey married the second baronet, Edward Dering (1625–1684), who later became better known as the "noble Silvander" of Philips's writings.[7] Within this marriage, Harvey gave birth to seventeen chil-dren, all but six of whom died before the age of four. Yet, from every account, Harvey spent her years happily among a caring family. In 1684, the year of her husband's death, sur-rounded by friends, children, and grandchildren at the cele-bration of their thirty-sixth wedding anniversary, Edward Dering toasted, "all I shall say upon this occasion is, that after 36 years I believe we are not weary of one another, nor our children weary of us."[8]

It is not known how many works Harvey actually com-posed. All that survive are the three songs—"When first I saw fair Doris' eyes," "And is this all? What one poor kiss?" and "In vain, faire Cloris, you design"—which appear to-gether on pages twenty-four and twenty-five of Lawes's 1655 songbook. One of the pieces, "In vain, faire Cloris, you design," became considerably popular, as is evidenced by its inclusion in two later publications of John Playford: *Select Ayres and Dialogues,* 1659, and *The Treasury of Music,* 1669.[9]

Harvey's songs are in the simple lyric style frequently found in the home music making of the day. Like her con-temporaries in the genre, she approaches her compositions as devices for enhancing lyrics. In order for the music to suit the text, Harvey employs word painting, but more impor-tantly, she focuses on the rhythmic speech patterns of the verses—verses she must have heard recited by the poets of Philips's circle—and then reproduces the patterns musically. This follows the practice of her teacher, Lawes, who in the introduction of his second book of *Ayres* states, "the way of composition I chiefly profess (which is to shape notes to the words and sense) is not hit by too many." As Lawes suggests in his dedication to Harvey, she was one of the few who "hit." Her attention to the text, coupled with her melodic gift, produce both well-crafted and charming compositions. Although slight, Mary Harvey's songs are some of the best of their kind, and neither they nor the pioneer composer should be forgotten.

Notes

1. For further information on Katherine Philips and the mem-bers of her coterie, see Philip Souers, *The Matchless Orinda* (Cam-bridge: Harvard University Press, 1931).

2. A survey of Lawes can be found in Willa McClung Evans, *Henry Lawes: Musician and Friend of Poets* (London: Oxford Univer-sity Press, 1941).

3. More detailed biographical information on Harvey and her family is disclosed in Jessica Kerr's exemplary article, "Mary Har-vey—The Lady Dering," *Music and Letters* 25 (1944): 23–33. For personal information on the Harvey family see William Harvey, *The Diary of William Harvey,* ed. Jean Hamburger, trans. Barbara Wright (New Brunswick: Rutgers University Press, 1992).

4. As Lawes remarks in the introduction to his *Ayres,* Harvey's mother died the year the songbook was published.

5. John Aubrey, "Katherine Philips," in *Brief Lives,* ed. Richard Barber (New Jersey: Barnes and Noble, 1982), p. 248.

6. Roger Twysden, [Notebook] Add. MS 34, 164, f.95b, British Library, London: quoted in Wilmot Herringham, "The Life and Times of Dr. William Harvey," *Annals of Medical History* 4 (1932): 586.

7. Harvey probably began her music lessons shortly after her marriage. As noted in Edward F. Rimbault, "Sir Edward Dering's Household Book, A.D. 1648–52," *Notes and Queries* (January 12, 1850): 161–62, Dering's household book dated June 1, 1949, reads: "Paid Mr Lawes, a month's teaching of my wife 11 [pounds] 10s [shillings]." Women usually relinquished their musical endeav-ors after they became wives. The coinciding of Harvey's serious musical study with her marriage attests to the open thinking of both Harvey and her husband.

8. Maurice F. Bond, ed., *The Diaries and Papers of Sir Edward Dering Second Baronet* (London: House of Lords Record Office, 1976), pp. 3, 28, and accompanying genealogical table prepared by Philip Blake.

9. This song is recorded on *Non Tacete! (I'll Not Be Silent!),* Ars Femina Ensemble, Nannerl Recordings, 1991. A modern edition of the piece is included in Ian Spink, ed., *English Songs, 1625–1660,* vol. 33, *Musica Britannica* (London: Stainer and Bell, 1971), p. 176.

Bibliography

Aubrey, John. "Katherine Philips." In *Brief Lives,* edited by Richard Barber. New Jersey: Barnes and Noble, 1982.

Bond, Maurice F., ed. *The Diaries and Papers of Sir Edward Dering Second Baronet.* London: House of Lords Record Office, 1976.

Evans, Willa McClung. *Henry Lawes: Musician and Friend of Poets.* London: Oxford University Press, 1941.

Harvey, William. *The Diary of William Harvey.* Edited by Jean Hamburger. Translated by Barbara Wright. New Brunswick: Rutgers University Press, 1992.

Kerr, Jessica M. "Mary Harvey—The Lady Dering." *Music and Letters* 25 (1944): 23–33.

Rimbault, Edward F. "Sir Edward Dering's Household Book, A.D. 1648–52." *Notes and Queries* (January 12, 1850): 161–62.

Souers, Philip. *The Matchless Orinda.* Cambridge: Harvard University Press, 1931.

Twysden, Roger. [Notebook] Add. MS 34, 164, British Library, London; quoted in Wilmot Herringham, "The Life and Times of Dr. William Harvey." *Annals of Medical History* 4 (1932): 575–89.

Compositions

Lawes, Henry. *Second Book of Ayres and Dialogues for One, Two, and Three Voyces.* Vol. 2. London: Printed by Thomas Harper for John Playford, 1655.

Playford, John. *Select Ayres and Dialogues for One, Two and Three Voyces to the Theorbo-Lute or Basse-viol.* London: Printed by William Godbid for John Playford, 1659.

———. *The Treasury of Music.* London: Printed by William Godbid for John Playford, l669.

Spink, Ian, ed. *English Songs, 1625–1660.* Vol. 33, *Musica Britannica.* London: Stainer and Bell, 1971.

Discography

"In vain, faire Cloris," in *Non Tacete! (I'll Not Be Silent!).* Ars Femina Ensemble. Nannerl Recordings, 1991.

When First I Saw Fair Doris' Eyes

Mary Harvey, *The Lady Dering*
Lisa Urkevich, editor

3. Since which allowed, on thy free lip
   To story out my hopes and love
   Immortal grown, I held aloft
   The mansion of dethroned Love

4. But when ruled by my kinder stars
   Thy nameless tresures crown my pain,
   Love and his empty joys despised,
   I Shepherd turned on earth again.

𝄋 Gods, take your own, said I, vain alters now,
   I choose a happy fate with her below.

And is this all? What one poor kiss?

Mary Harvey, *The Lady Dering*
Lisa Urkevich, editor

Antonia Bembo

(ca. 1643–ca. 1715)

CLAIRE A. FONTIJN

Antonia Bembo was the only child of Giacomo Padoani, a medical doctor, and Diana Paresco. Thanks to an arrangement made by her father, she studied music in the 1650s with the renowned composer Francesco Cavalli. Although the record of her birthdate has not yet been located, documents concerning her father and her marriage in 1659 to Lorenzo Bembo, a Venetian nobleman, place it around 1643 in Venice. She herself was not noble by birth, and therefore her marriage was somewhat unusual. During the 1660s, Lorenzo and Antonia had three children, a daughter and two sons. Sometime before 1676, Antonia Bembo left her family to go to France. Prior to her departure, she deposited her valuables and her daughter, Diana, at the convent of San Bernardo of Murano for safekeeping. The sons remained with their father in Venice.

Documents preserved in the San Bernardo archive reveal part of Antonia Bembo's intriguing story. Two of these are letters that she wrote from Paris in 1682 concerning the regulation of her affairs. Since by then Diana had been living at the convent for at least six years, a considerable debt had incurred, which Antonia's initial arrangement no longer covered. Lorenzo was either unwilling or unable to pay. By 1685, the Council of Ten, the noble's ruling body, ordered an appraisal of Antonia's valuables, mostly jewels, in order to sell enough to settle accounts with the convent.[1]

The San Bernardo archive also preserves a journal written by Maria Giordana Gozzi, a friend of Bembo's at the convent, who gave the Petite Union Chrétienne des Dames de Saint Chaumont on the rue de la Lune as Bembo's Parisian address. This information is confirmed by the dedication to *Produzioni Armoniche,* in which Bembo wrote that she composed her music in the refuge of a religious community at Notre Dame de Bonne Nouvelle. The dedicatee of this volume was King Louis XIV, whom she thanked for a pension that enabled her to live there. Situated in the parish of Notre Dame de Bonne Nouvelle, the community lodged a number of *dames pensionnaires.*

Produzioni Armoniche, designated here as Book 1, is a compilation of forty-one arias, cantatas, motets, and a serenata (*PA 1–41*), most of which are scored for soprano and *basso continuo.* Bembo stated in her dedication that she was a singer; it is likely that she performed these pieces and wrote many of their texts. She dedicated to the king four more volumes of musical manuscripts in which she worked with larger media. Book 3 contains two motets: a *Te Deum* set as a *grand motet* for five voices and orchestra and a three-voice setting of Psalm 19, with a three-part instrumental ensemble. This instrumental trio, two treble instruments with *basso continuo,* was standard during the period, and Bembo employed this combination to some extent in all of her works. Books 4 and 5 comprise the opera of 1707, *Ercole Amante,* her largest and only dated work. Book 6 sets the seven penitential psalms paraphrased by Élisabeth Sophie Chéron (1648–1711) in her *Essay de Pseaumes* of 1694. These call for various solo voices or vocal ensembles accompanied throughout by the instrumental trio.

Bembo's compositions reveal an explicit interest in the lives and work of women. She dedicated Book 2 to Louis XIV's granddaughter-in-law, Marie-Adélaïde of Savoy, Duchess of Burgundy (1685–1712), on the occasion of the birth of the Duke of Brittany in 1704. The volume consists of two works: the first, a *Te Deum* for three voices and instrumental trio; the second, a serenata for five voices and instrumental trio that extols the boy and his mother. Earlier, in Book 1, Bembo had honored the duchess with a cantata, an epithalamium, and a serenata for her wedding in 1697. Three poems in Book 1 are attributed to Aurelia Fedeli, the pen name of Brigida Fedeli (ca.1615–1704), an Italian actress and writer who also lived in the parish of Notre Dame de Bonne Nouvelle; one of these (*PA 18*) is narrated by a female voice. Three *cantate spirituali* (*PA 5–7*) dramatize from an unmistakably female point of view the lives of the Virgin Mary and of Saint Regina. Book 6 offers one of the few extant musical settings of Elisabeth Sophie Chéron's writing.

The selections provided in this edition are representative of the chamber music of *Produzioni Armoniche.* They include vocal music in all languages in which Bembo composed and provide examples of her sacred and secular compositions: an Italian aria, a Latin motet, and a French air. Titles have been assigned according to the first lines of text. Each piece treats the theme of love from a different perpective: the mutual love of a couple (*PA 20*), the lover's admiration of his beloved (*PA 39*), and unrequited love (*PA 41*).

PA 20, a *da capo* aria in Italian for two sopranos and *basso continuo,* is titled *Affettuoso* in the compilation. Its poem celebrates the joys of a couple in love. The rhyme scheme symbolizes the reciprocal nature of their affection: the first stanza has two mirroring couplets (in *rima baciata*), while the anagram *e me teco, e te meco* forms the centerpiece of the second stanza's two reflecting tercets. In the final line, *tenace* rhymes with *pace,* thus signalling the return to the beginning.

The opening of the piece features a duet between the sopranos in unisons, thirds, or sixths, while the bass provides an accompaniment of fluid line (mm. 1–5, 17–19) and gentle arpeggiated chords (mm. 5–16). Beginning with the first soprano in m. 19, an imitative trio texture dominates until the close of the A section. Just before the double bar at m. 34, the bass leaps downward from d to D, a typical figure that recurs in much of Bembo's music.

Section B continues the imitative interplay among the three parts, in which the bass takes up the motive introduced by the sopranos (mm. 35–37), provides harmony for their duet (mm. 37–39), and initiates a new motive that the voices pick up (mm. 39–41). On the text *nodo d'amor tenace,* the imitation is especially exciting: the tied notes (*Augenmusik,* in mm. 44–47, 56–58) and lengthened, "tenacious" notes symbolize the tying of the firm knot of love. Indeed, word painting abounds in Bembo's compositions, as it does for much *seicento* music. An earlier instance occurred in Section A, where on the words *in pari ardore* the two voices confirm their equal desire with identical rhythms and felicitous intervals of thirds or sixths (mm. 6–7, 12). Section B builds to a powerful climax with the superimposition and overlapping of *nodo d'amor* and *tenace* in an increasingly chromatic texture, concluding with a cadence in the relative minor key.

The text of *PA 39* is derived from the *Song of Solomon* (4: 7–8, 11) which, though a sacred text, is probably the most worldly of biblical books; it expresses a lover's admiration of a woman's beauty, celebrating her purity and the comeliness of her lips and tongue. Two passages in the text required emendation and have been corrected: in line 2, the music manuscript gave *es,* but a *t* is required for the third-person singular. Line 3 contained the incomprehensible words *non a mea*—these probably should read *sponsa mea,* the appellation of the beloved.

Certain ambiguities in the manuscript raise questions concerning the correct manner of execution. The bass in m. 23 presents a tag that leads from g to f♯ (beats 3–4) to an implied e. In performance, one can either repeat the entire piece, go back to the editorial sign at m. 21 (*a petite reprise*), or do both. In any case, the motet ends on the fermata.

On the words *Tota pulcra es,* the soprano outlines an inverted E-minor triad with the poignant intervals of a falling fourth and a rising minor sixth, then proceeds stepwise down to d♯². The bass line supports the voice with a steady stream of eighth notes throughout the piece, a walking ostinato from which it occasionally departs in order to imitate the voice. One such instance occurs on the third beat of m. 3, where the bass echoes the soprano's first statement of the word *amica* (m. 2) at the octave, e-d-c-B.

After the somewhat ponderous nature of the soprano's *amica mea* (mm. 3–5), the melodic motion accelerates (mm. 5–9). *Et macula non est in te* is rapid and straightforward. Anapestic rhythms on *veni, veni de Libano* occasion imitation in the bass—together, the two parts depict the textual implication of motion. With g-a-b-a-g in m. 8 (beats 1–2), the bass mimics the rising and falling of the soprano in mm. 6–7. Bembo wrote a stepwise descending scale for the soprano in mm. 13–15, 17–18, and 21–23, as if to illustrate the flow of honey and milk under the tongue that is suggested by the phrase *mele et lac sub lingua tua.*

PA 41, "Air," is the last piece of *Produzioni Armoniche* and the only one with a French text. Based on a poem of two quatrains, its scansion is typically Gallic: one alexandrine followed by seven hemistichs. The first stanza rhymes *abba;* the second uses the same rhymes in the pattern *abab.* The subsequent repetition of the first quatrain is inherent in the poem: *love inspires us often to* repeat: / 'Ah, *absence is a cruel martyr'* [emphasis mine].

The manuscript bears the marking *L'on se plaint* after its final double bar; this indicates a return not to the beginning but to the second verse. The poem is thus set in strophic rondo form: A ‖: BAA′:‖. The last three-measure phrase, *est un cruel martire,* is marked *Doucement* to indicate that it should be a softer repetition of the nearly identical music in mm. 22–24, a common practice in France at the time. The final measure notates the return to Section B on a descent from A to F; when one goes back to m. 8, however, the bass note is not the expected E but rather an e. The most expedient solution is to fill in the descending fifth by changing the half note e in m. 8 to an E, and then to continue as written thereafter.

In addition to the dynamic indication in m. 25 discussed above, several other French characteristics are present in this air. In mm. 6–7, the soprano descends stepwise from c² to e¹ in a decorated line, approaching the cadence with an implied trill on the f♯¹ in m. 6. The f♯¹–b¹-g♯¹ passage of the preceding phrase (m. 5) consists of a rising fourth over V of V (B major in first inversion) falling to the major third of the dominant (E major)—the same harmonic procedure occurs in other French airs, notably one by a certain "Mademoiselle H.," that was published in Paris in 1713.[2]

The variety of styles in Bembo's music shows the confrontation of her Venetian musical mind with the French soundscape in which she was immersed; her oeuvre compares favorably with that of her contemporaries in Italy and France. *PA 20* resembles the chamber duets of Steffani, also a native of the Veneto. *PA 39* belongs alongside works in this genre by Lully and Charpentier. *PA 41* bears some similarity to the popular airs that were sung in Paris at the turn of the century. Bembo's larger motet settings sound somewhat akin to those of Michel Lalande. Her opera testifies to her training with Cavalli, but is closer in style to compositions by Giovanni Legrenzi, Antonio Sartorio, André Campra, and Lully. The exquisite pieces included here give a taste of the talent that would later blossom in Bembo's large-scale works.

Notes

1. The first chapter of my dissertation treats these biographical matters in detail; see "Antonia Bembo: *Les goûts reunis,* Royal Patronage, and the Role of the Woman Composer during the Reign of Louis XIV," (Ph.D. diss., Duke University, 1994), pp. 8–43. On Bembo's valuables in particular, see pp. 14–20 and 409–26.

2. For more about Mademoiselle H's *air,* see my dissertation, pp. 174, 278–80, and 562.

Works List

Extant works

All manuscripts in unica are at the Bibliothèque Nationale, Paris, France.

Shelf number Rés.Vm^{1}117: "Produzioni Armoniche Della Dama Bembo Nobile Veneta Consacrate al Nome Immortale Di Luigi XIIII Il Grande Rè di Francia, e di Navarra" [Book 1, ca.1697–1701]

Shelf number Rés.Vm^{1}112–113: "Te deum per render gratie a Sua Divina Maesta del Glorioso Parto di Vostra Altezza Reale che a dato al mondo un Principe cosi aggradito a tutto l'Universo et in particulare à Sua Maesta. Con l'aggionta d'un picciolo divertimento, per la Nascita del medesimo Principe. Musica di Antonia Bembo N.^{ble} V.^{ta}" [Book 2, ca. 1704]

Shelf number Rés.Vm^{1}114–115: "Te deum per Impetrar da Sua Divina Maesta la conservatione d'un Monarcha cosi Grande come Luigi quattordice, è tutta la Sua Familia Reale. accompagnato d'un Exaudiat. Compositione di Antonia Bembo N.^{ble} V.^{ta}" [Book 3, ca.1707]

Shelf number Rés.Vm^{4}9–10: "L'Ercole Amante Tragedia Nuovamente Posta in Musica, da Domina Antonia Bembo No.^{le} Ve.^{ta} E Consacrata alla Majesta Christi.^{ma} Di Luigi quarto Decimo L'anno 1707" [Books 4 and 5, 1707]

Shelf number Rés.Vm^{1}116: "Les sept Pseaumes, de David, Mis en air. Par Mme Bembo, N.^{ble} Ve.^{ne} Dédiez a sa Majesté Tres Chrêtienne Louis Quatorze" [Book 6, after 1707]

Modern edition

"In amor ci vuol ardir," PA 17 from *Produzioni Armoniche* on a text by Aurelia Fedeli. In *Italian Arias of the Baroque and Classical Eras,* John Glenn Paton, ed. Van Nuys, CA: Alfred, 1994, pp. 55–59.

Bibliography

Fontijn, Claire A. "Antonia Bembo: *Les goûts réunis,* Royal Patronage, and the Role of the Woman Composer during the Reign of Louis XIV." Ph.D. diss., Duke University, 1994.

——— and Marinella Laini. "Bembo, Antonia." In *The New Grove Dictionary of Women Composers,* edited by Julie Anne Sadie and Rhian Samuel. London and New York: W. W. Norton, 1994.

Laini, Marinella. "Bembo, Antonia." In *The New Grove Dictionary of Opera,* edited by Stanley Sadie. London: Macmillan, 1992.

———."Le 'Produzioni Armoniche' di Antonia Bembo." Ph.D. diss., University of Pavia, 1987.

Rokseth, Yvonne. "Antonia Bembo, Composer to Louis XIV." *Musical Quarterly,* 23 (1937): 147–69.

Editorial Procedures

In the text, line one, *Faccian* appears as an alternate spelling for *facciam* in the manuscript.

I am grateful to Lorenzo Muti of Duke University for assistance with this translation. The translation of the *Song of Solomon* 4:7–8, 11 is from the King James version of the Holy Bible (London: Samuel Bagster & Sons; New York: Harper & Brothers Publishers, n.d.), p. 725. The emendations to the Latin verse are explained in my article. The text for *Ha, que l'absence est un cruel martire* includes modern accents that are not in the manuscript; however, the original old French spellings have been retained. I would like to thank Penka Kouneva for her assistance with the transcription of the music and Zvi Meniker for his basso continuo realizations.

Amor mio, "Affettuoso," *PA 20* (pp. 170–78)

Amor mio, facciam la pace,	My love, let us make peace,
Dammi il tuo, prendi il mio core,	Give me your heart, take mine,
Et accesi in pari ardore;	And, ignited with equal fire,
Adoriam d'amor la face.	Let us adore the torch of love.
Vada lungi il sospetto,	Do away with suspicion,
Pera la gelosia,	Let jealousy perish,
E me teco,	And I with you,
E te meco,	And you with me,
Anima mia,	My darling,
Stringa con dolce affetto	Tie with sweet affection
Nodo d'amor tenace.	A firm knot of love.

Tota pulcra es, PA 39 (pp. 261–62)

Tota pulcra es, amica mea,	Thou art fair, my love;
Et macula non est in te.	There is no spot in thee.
Veni de Libano, sponsa mea.	Come with me from Lebanon, my spouse;
Favus distillans labia tua,	Thy lips drop as the honeycomb:
Mele et lac sub lingua tua.	Honey and milk are under thy tongue.

Ha, que l'absence est un cruel martire, "Air," *PA 41* (pp. 267–68)

Ha, que l'absence est un cruel martire,	Ah, absence is a cruel martyr,
Lorsqu'on aime tendrement	When one loves tenderly
Un objet tout charmant	A charming object
Et qu'on ne l'ose dire.	And one does not dare say so.
L'on se plaint, l'on soupire,	One complains, one sighs,
L'on chéri le tourment;	One cherishes the torment;
Et l'amour nous inspire	And love inspires us
De répéter souvent:	Often to repeat:
Ha, que l'absence est un cruel martire . . .	Ah, absence is a cruel martyr . . .

Amor mio

PA 20. "Affettuoso"

Antonia Bembo
Claire Fontijn, editor

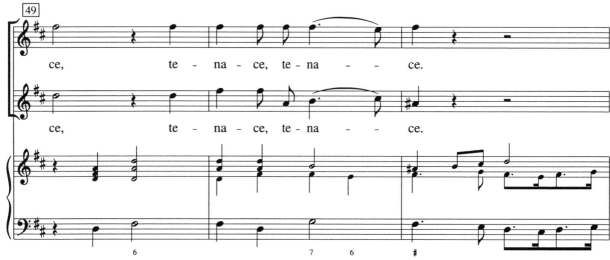

Tota pulcra es
PA 39

Antonia Bembo
Claire Fontijn, editor

Ha, que l'absence est un cruel martire

PA 41, "Air"

Antonia Bembo
Claire Fontijn, editor

Ha, _____ que l'ab- sen-ce est un cru-el _____ mar-ti- re, lors-qu'on ai- me ten- dre-ment un ob- jet _ tout char-mant, et qu'on ne l'o-se di-- re. L'on se plaint, l'on sou- pi- re, l'on se plaint, l'on sou- pi- re, l'on ché-ri _ le tour- ment; et l'a- mour nous ins-pi- re de

Diacinta Fedele, Romana

(fl. 1628)

SALLY CATLIN PARK

Listings of the octavo print *Scelta di vilanelle napolitane bellissime*[1] are found in at least four bibliographies of music printed before 1800.[2] The folk poetry in this volume, an ancient form of Italian, should not be attributed to Diacinta Fedele, Romana, because it predates the seventeenth century. The third song in the collection in particular is related neither to Neapolitan nor Sicilian dialect, but has a Venetian sound. Rather than Diacinta, the name would be "Giacinta," which is supported by the print's entry as such in *Il Nuovo Vogel*.[3]

Fedele's contribution to music history consists of making available to the public a heritage of "very beautiful villanelle from Naples with some stanzas from Sicily."[4] There are six poems; five have *alfabeto* tablature above the text of the first stanzas. Four are included in this volume.

To execute *alfabeto* tablature, all courses were strummed at once in upward and downward sweeps of the right hand in a new style, *rasqueado,* another manifestation of the early Baroque obsession with vertical aspects in music. The letters of the *alfabeta* tablature represent left-hand fingerings for each specific guitar chord. For example, the fret pattern 0–2–2–1–0 on courses tuned A d g b e′ (sounding A e a c e′) symbolized by *d,* is realized as an A-minor chord

In *punteado* performance on lute, vihuela, or guitar, one or more strings are plucked with the fingers of the right hand. Tablature on lines corresponding to the courses of the instrument identified the frets to be covered by the fingers of the left hand. Tablature notation was used for all guitar music until the end of the eighteenth century. Stems with one or more flags above the tablature identified note values. Music for the guitar was included in vihuela and lute tablature books of contrapuntal music from the sixteenth century.

During the first decades of the seventeenth century, guitar playing became exclusively *rasqueado*. By means of numbers in Spain and letters in Italy, guitar tablatures indicated which chords were to be strummed. Melodies that would have been sung are not part of the tablature. In Italy, *alfabeto* was inscribed above the figured bass line in the most elegant collections of vocal compositions for one or more voices. Tablature was written above texts, in the absence of any other musical symbols, as in Fedele's print. *Rasqueado* prints and manuscripts introduced dance patterns of many different origins, with vertical lines added above and below a horizontal line to indicate the direction of the strum. Early books of sonatas, the instrumental form most widely published, used *alfabeto* tablatures.[5] It was not until around 1629 that mixed tablatures for both *punteado* and *rasqueado* styles, or guitar tablatures entirely in frets, appeared.

Girolamo Montesardo,[6] Italian composer and singer, invented *alfabeto* tablature. Letters and signs symbolized the twenty-four major and minor triads for the Spanish guitar.[7] Besides popular songs and dances, his volume included *ritornelli* that were to be interspersed before and between stanzas of songs.[8] Montesardo introduced capital letters, but among refinements made over the years was the change to small letters; capital letters indicated notes of double length. Actual notes or simply stems and flags were also used above the chord symbols and text with *alfabeto* to indicate time values.

The name *Spanish guitar* was first used in an earlier Spanish treatise by Juan Carlos y Amat,[9] that aimed at popularizing the instrument in the playing of accompaniments. Amat's method did not depend on a knowledge of music or the expertise required to realize a figured bass. Unlike most instructions provided in treatises on the style, those of Amat gave vital information for tuning, specifing actual pitch and octave tuning of the fourth- and fifth-course strings. Amat, a doctor by profession, employed numbers one through twelve to represent triads of all keys, without differentiating between major and minor. His treatise was very successful and was reprinted for two hundred years. Although he wrote for the five-course guitar, a chapter on music for four-course instruments was also included.[10] The guitars of the sixteenth century had four and five courses, movable gut frets, and were double strung. Five-course instruments were at first less common, but by the end of the century, as the Spanish guitar gained in importance along with the new style of playing, that situation was reversed.[11]

In the novels and poems of a famous performer on the Spanish guitar, Vicente Espinel (1551–1624),[12] the amazing popularity of *rasqueado* is depicted in outdoor scenes of convivial singing and playing. It is known that Espinel, a skilled vihuela player, was employed for many years as a director of church music in Madrid. But it was his guitar accompaniments that brought him fame in fashionable musical circles. Espinel established the preference for octave tuning on the lowest course of the five-coursed instrument.[13]

The Spanish guitar was provided with ten tuning pegs, although only nine strings are accounted for. It is thought that the tenth may have been used as a spare string or a bourdon. The highest string was known as the *chanterelle,* strung singly for ease in the playing of ornaments, as was the lute custom. The remaining courses were double strung. There were at least two Spanish guitar tunings, one of which used the same pitches as the upper five strings of the modern guitar. The low notes in octave tuning, muffled and unclear, were put to good use as a bourdon and gave fullness to *rasqueado* performance. Were that not needed, the courses were tuned in unison at the higher octave, with the result that the strings of the third course were at the lowest pitch.[14] This was known as "re-entrant" tuning. Because of the predominance of the upper three notes in *rasqueado,* this style allowed first- and second-inversion chords.[15] This system supported originality and invention in the repeats of popular variation dances.[16] Rhythmic techniques for the right hand presented guitar players of the early Baroque with opportunity to display amazing skill. As the century progressed, *rasqueado* music lost its independence, but passages using its techniques remained an integral part of guitar style.

For modern performance, the *alfabeto* letters in the print have been transcribed into our system of chord names[17] and put below the chords. Accompaniments published by Giacinta Fedele are variations of the *ciaccona* pattern, I-IV-V-I. Pitch centers of the music are the major modes, F, G, C, and d minor, respectively. The *alfabeto* letters *c* and *e,* when transcribed, are chords of D major and minor in the second inversion. Their fret patterns are (low to high) 0–0–2–3–2 and 0–0–2–3–1.

Fine points in methods of performance and ornaments that were part of *rasqueado* style are described in both ancient and modern literature of the Spanish guitar.[18]

Notes

1. Diacinta Fedele, Romana, *Scelta di vilanelle napolitane bellissime Con alcune Ottave Siciliane nove, con le sue intavolature di guitarra alla Spagniola* (Vicenza: Francesco Grossi, 1628). (The original print

users the spelling *Siciliane* and *quittara.*) A copy of the print is bound in the volume, *Italian Poetry 1627–1628* (British Library, London, Great Britain: 1071 g 16 [18]). *RISM* F 150.

2. Aaron I. Cohen, *International Encyclopedia of Women Composers,* 2nd edition (New York: Books and Music Inc., 1987), p. 231, gives a selection of listings.

3. Emil Vogel, Alfred Einstein, François Lesure, Claudio Sartori, eds., *Il nuovo Vogel: Bibliografia della musica italiana vocale profana pubblicata dal 1500 al 1700,* vol. 1 [Pomezia?] (Staderini-Minkoff Editore, 1977): 918. Complete titles and first lines of stanzas are included.

4. Jane Bowers, "The Emergence of Women Composers in Italy, 1566–1700," in *Women Making Music: The Western Art Tradition, 1150–1950,* ed. Jane Bowers and Judith Tick (Urbana: University of Illinois Press, 1986), p. 118.

5. William S. Newman, *The Sonata in the Baroque Era* (New York: W. W. Norton, 1983), p. 45. Composers of the early sonata are listed on pp. 97–98.

6. Girolamo Montesardo, *Nuove inventione d'intabolatura per sonare la balletti sopra la chitarre spagnuola, senza numeri e note* (Florence, 1606).

7. Johannes Wolf, *Handbuch der Notationskunde,* vol. 2 (Leipzig, 1919). Reprint (Hildesheim: Georg Olms Verlag, 1963), pp. 171–175. *Alfabeto* transcription is given for both G c f a d′ and A d g b e′ tunings.

8. Lorenzo Bianconi, *Music in the Seventeenth Century,* trans. David Bryant (Cambridge University Press, 1987), p. 103. A list of composers for Spanish guitar is found on p. 100.

9. Juan Carlos y Amat, *Guitarra española y vandola, en dos maneras de guitarra, castellana y valenciana, de cinco ordenes; la qual enseña a templar, y tañer rasgado todos los puntos naturales y b mollados, con estilo marvilloso* (Barcelona, 1596). The work was available in reprints until 1758.

10. Neil Pennington, *The Baroque Guitar in Spain* (Ann Arbor, Michigan: UMI Research Press, 1981), pp. 48–49, 80–89. Strings, tunings, notation, ornaments, technique, and so forth, from 1552 (Diego Pisador) to 1799 (Rubio, Moretti, and Fernandière) are discussed.

11. James Tyler, "The Renaissance Guitar 1500–1650," *Early Music* 3 (October 1975): 341–47, lists sources in which descriptions of early guitars or guitar repertoire may be found. He states that the string length of the two sixteenth-century guitars in existence are not much longer than fifty-five centimeters, in contrast to the six-coursed vihuela with strings over eighty centimeters long. The backs of Spanish guitars could be either flat or vaulted, but their sides were very shallow.

12. See Neil Pennington, *The Baroque Guitar in Spain,* pp. 45–46, 173.

13. Johannes and Ingrid Hacker-Klier, *Die Gitarre* (Bad Buchau: A. Sandmaier & Sohn, 1980), p. 115.

14. Sylvia Murphy, "The Tuning of the Five-course Guitar," *Galpin Society Journal* 23 (August 1970): 49–63. The many variations in the tuning of the fourth and fifth courses are explained.

15. Donald Gill, "The stringing of the five-course baroque guitar," *Early Music* 3 (October 1975): 370–71. If a modern guitar is tuned with the fifth string an octave higher, this effect can be partially realized.

16. Richard A. Hudson, *The Folia, the Saraband, the Passacaglia, and the Chaconne*, vols. 1–4, Musicological Studies and Documents 35 (American Institute of Musicology, 1982).

17. The tuning used is A d g b e′, as realized in Wolf, *Handbuch*, vol. 2, pp. 171–72. Italian lute tablature represented the highest strings of the guitar with the lowest lines of the tablature and identified the frets by numbers. The same applies to *alfabeto* chords.

18. Murphy, Sylvia, "Seventeenth-Century Guitar Music: Notes on *Rasqueado* Performance," *Galpin Society Journal* 31 (March 1968): 24–32. Strizich, Robert, "Ornamentation in Spanish Baroque Guitar Music," *Journal of the Lute Society of America,* 5 (1972): 18–39.

Bibliography

Amat, Juan Carlos y. *Guitarra española y vandola, en dos maneras de guitarra, castellana y valenciana, de cinco ordenes; la qual enseña a templar, y tañer rasgado todos los puntos naturales y b mollados, con estilo marvilloso.* Barcelona, 1586.

Bianconi, Lorenzo. *Music in the Seventeenth Century.* Translated by David Bryant. Cambridge University Press, 1987.

Bowers, Jane. "The Emergence of Women Composers in Italy, 1566–1700." In *Women Making Music: The Western Art Tradition, 1150–1950,* edited by Jane Bowers and Judith Tick. Urbana: University of Illinois Press, 1986.

Cohen, Aaron I. *International Encyclopedia of Women Composers.* 2d. ed., 2 vols. New York: Books and Music Inc., 1987.

Fedele, Diacinta, Romana. *Scelta di vilanelle Napolitane bellissime Con alcune Ottave Siciliane nove, con le sue intavolature di quitarra alla Spagniola.* Vicenza: Francesco Grossi, 1628.

Gill, Donald, "The stringing of the five-course baroque guitar." *Early Music* 3 (October 1975): 370–71.

Hudson, Richard A. *The Folia, the Saraband, the Passacaglia, and the Chaconne.* 4 vols. Musicological Studies and Documents 35. American Institute of Musicology, 1982.

———. *Italian Poetry 1627–1628.* British Library, London, Great Britain. 1071 g 16, (8).

Hacker-Klier, Johannes and Ingrid. *Die Gitarre.* Bad Buchau: A. Sandmaier & Sohn, 1980.

Montesardo, Girolamo. *Nuove inventione d'intabolatura per sonare la balletti sopra la chitarre spagnuola, senza numeri e note.* Florence, 1606.

Murphy, Sylvia, "Seventeenth-Century Guitar Music: Notes on *Rasqueado* Performance." *Galpin Society Journal* 21 (March 1968): 24–32.

———, "The Tuning of the Five-course Guitar," *Galpin Society Journal* 23 (August 1970): 49–63.

Newman, William S. *The Sonata in the Baroque Era.* New York: W. W. Norton, 1983.

Pennington, Neil. *The Baroque Guitar in Spain.* Ann Arbor, Michigan: UMI Research Press, 1981.

Strizich, Robert. "Ornamentation in Spanish Baroque Guitar Music." *Journal of the Lute Society of America* 5 (1972): 18–39.

Tyler, James. "The renaissance guitar, 1500–1650," *Early Music* 3 (October 1975): 341–347.

Vogel, Emil, Alfred Einstein, François Lesure, and Claudio Sartori, eds. *Il nuovo Vogel: Bibliografia della musica italiana vocale profana pubblicata dal 1500 al 1700.* Vol. 1, [Pomezia?]. Staderini-Minkoff Editore, 1977.

Wolf, Johannes. *Handbuch der Notationskunde,* vol. 2. Leipzig, 1919. Reprint, Hildesheim: Georg Olms Verlag, 1963.

Choice of Villanelle

**Very beautiful, from Naples
With some new Ottave from Sicily, with its tablature
for the Spanish guitar
Brought to light by me, Giacinta Fedele, Romana
In Vicenza: Appresso Francesci Grossi. 1628.**

1 Gite hardenti sospiri hà Colei hà Colei
Che è cagion del mio male è miei martiri
Sà pietà non si move dite che io
Repr. Andrò gridando con ragione, à torto
Voi Fili mia voi sol mi havete morto.

Go, (my) burning sighs to Her, to Her
Who is the cause of my suffering and my martyrdom
If she is not moved to pity, tell her that I
Refrain: Will be crying with good reason—wrongly
You, my child, only you, have killed me.

2 Che dirrà se, io moro la crudel' nemica mia
Che il mio mal táto desia, che il mio mal táto desia
Si, si, sò ben che dirà
Amela sperala un tempo chi sà, chi sà
Se movesse se movesse à pietà.

What will she say, if I die, my cruel enemy
Who so greatly desires my suffering, who so greatly desires
my suffering
Yes, yes, I know well what she'll say
To me (there is) the hope (that) one day, who knows, who knows
She could be moved to pity.

3 Bona sera sia donna Zezza, bona sera siz donna Zezza
Me venuta una fantasia de te fare una Bisscazzia
E dapoi te pago una meza bona sera sia donna Zezza
Col' lu, ia, ia, col', lu, ia, ia, ha, ha, ha.

Good evening, Donna Zezza, may it be a good evening to you,
Donna Zezza.
An impulse came upon me, to do a . . . (?) to you
and then I'll pay you a half. Good evening, Donna Zezza, may it
be a good evening to you, Donna Zezza.
(Fa la la la, fa la la la, ha ha ha.)

4 No vedi tu Come, io per te, i tengo à morte
Ferito il mio Cuore ferito si
Che languendo, per te si muore si muore
Tu fusti lummecida e tu ben poi
Repr. Sanar la piagha de i belli occhi tuoi
Sanar la piagha sanar la piagha de i bel'occhi tuoi.

Don't you see how I for you,
I have my heart wounded to death,
so that, languishing, for you it dies, it dies
You were the killer, and you well can (be)
Refrain: To heal the wound of your beautiful eyes.
To heal the wound, to heal the wound of your beautiful eyes.

From British Library 1071 g 16 [18] A1ᵛ–A2. Reproduced by permission of the British Library.

Scelta Di Villanelle

Napolitane bellissime
Con alcune Ottave Siciliane nove, con le sue intavolature
di guitarra alla Spagniola

Posta in luce da me Diacinta Fedele, Romana
In Vicenza: Appresso Francesci Grossi. 1628.

Giacinta Fedele
Sally Park, editor

Gite hardenti sospiri hà Colei

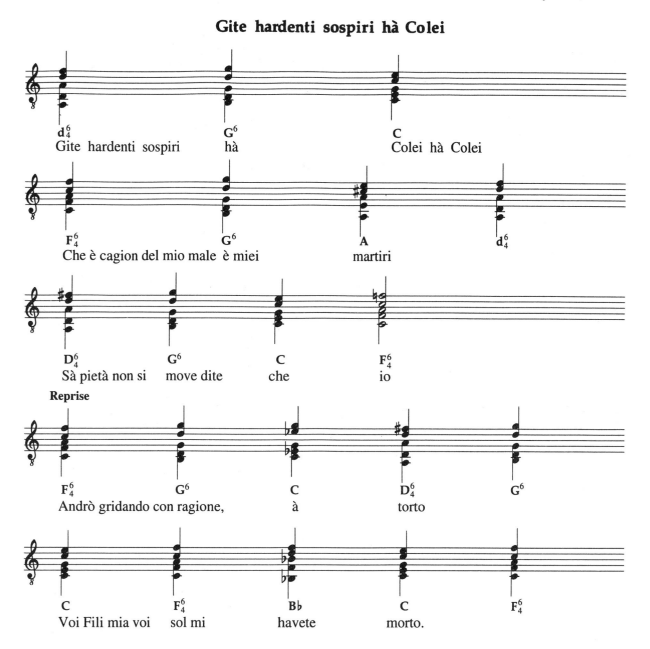

Che dirrà se

G⁶ — Che D₄⁶ — dirrà se, G⁶ — io moro d₄⁶ — la crudel' nemica G⁶ D₄⁶ — mia G⁶

G⁶ — Che il C — mio mal táto D₄⁶ G⁶ — desia, che il mio mal C D₄⁶ — táto G⁶ — desia

G⁶ — Si, D₄⁶ — si, A — sò ben che D₄⁶ — dirà

D₄⁶ — Amela sperala G⁶ — un tempo A — chi d₄⁶ — sà, chi d₄⁶ — sà

C — Se moresse se D₄⁶ — moresse à G⁶ — pietà.

Bona sera sia dóna Zezza

C   F$_4^6$ G^6 C   F$_4^6$ G^6 C

1. Bona sera sia dóna   Zezza,   bona   sera sia   dóna   Zezza

C   G^6 C   F$_4^6$ G^6 C

Me venuta una fantasia   de te   fare una   Bisscazzia

C   F$_4^6$ G^6 C   F$_4^6$ G^6 C

E dapoi   te pago   una meza   bona   sera sia   dóna   Zezza

C   E$_4^6$ a   F$_4^6$ G^6 C

Col',   lu, ia, ia,   col',   lu, ia,   ia, ha,   ha, ha.

No vedi tu Come

Maria Xaveria Peruchona

(ca. 1652–after 1709)

JANE BOWERS

Suor (sister) Maria Xaveria Peruchona, as she is known from her only musical publication, was born around 1652 to Carlo and Margarita Parruchono, according to convent visitation records housed in the archives of the diocese of Novara.[1] In an early study of illustrious Novarese figures, Lazaro Agostino Cotta reported that on May 6, 1668, at the age of sixteen, Peruchona took the veil in the Collegio of Sant'Orsola in Galliate, a town just a few miles northeast of Novara. Describing her as an excellent *Maestra* of music and an esteemed singer, Cotta stated that Peruchona had already been well schooled in the art of music, playing, and singing by Francesco Beria and Antonio Grosso before entering the convent.[2] Although Cotta thought Peruchona was a native of Gozzano, she is mentioned as *novariensis* in a *status personalis* drawn up on the occasion of a pastoral visit to Sant'Orsola in 1678.[3] Moreover, in the dedication of her only work to Donna Anna Cattarina della Cerda, wife of the governor of Novara, Peruchona wrote of the "blessed Government, by which your Grand Consort and Your Excellency ensure that my fortunate Country enjoys in this century of iron an age of gold."[4] Thus, Peruchona would appear to have been a native of Novara, as was the most prolific nun composer of the preceding generation, Isabella Leonarda (1620–1704), and like Leonarda, she chose to enter an Ursuline convent. While the Ursulines were initially exempt from the monastic enclosure decreed for other orders by Pope Pius V's *Circa pastoralis* constitution of 1566, this was no longer the case by the time Leonarda and Peruchona joined the order.

In 1675, when Peruchona was around twenty-three years old, her only work, a collection of *Sacri concerti de motetti a una, due, tre, e quattro voci, parte con violini, e parte senza,* was published by a small publisher in Milan, Francesco Vigone. Peruchona's dedication of this collection supplies us with little information about herself or her convent. We learn only that her sacred concertos, or motets as they might equally be called, were the "first-born of my poor talent"; that the dedicatee, Anna Cattarina della Cerda, had shown her some af-

fection; and that Anna Cattarina had made substantial gifts to Sant'Orsola. Graziano Sanvito has suggested that Peruchona (or Parruccona, as her name appears in some documents) probably did not actively pursue the study and composition of music after the publication of her *Sacri concerti,* because the *status personalis* drawn up at the time of the 1678 pastoral visit to Sant'Orsola reported only that she was in mediocre health, possessed a dowry of 2,000 *lire,* was able to write sufficiently, and was familiar with *canto figurato* (polyphonic music). In 1690, at the time of another pastoral visit, nothing was said about her musical gifts, and she had assumed the office of *Prefectae educandarum.* Although she was still listed at the convent in 1709, her status was not mentioned.[5] She has not been traced further.

Peruchona was but one of many Italian nun composers active during the seventeenth century. The dramatic growth of convents, of music study by young women before taking the veil, and of the performance of polyphonic music in female monastic institutions—the latter despite considerable opposition by a number of church fathers—led to a marked increase in compositional activity by nuns or young women preparing for the convent. As a result, more than half of the Italian women whose music was published between 1566 and 1700 were nuns.[6] Yet, most Italian nuns of the seventeenth century published only one or two collections of music and were then heard from no more. Like so many of her counterparts, Peruchona studied music seriously before entering the convent, and she had probably begun composing her sacred concertos before she took her final vows. Continuing work on these compositions and arranging for their publication while she was still in her first years at the convent, she later lost her momentum and "disappeared" into the convent with scarcely any further trace.

What sort of musical establishment did the Collegio of Sant'Orsola in Galliate have? Was it one that specialized in polyphonic music and was known, as some convents were, for the excellence of its music?[7] Apparently there was an organ at Sant'Orsola at least from 1657, since in that year a *status personalis* of Francesca Caterina Cellana described her as an organist as well as a composer. Cellana remained in the post of organist at Sant'Orsola through 1690, when she was also said to teach *canto figurato*. Apparently, none of her compositions are extant. Records of visitation to Sant'Orsola in 1678 indicate that another organist, Paola Maria Caroella, was also active at that time, although by 1690 she was employed in taking care of the sick. In 1678, at least six nuns were familiar with *canto fermo* (plainsong) and *canto figurato* (polyphonic music), including Peruchona.[8] That would not have made for a very big choir, but it would have been sufficient for the performance of the sacred concertos in Peruchona's publication of 1675, at least for works in which the voice ranges corresponded to those of the singers in the convent. Still, Peruchona's collection apparently constitutes the only musical print to have come out of her convent, and it reveals the names of no other singers or musicians there. Perhaps the musical establishment at Sant'Orsola was at its high point around 1678—although it was not very strong even then—and later lost numbers. If so, it would not be surprising if Peruchona had lost interest in composing, even if she had had the opportunity to continue her work. It is possible, however, that she continued to write music but that none survived.

Peruchona's book of *Sacri concerti* contains eighteen motets, all of which are accompanied by a basso continuo part for organ. There are two solo motets for soprano and two violins; one duo for two sopranos (or tenors) and two violins; two duos for two sopranos (or tenors) without violins; two duos for soprano and bass; two trios for two sopranos (or tenors) and bass; three duos for soprano, tenor, and bass; four quartets for soprano, alto, tenor, and bass; and two quartets for two sopranos, alto, and bass. Five partbooks—for canto (or soprano), alto (including the first violin part), tenor, bass (including the second violin part), and organ—contain music.

Only one motet is a setting of a liturgical text, that of the antiphon *Regina caeli*. The other texts appear to have been newly written, and they are anonymous. While these texts are nonliturgical, they may very well have been introduced into religious services as replacements of liturgical items, especially those of the Proper, as well as into paraliturgical and private devotional services.[9] It seems likely that Peruchona intended her works to be used within the framework of liturgical services, because in the table of contents of several of the partbooks, there are rubrics specifying the suitability of each nonliturgical motet for a particular feast or type of feast. Isabella Leonarda made use of this practice too, although not as systematically as Peruchona.[10] Three of Peruchona's motets specify *Per un Santo* (for a saint) or *Per qualsivoglia Santo* (for any saint); in the latter case, the name of a saint could be inserted where the text reads *Beata N. (N.* stands for *nome,* or name). Robert Kendrick has indicated

that this sort of generic sanctoral motet had already become increasingly important in the midcentury musical repertory of Milan.[11] Five of Peruchona's motets specify *Del Signore* (of the Lord); two, the nativity of the Lord; and two, the resurrection. Thus, there is a preponderance of Christological texts. There are also motets for the Holy Ghost and the Holy Virgins and Martyrs. Surprisingly, only two motet texts have to do with the Virgin Mary: one is specified for the assumption of the Madonna; the other, *Quid pavemus sorores* transcribed here, is simply labeled *Della Madonna*. The small number of texts praising the Virgin seems to contrast with the large number of such texts among the works of Leonarda.[12] Finally, one of Peruchona's motets is designated *De comune*.

The strong image of the Virgin Mary presented in the text of *Quid pavemus sorores,* however, seems to make up for the small number of texts devoted to her in the collection. The motet begins by evoking the fear sisters have of the religious life, which it likens to a painful battle in which the enemies are the devil, the flesh, the world, and sloth. (One wonders just how closely this describes the way many seventeenth-century nuns felt about their lives.) But there is reason to be comforted and to rejoice, because the Virgin Mary has come to overcome all of their battles. This is not Mary the intercessor, but Mary the invincible warrior; she will fight bravely in the world, she will be victorious, and she will shine surrounded by stars. Not only will the sisters triumph with her, they "will shout with her in triumph." The text of *Quid pavemus sorores* appears very personalized: it seems to speak directly for Peruchona and her religious sisters. One can easily imagine how those nuns identified with Mary, borrowed strength from her perceived strength, and considered her adornment with stars to shine light on them too. Peruchona's other motet devoted to Mary, *Congaudete mecum gentes,* also focuses on the idea of the triumphant Mary.

The same sort of idea is explored in one of Leonarda's Op. 10 motets (1684), *Surge Virgo* (also included in this volume), whose text in translation reads, "Arise happily, oh Virgin, arise to arms. / Arise happily to the struggle" (see article on Leonarda for remainder of translation).[13] In a different, though related, way, another motet from Leonarda's Op 13 (1687), *Ad arma, o spiritus,*[14] centers on battle, victory, and a virgin's overcoming fear, although in this case the concepts are not related directly to the Virgin Mary. Thus, it appears that there may have been a subgenre of triumphant Mary/triumphant virgin texts in the works of seventeenth-century nuns that is awaiting systematic exploration. Peruchona's text, however, seems more individualized than Leonarda's and Peruchona seems less bent on exploring in her music what Carter calls the "military style" in connection with such texts than does Leonarda.

The text of *Quid pavemus sorores* lies somewhere between prose and poetry. It exhibits both frequent poetic rhyme and groupings of adjacent lines of text with the same or nearly the same numbers of syllables. Yet, there is no overall regularity of rhyme scheme or line length. The text is therefore sectional, and the musical structure of the motet, responding to the verse structure of the text, is also sectional. Furthermore, a number of different, though related, ideas are expressed in the text, and a number of contrasting musical ideas are devised to set them. An irregular plan of alternating meters is used in the motet, similar to that in most of Leonarda's four-voice nonliturgical motets.[15] An overview of the structure of *Quid pavemus sorores* is given below. (The subsections connected with brackets share the same meter and tempo and make use of related or complementary melodic material.)

The opening four lines of text, as I have arranged them on page 231 so as to allow the text's parallel construction and rhyme to stand out, are set in common time as a splendid arioso for bass voice. This solo demonstrates subtle word painting—a sequential figure based on a sharply articulated falling triad (in a brief patch of "military style") for *est quasi pugna* (is like a battle) and a smooth, stepwise descent through an octave on the word *dolorosa* (painful). The next four lines of text are set as a lyrical miniature aria in 3/2 for bass voice. These lines are strongly poetic: except for the last, they each have eight syllables; the rhyme scheme is aabb; and three of the four lines begin in parallel fashion with the word *ubi* and include the word *semper*. Thus, the poetic structure of the text gives rise to the aria style of the music as well as to rhythmic similarities between musical phrases. The composer takes the liberty of repeating the first two lines of text after the second two in order to extend the musical structure; the fourth line, *et accidia nos tormentat* (and sloth torments us) ends with a strong cadence on B in m. 12. The first two lines of text are repeated, musically returning to the tonic, E minor, where the final cadence is beautifully emphasized by a melisma on the word *perit* (perishes).

Following, the other voices join the bass at *consolemur et laetemur* (let us be comforted and let us rejoice) in a prolongation of the 3/2 meter, which suggests a slow lilting dance, with long-short (whole–half note) rhythms. Repeating the text twice, the voices take up a circular motive (m. 22) in a lightly imitative texture in which voices are paired in parallel thirds and sixths. All of these features serve to enhance the idea of *consolemur*. There is interesting harmonic variety within this section: after a cadence on B, followed by one on D, two imitative passages briefly move sequentially through a portion of the circle of fifths (mm. 22–24 and 25–27), coming to a forceful cadence on e, which concludes the section (m. 30).

A marked change on *ad superanda omnia bella* (to overcome all of our battles) follows. Although the key signature does not change, there are frequent accidentals on the third, sixth, and seventh degrees of the scale, which convert the previous tonality of E minor to E major. Accidentals are inconsistently placed, however. In the opening fugal motive, for example, only the bass has a sharped third note (on *per* of *superanda*), and although the soprano, alto, and bass all have sharped fifth notes (on *da* of the same word), the tenor does not (see mm. 31–32). Moreover, when the bass reenters with the same motive in m. 34, neither the third nor the fifth note is sharped. This is not the place to survey the problems of interpreting accidentals in seventeenth-century music, but it is obvious that some decisions must be made by performers. In this edition editorial accidentals placed over certain notes present one possible reading, but some performers might well find other solutions. Then, too, errors in the parts present challenges: for example, an accidental clearly placed in one or several of the vocal parts may not correspond to the pitches indicated in another part or in the organ figures. Thus, I have made some corrections here too. Besides the change of mode, the *ad superanda* section introduces contrasting texture, becoming decidedly fugal, as well

Text Incipit	Meas.	Meter	Key	Voices	Style and Texture
Quid pavemus	1	C	e	B	Arioso
⌠ Ubi demon	7	3/2	e	B	Aria
⌊ Consolemur	18	3/2	e	SATB	Homophonic→imitative
ad superanda	31	C	E	SATB	Fugal
Ecce iam nobis	39	C	e	SB	Quasi-imitative
⌠ Si iam virgo	45	6/4	e–E	AT–S–TB–SATB	Mainly homophonic
⟨ et nos cum ipsa	60	6/4	E	SATB	Completely homophonic
⌊ ergo sint jubila	68	6/4	E	SA–TB–SATB	Homophonic
ergo sint jubila	77–79	C	E	SATB	Fugal

as contrasting character, with fast, jagged, and strongly rhythmic motives. No doubt Peruchona calculated these effects to contribute to the sense of doing battle.

A lovely soprano and bass duet in E minor on *Ecce iam nobis presentatur* (behold she is shown to us) follows. Notable instances of coloratura first appear on *praeliabitur* (she will fight) and then are more fully developed imitatively on *dominabitur* (will dominate).

The change to 6/4 meter at m. 45 initiates the longest section of the motet. *Si iam virgo fuit cara* (since she has been a virgin) returns to the pattern of long-short rhythms (here notated as half and quarter notes) that were used for *consolemur* but now in a presumably quicker tempo and of dance character. The scoring is imaginative: two inner voices (alto and tenor) replace the two outer ones of the previous duet; and with the organ part frequently sounding a high bass line, they make a sweet trio in close harmony. A soprano solo enters abruptly (m. 50) and alludes again to Mary—*si Maria stellis est adornata* (if Mary has been adorned with stars); the mode returns to major. A tenor and bass duet on *astris dilecta vincta fulgebit* (she, beloved, will shine surrounded with stars) overlaps with the end of this brief solo, following which all four voices enthusiastically sing *vincta fulgebit*. The tutti passage evokes the fullness of the celestial firmament, in contrast to the lone solo voice that represents Mary. Then, suddenly, without a break, all voices fuse homophonically on *et nos cum ipsa triumphabimus* (and we will triumph with her), which suggests the collectivity of "we." Dotted rhythms on *pha-bi-mus* of *triumphabimus* (we will triumph) and *ma-bi-mus* of *acclamabimus* (we will shout) convey the meaning of the text in a particularly forceful way. Without any pause before the penultimate line of text, *ergo sint jubila in nostris cordibus* (therefore let there be joy in our hearts), the texture changes to paired voices (SA and TB), following which all four voices together proclaim the final line of text, *ergo sint cantica in nostris oribus* (therefore let there be songs in our mouths). The dotted rhythmic pattern is sustained to create the feeling of joyfulness. The last line of text is repeated imitatively and in stately common time for a brief but powerful coda.

The use of contrasting meters, textures, and performing forces is an important means of formal articulation in *Quid pavemus sorores*. Indeed, all Peruchona's motets are typically sectional and include metric contrast. The most frequently used meters are C and 3/2; others include C3/2 and C6/4, 6/4, 6/8, and 3/4. In some motets changes of tempo are explicitly indicated, as, for example, in *Vos aure suaves*, where there appear such markings as adagio and prestissimo. Occasionally, the ends of sections are delineated by piano repetitions of material. Contrasts in texture and numbers of voices are also apparent. Few of Peruchona's motets, with the exception of her solo motets, however, make as expressive a use of solos as *Quid pavemus sorores*. Nevertheless, *O superbi mundi machina*, also opens with an impressive, florid bass solo.

There are no recurrent refrains in *Quid pavemus sorores*, nor are there tutti sections that merely repeat material from solos or duets. There are also no lengthy coloratura passages on individual words, aside from the moderately melismatic *dominabitur*, nor extended sections based on one or two lines of text. On the whole, the text is declaimed at a relatively quick pace. Melodically, an attractive lyricism abounds, except for the deliberately rougher *ad superanda*. In addition to the instances of word painting mentioned above, perhaps the most striking pictorialism is the turn to the major mode whenever the Virgin Mary's name is mentioned (see mm. 31ff. and 50ff.).

Peruchona shows herself to be in relative, if occasionally awkward, command of the harmonic vocabulary of her time, including the use of secondary dominants. Her principal chords correspond to root-position triads and sixth chords with occasional 4-3 suspensions. There is only one 7-6 progression. There are, of course, few tonal centers explored. The motet centers very much around the tonality of E, although it should be noted that there is no key signature in the original print; the F♯s as well as all other accidentals were printed in the original parts. The edition included here uses an E-minor key signature. Besides cadences on E, there are occasional cadences on B and several on D, the latter lending a somewhat modal flavor to the harmony. Peruchona seems to strive for colorful harmony in the 6/4 section, where she moves from E minor to E major (m. 51) and then B (m. 57), passes quickly through A (m. 59) back to E (m. 60), stretches up to F-sharp (m. 64), falls by fifth to B (m. 66), and then by the same means arrives back in E (m. 68). This degree of modulation is occasionally awkwardly controlled, particularly in mm. 58–59 where, following the subcadence in B major, the music without preparation suddenly drops down to A. The final three measures of the motet also move in a somewhat awkward fashion harmonically. It appears that Peruchona was striving for a greater degree of tonal variety than she had fully mastered. There are also locations in the score where the sparseness of figures in the organ part prevents a clear understanding of the composer's precise harmonic intentions. I have made specific suggestions by inserting figures within brackets under the bass line, but in some passages alternative readings may be justified (for example, a minor, rather than major, third may be played over the bass note). Thus, performers are urged to find their own solutions in these passages. Performers should also be advised that, in accord with the convention of the period, a flat in the figures indicates that a minor third, not a flatted third, is to be played over the bass note, while a sharp indicates that a major third is to be played over the bass note.

Finally, how might *Quid pavemus sorores* most appropriately be performed? In terms of tempo, proportional relationships between different meters seem to work reasonably well. A tactus of moderate speed may be adopted and retained nearly steadily throughout the motet. At the 3/2, taking three half notes in the time of two previous half notes works well; at the 6/4, taking six quarter notes in the time of four previous quarter notes produces a suitably lilting dance character; and all sections in common time are effective at the same basic tempo. (It is important to note that the sections marked C must not be beat at the speed of the quarter note, for the tempo would be unbearably slow. Since all measures in common time contain four half notes, these measures must be beat at the speed of the half note.) My recommendation to consider proportional relationships between sections, however, should not stop performers from taking other factors into consideration when determining suitable tempi.

Regarding performing forces, when a part is marked "solo"—as in the opening arioso for bass—obviously the intention is clear. At m. 18, however, the mark tutti in the bass voice and organ parts may merely indicate the entrance of the other solo voices, as none of the other parts contain this marking. Nowhere else in any of the parts is there an indication of solo or tutti passages, except at m. 39, in which reduced scoring is signalled in the organ part by the letters C. and B., for the respective entries of the soprano and bass voices. Similarly, the reentry of the soprano at m. 50 is signalled by the letter C. Thus, no distinction between choral and solo sections seems intended. Although Stewart Carter suggests that Leonarda's four-voice nonliturgical motets should be sung chorally, except for obvious solo and duet passages, by his own admission the evidence is rather weak for this practice. He also points out that whether or not a solo ensemble or a chorus was used for a performance would have depended to a large extent on the resources of a given religious institution.[16] In Perochona's four-voice motets, there seems to be no specific evidence to encourage choral performance, and I believe that a solo ensemble suits the music better than a chorus. In *Quid pavemus sorores,* for example, performance by a solo ensemble would mean that the performers would not have to decide where the chorus should reenter after the soloistic soprano-bass duet at m. 39. Should the choral altos and tenors come in at m. 45? I would argue not, since a more appropriate contrast to the sonority of the SB duet would be made by the sonority of solo alto and tenor voices here. There is no very satisfactory place for the chorus to enter before m. 60, when all four voices begin to sing together in homophony; yet, nothing indicates that any change in performing forces should take place here. Thus, the simplest solution is probably the best: perform the music with only one singer on a part throughout. Still, a small chorus might perform this motet if it wished, except for the opening bass solo and the SB duet, without spoiling the proportions of the music. For the accompaniment, the organ is clearly the appropriate instrument and should probably be played without reinforcement, as there is no separate part for another bass-line instrument.

This position concurs with that of Tharald Borgir, who maintains that the absence of extra bass parts suggests that "throughout the baroque period the bulk of Italian sacred music was performed without any other accompaniment than the organ."[17]

Aside from decisions concerning the size and appropriateness of performing forces, what are we to make of so prominent a bass solo in the work of a nun composer? How might this piece have been performed in Peruchona's convent? It is important to note that the effect of this solo seems dependent on the specific sonority of the bass voice. Moreover, even though the text is spoken from the point of view of a nun, the bass voice does not seem wildly out of place, because it suggests the "lower" region of the religious life with its painful battles, temptations, and torments. When all four voices enter at *consolemur et laetemur,* the marked change in pitch level parallels the shift of the text to a "higher" region, focussing on the Virgin Mary who has come to help the sisters. But could the bass part have been negotiated by a nun? Only a rare female singer could have successfully sung the solo at written pitch—and this would hold true today as well—even if the pitch in use at a particular convent were somewhat higher than modern pitch or the entire motet were transposed upwards. In either case, the motet could not have been sung at a much higher pitch level since the range of the soprano part is already elevated (witness the frequent f-sharps, not to mention the two g's, one of which should probably be sharped, in m. 26).[18] Thus, some adjustment of the bass part would probably have had to be made when the motet was performed in a convent. Certainly, there could be no question of substituting a bass instrument for the bass voice, as might be done in some nuns' repertory, because crucial elements of the text would be missing. Because the inclusion of men in music making at convents would probably have been considered scandalous,[19] the most frequent solution to performing this motet in a convent may have been to use an alto to sing the bass part up an octave. Ideally, of course, a true bass voice is preferable, not only for the opening solo, but for the passages in four-part counterpoint as well. A further conclusion that may be drawn from this example is that when composing music, nuns must have thought beyond the immediate circumstances of their female institutions to a potentially broader audience.

Notes

1. Graziano Sanvito, "Organi, organisti, organari della Diocesi di Novara nel secolo XVII," *Novarien* 12 (1982):136.

2. Lazaro Agostino Cotta, *Museo Novarese di Lazaro Agostino Cotta accresciuto di nuove biografie d'illustri novaresi e di altri notizie* (Novara: Francesco Merati, 1872), p. 283.

3. Sanvito, "Organi, organisti," p. 137.

4. Maria Xaveria Peruchona, *Sacri concerti de motetti* (Milan: Francesco Vigone, 1675), dedication.

5. Sanvito, "Organi, organisti," pp. 137–38.

6. The first compositions by an Italian woman appeared in print in 1566; these were four madrigals by Madalena Casulana in Giulio Bonagionta's *Il Desiderio*. For more detailed information about the development of nun composers in Italy during this period, see Jane Bowers, "The Emergence of Women Composers in Italy, 1566–1700," in *Women Making Music: The Western Art Tradition, 1150–1950*, ed. Jane Bowers and Judith Tick (Urbana: University of Illinois Press, 1986), pp. 116–67; Robert L. Kendrick, *Genres, Generations, and Gender: Nuns' Music in Early Modern Milan, c. 1550–1706*, 2 vols. (Ann Arbor: University Microfilms International, 1993). Craig A. Monson, *Disembodied Voices: Music and Culture in an Early Modern Italian Convent* (Berkeley: University of California Press, 1995).

7. For a study of one of the most important centers of nuns' music making in Milan, see Kendrick, *Genres*.

8. Sanvito, "Organi, organisti," pp. 135–36.

9. For a discussion of such uses of motets, see Stewart Carter, *The Music of Isabella Leonarda (1620–1704)* (Ann Arbor: University Microfilms International, 1982), pp. 185–88.

10. See Carter, ibid., pp. 186–87.

11. Kendrick, *Genres*, pp. 300–301.

12. See Carter, *Music of Isabella Leonarda*, p. 189.

13. Carter, ibid., p. 390; modern edition, Isabella Leonarda, *Selected Compositions*, ed. Stewart Carter, Recent Researches in the Music of the Baroque Era, vol. 56 (Madison: A-R Editions, Inc., 1988), pp. 365–89.

14. Leonarda, *Selected Compositions*, pp. 57–69; translation of text, xxi–xxii.

15. See Carter, *Music of Isabella Leonarda*, p. 246.

16. Carter, ibid., pp. 251–53.

17. Tharald Borgir, *The Performance of the Basso Continuo in Italian Baroque Music* (Ann Arbor: UMI Research Press, 1987), p. 45. For a fuller discussion of this question, see ibid., pp. 45–50.

18. For a useful discussion of voice ranges, pitch levels, and transposition in the polyphony of Milanese nuns, see Kendrick, *Genres*, pp. 326–58.

19. See, for example, Craig A. Monson, "Disembodied Voices: Music in the Nunneries of Bologna in the Midst of the Counter-Reformation," in *The Crannied Wall: Women, Religion, and the Arts in Early Modern Europe*, ed. Craig A. Monson (Ann Arbor: University of Michigan Press, 1992), p. 195, who cites

such reactions to performances by outside musicians at convent feast days in Bologna.

Bibliography

Extant Works

Sacri concerti de motetti a una, due, tre, e quattro voci, parte con Violini, e parte senza di Suor Maria Xaverona Peruchona Monaca nel Collegio di S. Orsola in Galiate. Opera prima. Milano: Appresso Francesco Vigone, à S. Sebastiano, 1675. I Bc.

Ad gaudia, ad [j]ubila (from op. 1). Louisville: Editions Ars Femina, 1993.

Books and Articles

Borgir, Tharald. *The Performance of the Basso Continuo in Italian Baroque Music.* Ann Arbor: UMI Research Press, 1987.

Bowers, Jane. "The Emergence of Women Composers in Italy, 1566–1700." In *Women Making Music: The Western Art Tradition, 1150–1950,* edited by Jane Bowers and Judith Tick, pp. 116–67. Urbana: University of Illinois Press, 1986.

Carter, Stewart. *The Music of Isabella Leonarda (1620–1704).* Ann Arbor: University Microfilms International, 1982.

Cotta, Lazaro Agostino. *Museo Novarese di Lazaro Agostino Cotta accresciuto di nuove biografie d'illustri novaresi e di altri notizie.* [1701.] Novara: Francesco Merati, 1872.

Kendrick, Robert L. *Genres, Generations, and Gender: Nuns' Music in Early Modern Milan, c. 1550–1706.* 2 vols. Ann Arbor: University Microfilms International, 1993.

Leonarda, Isabella. *Selected Compositions,* edited by Stewart Carter. Recent Researches in the Music of the Baroque Era, vol. 56. Madison: A-R Editions, Inc., 1988.

Monson, Craig A. *Disembodied Voices: Music and Culture in an Early Modern Italian Convent.* Berkeley: University of California Press, 1995.

———. "Disembodied Voices: Music in the Nunneries of Bologna in the Midst of the Counter-Reformation." In *The Crannied Wall: Women, Religion, and the Arts in Early Modern Europe,* edited by Craig A. Monson, pp. 191–209. Ann Arbor: University of Michigan Press, 1992.

New Catholic Encyclopedia, s.v. "Ursulines." 15 vols. New York: McGraw-Hill Book Co., 1967–74.

Sanvito, Graziano. "Organi, organisti, organari della Diocesi di Novara nel secolo XVII." *Novarien* 12 (1982): 105–47.

Quid pavemus sorores

Quid pavemus sorores	What do we fear, sisters,
quid timemus	what are we afraid of?
quia vita religiosa	Because the religious life
est quasi pugna dolorosa	is like a painful battle
Ubi demon semper ferit	where the devil always wounds
ubi caro semper perit	where the flesh always perishes
ubi mundus semper tentat	where the world always tempts
et accidia nos tormentat	and sloth torments us.
Consolemur et laetemur	Let us be comforted and let us rejoice.
ad superanda omnia bella	To overcome all of our battles
Virgo Maria vinci bella	the beautiful Virgin Mary has come.
Ecce iam nobis presentatur	Behold she is shown to us,
gratis nobis aggregatur	she approaches us freely,
fortis in orbe praeliabitur	she will fight bravely in the world,
in victoria Maria dominabitur.	in victory Mary will dominate.
Si iam virgo fuit cara	Since she has been a virgin
erit in Caelis coronata	she will be crowned in heaven.
Si Maria stellis est adornata	If Mary has been adorned with stars,
astris dilecta vincta fulgebit	she, beloved, will shine surrounded with stars,
et nos cum ipsa triumphabimus	And we will triumph with her
cum triumphanti acclamabimus	we will shout with her in triumph.
ergo sint jubila in nostris cordibus	Therefore let there be joy in our hearts,
ergo sint cantica in nostris oribus.	Therefore let there be songs in our mouths.

Translation by John Trudeau with some modifications by Steven Beall.

Quid pavemus sorores
(Della Madonna)

Maria Xaveria Peruchona
Jane Bowers, editor
Basso continuo realization by Peter Wolf

pe – rit u – bi mun-dus sem-per ten – tat et ac-ci – di – a-nos tor-men – tat __ u – bi

[#] [6] [#6] # [6] b[♮] 4 #3 [#]

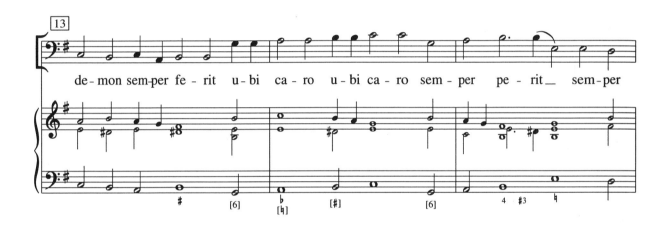

de – mon sem-per fe – rit u – bi ca – ro u – bi ca – ro sem – per pe – rit __ sem-per

[6] b[♮] [#] [6] 4 #3 ♮

Tutti

Con – so – le – mur

Con – so – le – mur

Con – so – le – mur

pe – – – – – rit __ Con – so – le – mur

[#6] b[♮] #

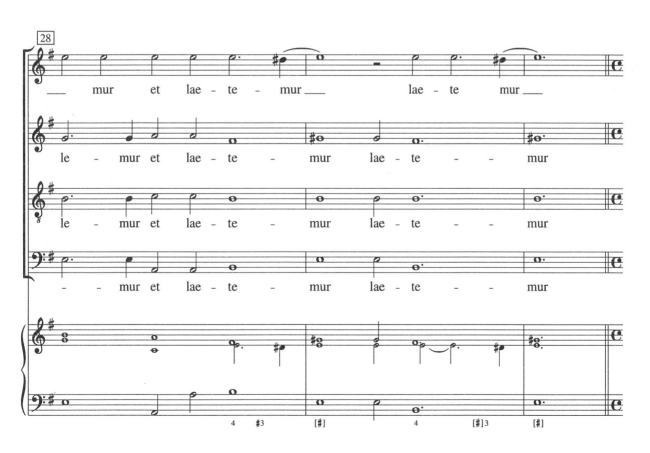

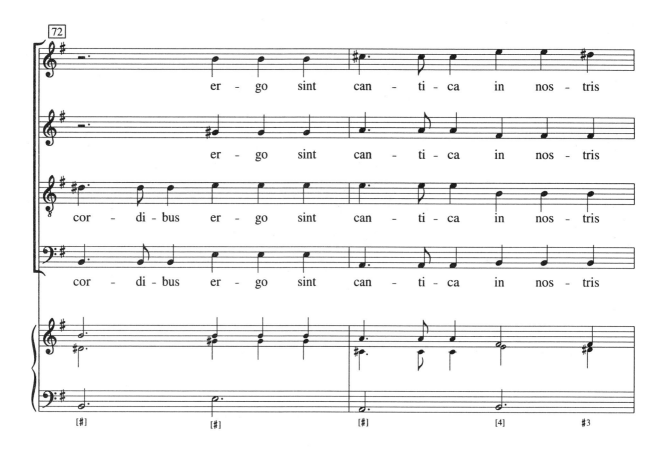

Maria Francesca Nascinbeni

(b. 1657/1658–?)

BARBARA GARVEY JACKSON

All that is known of the life of Maria Francesca Nascinbeni is on the title pages and in prefaces of two volumes of music published in 1674 that include her compositions. Her motet for two sopranos and bass was published in Scipione Lazzarini's *Motetti a due e tre voci* (Motets for two and three voices) in Ancona. Lazzarini was an Augustinian monk who taught theology and music. It was common practice to introduce the works of students in a teacher's publication. In this volume, there are works by three of Lazzarini's students, whom he identifies with the terms *discepola* and *discepolo* (female and male students). Signora Maria Francesca Nascinbeni d'Ancona and Signor Antonio Giuseppe Giamaglia are each represented by a motet for two sopranos and bass with organ continuo. Signor Filippo Giamaglia, perhaps a brother of Antonio Giuseppe, contributed a motet for three sopranos and continuo, the only three-voice work in the volume that does not require bass or tenor voices. Nothing else is known of the Giamaglias, and no other works by them seem to have survived.

On December 15 of the same year, Nascinbeni published a complete volume of her own music, *Canzoni e madrigali morali e spirituali a una, due e tre voci e organo* (Moral and spiritual canzonas and madrigals for one, two, and three voices and organ). She describes herself in the preface as "a young girl of sixteen years," so a birth year of 1657 or 1658 may be established for her. Her birthplace is indicated by the appellation "d'Ancona," and her studies were with a teacher in her home city. No further works are known after the *Canzoni e madrigali.*

There is no indication that she was in any way related to Stefano Nascinbeni, a late sixteenth-century Mantuan church composer with a similar, but not identical surname. The spelling used for Maria Francesca Nascinbeni's name in this anthology is that printed in both surviving publications of her music. Although the spelling "Nascimbeni" is handwritten on the outer binding of the copy of *Canzoni e madrigali* in the Civico Museo of Bologna, this is probably the mistake of a previous owner or librarian who confused Nascinbeni with the sixteenth-century composer of similar name. The ownership history of the volume is not known. Confusion in modern reference works has not been limited to the spelling of her surname. Both Fétis and MGG have given her male first names: Fétis thought she was François Nascimbeni, and in MGG she is referred to in an article on Lazzarini as Francesco Maria Nascimbeni.

Nascinbeni represents one of the many very talented young women who survive only through work representing the beginning of their careers. Her few works include settings of both Latin and Italian religious texts and show a fine grasp of a surprisingly wide variety of appropriate stylistic conventions. Her training was clearly professional, and her mastery of the craft makes it regrettable that no later works are known.

Nascinbeni's contribution to her teacher Lazzarini's *Motetti a due e tre voci* is a long sectional motet on a paraliturgical Latin communion text, *Sitientes venite ad aquas* (Come thirsting to the waters). The work alternates solo passages for each of the three singers with sections *à 3*. The *Canzoni e madrigali,* on the other hand, are all settings of Italian texts and represent the devotional or spiritual madrigal, all with continuo. It is the Italian devotional madrigal that has been chosen to represent Nascinbeni in this anthology, since these works are more numerous. Though the texts are all religious or devotional, they do not necessarily imply that the composer was, or later became, a nun; there is merely no information one way or another.

The publication is dedicated to Donna Olimpia Aldobrandini Pamphilii, Principessa di Rossano, an interesting and powerful Roman noblewoman whose important political and artistic connections include her sons, the librettist and lavish patron of music, Cardinal Benedetto Pamphili, and the Pamphili Pope, Innocent X. The poet or poets of the *Canzoni e madrigali* are not identified, but the two sonnets at the beginning of the book are by an Augustinian monk, Fra Giovanni Battista Sarri, who might also have been the poet for the musical texts. One of the sonnets is in praise of the patroness Olimpia Pamphilii, and the other alludes to "the virtue of music that is resplendent in [the composer] Signora Maria Francesca Nascinbeni."

Three of the *Canzoni e madrigali* are for a single soprano voice, four are for two sopranos, and six are for two sopranos and bass; the final piece, *Non tema nò di morte* ([One should] fear naught of death), is for three sopranos. All fourteen *Canzoni e madrigali* use images and devices from secular poetry and music, including a full-blown "battle canzona," which is replete with trumpet and drum effects in the voices. Unlike secular battle pieces, however, the warfare is neither military nor amorous, but a spiritual battle, against the fear of death, hell, and the serpent. The piece chosen for this anthology, *Una fiamma rovente* (A scorching flame), is one which borrows the theme of burning passion—"inflaming the breast and consuming the heart"—from secular love poetry. In this composition, however, the passion is for otherworldly love. The imagery of the text is mirrored musically through melismatic passages that tone paint such words as *fiamma* (flame), *m'infuoca* (inflames me), and *venti instabili* (unsteady winds).

Una fiamma rovente is in four sections, alternating common and triple time. In the first two, the theme is introduced by the first soprano and imitated by the second; in each of the last two sections the voices begin in parallel thirds, continue imitatively, and come together at the end. Although the piece begins, and each section ends, in C major, new sections always begin in a contrasting, even though closely related, key, suggesting the instability alluded to in the text. The passages in minor keys also contribute to the affect.

The sectional structure and continuo accompaniment of Nascinbeni's *Canzoni e madrigali* were typical of seventeenth-century motets and madrigals from the time of Monteverdi onward. The choice of two soprano voices was also a favorite of the period and may be found in countless examples of music by all composers, including the most famous and prolific woman composer of the period, Isabella Leonarda. Like the music of other Italian women composers, some of the pieces in the volume also require bass voice; and like all the other Italian women composers of the period, Nascinbeni rarely uses a setting for more than two treble voices. That so little music survives for ensembles of more than two treble voices is surprising, since many of the seventeenth-century women composers were nuns who wrote music for the convent.

Nascinbeni's talent and promise, as shown in her works of 1674, suggest a brilliant and creative future: unfortunately, no further evidence of her musical activity survives.

In this edition, spelling and capitalization of the original text have been preserved, although some commas have been added editorially in order to clarify the phrasing.

Bibliography

Principal sources of biographical information are title pages and prefaces of the composer's publications.

Sources

Nascinbeni, Maria Francesca (Anconitana). *Canzoni e madrigali morali e spiritual a una, due, e tre voci.* Ancona: Claudio Percimineo, 1674. Copies in Bologna: Civico Museo Bibliografico Musicale (BB 29); Oxford: Bodleian Library; Macerata, Italy: Biblioteca Comunale Mozzi-Borgetti (basso only, without title page); and Rome: Accademia Nazionale dei Lincei e Corsiniana and Biblioteca Vallicelliana.

Lazzarini, Scipione. *Motetti a due e tre voci,* opera seconda. Ancona: Claudio Percimineo, 1674. Includes Nascinbeni, Maria Francesca, "Sitientes venite (Per il Santissimo Sacramento)." Copies in Bologna: Civico Museo Bibliografico Musicale and Basilica di S. Petronio; Cesena: Biblioteca Comunale Matatestiana; Lucca: Seminario Vescovile.

The editor gratefully acknowledges the use of the copy of *Canzoni e madrigali* in the Civico Museo Bibliografico Musicale, Bologna (by microfilm) for the preparation of this edition.

Books and Articles

Répertoire International des Sources Musicales (RISM).

Einzeldrucke vor 1800. Kassel, 1971–. *Recueils imprimes XVIe–XVIIe siècles: Liste chronologique.* Ed. François Lesure. Munich-Duisburg: Henle, 1960.

Bertini, Argia. "Nascimbeni [sic], Maria Francesca." *The New Grove Dictionary of Music and Musicians,* edited by Stanley Sadie. London: Macmillan, 1992.

Cohen, Aaron. "Nascimbeni [sic], Maria Francesca." *International Encyclopedia of Women Composers.* 2d ed.

Eitner, Robert. "Nascimbeni [sic], Maria Francesca." *Biographisch-bibliographisches Quellen-Lexikon der Musiker und Musikgelehrten.*

Fétis, François-Joseph. "Nascimbeni, François [sic]." *Biographie universelle des musiciens.* 2d ed.

Sartori, Claudio. "Lazzarini, Scipione." *Die Musik in Geschichte und Gegenwart.* (Name given as Francesco Maria Nascimbeni).

Modern Edition

"Non tema nò di morte," from *Canzoni e madrigali morali e spiritual a una, due, e tre voci.* In *Two Sacred Works for Three Treble Voices,* edited and with preface by Barbara Garvey Jackson. Fayetteville: ClarNan Editions, 1990.

Una fiamma rovente

Una fiamma rovente, un fuoco fatale, un mongibello, ardente, m'infuoca il seno e mi consuma il core. Mi rapisce l'amore d'una beltà immortale, che questa vita frale o diare mi fà. E con taciti accenti suggerendo mi dice ch'adorare non lice, questi spasi quà giù questi contenti, che son ombre fugaci instabil venti.

A scorching flame, a fatal fire, a fiery volcano inflames my breast and consumes my heart. Love of such an immortal beauty so ravishes me that this frail life becomes hateful to me. And suggesting with quiet accents, says to me to adore, that it does not allow these pains here, these contentments there, which are ephemeral ghosts, unstable winds.

Una fiamma rovente
à due Canti

Maria Francesca Nascinbeni
Barbara Garvey Jackson, editor

E con ta - - - - - - - -

E con ta - - - -

- - - - citi ac-cen-ti sug-ge-ren - - do mi

- - - - citi ac-cen-ti sug-ge -

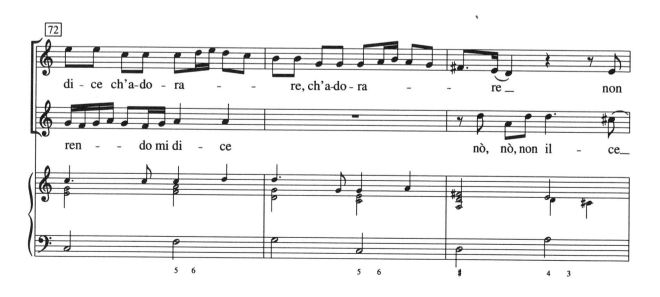

di - ce ch'a-do - ra - - re, ch'a-do-ra - - re _ non

ren - - do mi di - ce nò, nò, non il - ce_

che son om — bre fu — ga — ci,

ga — ci in — sta — — bil __ ven — — — — —

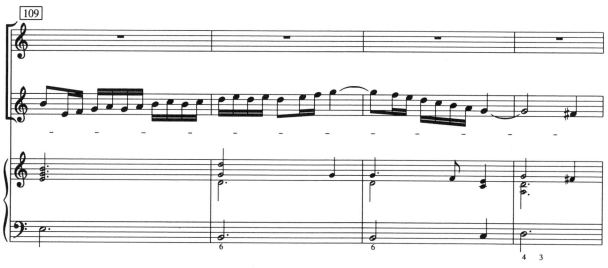

che son om — bre fu — ga — ci,

ti,

che son om — bre fu —

Rosa Giacinta Badalla

(ca. 1660–ca. 1715)

ROBERT L. KENDRICK

As much as we know of Cozzolani's life and career at Santa Radegonda, so much is mysterious concerning the monastery's second recorded composer, Badalla. No other member of her immediate family seems to have professed vows at the monastery, and Badalla herself appears on lists of nuns after 1678, which suggests that she took her vows around that year at Santa Radegonda and was born around 1660. She probably came from the nearby city of Bergamo. The preface to her motet book, *Motetti a voce sola* (Venice: Giuseppe Sala, 1684), mentions that she was *poco uscita dal quarto lustro,* that is, just over twenty years old, at the time of publication. Two secular—or quasi-secular—cantatas survive, one (*O fronde care*) in a French manuscript, one (*Vuò cercando,* edited here) in an English miscellany. Although she signed documents in the early 1710s, her name disappeared from Santa Radegonda's next preserved list from 1719. We have no idea whether she served as *maestra* of one of the house's two choirs, nor even which voice part she sang.

These lacunae are all the more unfortunate since Badalla's 1684 book of solo motets is perhaps the most interesting—and certainly one of the most virtuosic—of the late seventeenth-century Lombard repertory. *Pane angelico* is rubricated for the feast of Corpus Christi, which celebrates the Real Presence of Christ in the Eucharist. As the work of Caroline Walker Bynum has shown, the devotion to Jesus' suffering body in its Eucharistic incarnation was central to the religious experience of women in the later Middle Ages. Certainly this idea receives strikingly new expression in the music by and for nuns in the Milanese *Seicento.*

In contrast to some pieces in her book, this motet relies on abbreviated *da capo* forms for its two arias. The striking virtuosity and high tessitura of the *Fortunati mortales* section is without precise parallel among contemporary Lombard solo motets. Noteworthy also is the minor/major ambiguity in the aria "Tanto prodigio." At the same time, the more conventional harmonic language and greater regularity of musical forms, compared to solo motets earlier in the century, marks the generational difference in the development of the repertoire of Santa Radegonda that is typified by the contrasting works of Cozzolani and of Badalla. Contemporary evidence—travel reports and even printed manuals—suggests that the Elevation of the Host at Mass would have been the most likely occasion for this kind of solo motet.

The cantata *Vuò cercando,* although far simpler in vocal technique and formal structure, has been included here for its self-referential text, *'un mazzetto di Rose e di Hiacinte,'* a clear allusion to Badalla's own name. Indeed, the verbal content of this piece is infused with ambiguity, beginning with its addressee—God, a secular patron, or perhaps both—and including its speaker, presumably Badalla herself, who may or may not have written the text (the manuscript of her other cantata, now in Paris, states explictly *Poesia, e musica di D. Rosa Hiacinta Badalli*). The "garland of roses and hyacinths" may well refer to the composer's own musical talents. In any case, the explicitly self-revelatory nature of this short cantata is again rather a new feature of the musical repertory, one that testifies to Badalla's own personal and individual awareness of her place in the context of late seventeenth-century Milan. *Vuò cercando* itself is preserved in a post-1699 English cantata miscellany in the hand of Humphrey Wanley (Hughes-Hughes, 1908), where it is listed as "Cantata di D[on]na Rosa Hiacinta Badalli."

Bibliography

Hughes-Hughes, A. *Catalogue of the Manuscript Music in the British Museum.* London, 1908, p. 491.

Kendrick, Robert L. *Celestial Sirens: Nuns and their Music in Early Modern Milan* (Oxford: Clarendon Press, 1996).

Editorial Procedures

1. Time values and meter signatures have been left unaltered. Any variants in rhythm or pitch found in the source are noted as

follows: [measure number].[part-name, abbreviated].[note number (rests are prefixed with the letter *r*)]: [original reading]. Hence a given variant might be designated as: 34.CII.3–4: c♯″-b′, meaning m. 34, Canto II, notes 3–4 were originally c♯″ and b′.

2. Bar lines have been supplied when missing.

3. Clefs have been modernized; key signatures (actually indications of *cantus*) are as in the source.

4. Accidentals apply to the entire measure plus any notes tied into the next measure, as in normal modern notation. Editorial *musica ficta* is given above the staff; such *ficta* apply only to the note over which they are placed.

5. Text underlay is as in the original prints or manuscript; repetitions indicated by the abbreviation *ij* have been expanded and placed inside brackets < >. Punctuation is editorial and has been kept to a minimum.

6. All slurs are original.

7. Ligatures have been indicated by whole brackets, while *minor color* is set off by half brackets.

8. Continuo figures have been moved from above the staff to below; dashes have been added to suspensions (4–3). The continuo realization is only a guide and should be adopted to the actual chordal instrument used—organ, theorbo or chitarrone, or harpsichord, all of which were played by Milanese nuns in this period. The use of a string bass (violoncello/bass violin) to double the continuo line is generally anachronistic, at least before the generation of Badalla and Meda.

Abbreviations: C = Canto or Cantus; A = Alto; T = Tenor; Bc = Basso continuo; Vln = Violin; pitch designations employ the Helmholtz system (e.g. 440 Hz = a′). Sigla for music libraries are those found in *RISM Einzeldrucke*.

Sources

Pane angelico. Motetti a voce sola (Venice: Sala, 1684). Textual source: unknown.

Vuò cercando. GB-Lbl, Harley 1273, ff. 44–45r. Textual source: Unknown (?Badalla).

Critical Notes

Pane angelico. Variants: None

Vuò cercando. Variants: None; all the mid-bar *da capo* cues in the arias have been replaced by *dal segno* cues back to complete measures.

Pane angelico

"Per la Festa del Corpus Domini"
Pane angelico et divino
sacra mensa nostram famam satiat
et nectare celesti
animam fidelem recreat.

Aria: De coelo rapidi
o chori angelici,
venite volate.
Et Dei beneficii,
amore stupidi
sic exclamate.
De coelo rapidi . . .

O summi benefitii
o admirandi prodigii
inefabilis excessus
o incomparabilis divino amore
fragili creaturae honor concessus.

[Aria:] Tanto prodigio
triumpha amor;
exulta in gaudio
beatum cor.
Tanto prodigio . . .

Fortunati mortales,
mensae coelestis
gustate delitias,
et angelico pane refecti
cantando jubilate.
Alleluia.

For Corpus Christi
With angelic and divine bread
this sacred meal sates our hunger
and with celestial nectar
restores the faithful soul.

From heaven, quickly,
o angelic choirs,
come on wings.
And ecstatic with the love
of God's goodness,
cry out in this way.
From heaven quickly . . .

O highest gift
o marvelous prodigies,
indescribable surfeit,
o incomparable honor granted
by divine love to a fragile creature.

Love triumphs
through such a marvel;
a blessed heart
exalts in joy.

O lucky mortals,
enjoy the delicacies
of the heavenly supper,
and refreshed by angelic bread
rejoice in singing.
Alleluia.

Vuò cercando

Vuò cercando quella speme
che verdeggia per honor;
Questa sola mi da pace,
sol di questa si compiace
qual'or langue l'afflitto mio cor.

Ecco, ch'io gia la vedo,
spuntar dal tuo gran merto,
che fà del mio servir
ambito inserto.

Hiardiniera fortunata,
al fin ritrovo in grembo ai fiori
quel bel fior della speranza
che si nutre e più s'avanza
colle pioggia dei favori.
Hiardiniera fortunata . . .

Signor, se d'un tal fiore,
ne fai prodigo dono al mio desio
vò presentarti anch'io
benche vil contra cambio a tant'onore
un mazzetto di Rose e di Hiacinti
colti nei miei recinti.

Tù che sei la più bell'Aurora,
che risplenda nel Cielo d'Amor,
S'ancor l'Alba di Rose s'infiora
non sdegnar piccol dono di fior.

Tu che sei . . .

I seek that hope
which flowers in honor;
this alone gives me peace,
only from this is my anguished
heart pleased when it pines.

Behold, now I see that hope
flowing from your great merit,
one which makes good use
of my service.

Finally I, fortunate gardener,
find in a flowery lap
that lovely bloom of hope
fed and growing
with the moisture of your favors.
Fortunate gardener . . .

Lord, if with such a flower
you make a marvelous gift to my desires
I, too, would present you
(though slight recompense for such honor)
a garland of roses and hyacinths
plucked in my own cloistered keep.

You, the most beautiful dawn,
that glows in love's heaven,
though the sky still flowers with roses
do not disdain a small flowery gift.

You, the most beautiful . . .

Translation by Robert L. Kendrick

Pane angelico

Rosa Giacinta Badalla
Roberta Kendrick, editor

267

Vuò cercando

Rosa Giacinta Badalla
Robert Kendrick, editor

tro - vo in grem-bo ai fio - ri, al fin ri - tro - vo in grem-bo ai fio-ri, in grem bo ai fio -

ri,

quel bel _ fior del - la spe - ran - za, che si nut-re e più s'a - van - za
[second time: go to meas. 80]

col - le piog-gia dei fa-vo - ri, quel bel fior del-la spe-ran-za, che si nu-tre e più s'a-

Dal 𝄋 (m.57) alla fermata

Elizabeth-Claude Jacquet de la Guerre

(1665–1729)

CAROL HENRY BATES

Born in Paris in 1665,[1] child prodigy Elizabeth-Claude Jacquet received her early music instruction from her father, Claude Jacquet, organist at Saint-Louis-en-Île and a respected harpsichord and organ teacher. By the time Elizabeth was five, her harpsichord playing had attracted the attention of Louis XIV, who "honored her with his praise and told her that she ought to cultivate the marvelous talent Nature had given her."[2] In 1673, as a consequence of her first appearance at Versailles, Elizabeth was engaged by Mme de Montespan, the king's mistress, to provide musical entertainment for her and for her court visitors. During the three or four years in which she fulfilled this service, Elizabeth displayed extraordinary abilities as a singer, harpsichordist, and composer. Acclaimed "the marvel of our century,"[3] she soon became famous, even in foreign countries.

After being pensioned by the king, Elizabeth began composition studies. When the court moved to Versailles in 1682, she chose to remain in Paris where she earned great public acclaim, especially for her skillful harpsichord improvisations. On July 1, 1685, Elizabeth made her debut as a composer with the production of a short opera dedicated to Louis XIV. Presented at the Dauphin's apartment in Versailles, this composition so pleased the king that he not only requested but also attended additional performances.[4] In the years that followed, Louis XIV continued to honor Elizabeth by permitting her to dedicate her music to him and by attending performances of her works.

In 1684, Elizabeth married Marin de la Guerre, distinguished organist of the Jesuit Church on the rue Saint-Antoine and, later, of Saint-Séverin and the Sainte-Chapelle. Her happiness was to be short-lived, however, for Elizabeth and Marin's only child, a son, died at the age of ten.[5] Additional losses followed with the deaths of her father in 1702 and of her husband in 1704. These years of compounded bereavement impelled Elizabeth—now known as Mlle de la Guerre—to even greater creative activity. She published extensively between 1707 and 1715, contributed music to productions at the Théâtre de la Foire, and regularly presented public harpsichord recitals at her home on the rue Regrattière, Île Saint-Louis. These recitals were widely acclaimed; indeed, "all the great musicians and fine connoisseurs went eagerly to hear her."[6] Sometime after her retirement from public life in 1717, La Guerre moved to the rue de Prouvaires in the parish of Saint-Eustache. Her last composition, an unpublished *Te Deum* (now lost) that was written to give thanks for Louis XV's recovery from smallpox, was performed in the chapel of the Louvre in August 1721. By the time of her death on June 27, 1729, La Guerre was considered one of the great musicians of her day whose remarkable achievements merited lasting recognition.[7]

La Guerre's compositions include dramatic music, cantatas, popular songs, harpsichord pieces, and sonatas. Presumably inspired by the stage works of Jean-Baptiste Lully, as well as by her own participation in opera productions at the court, La Guerre early showed interest in writing dramatic music. The surviving portion of the dedication in her harpsichord book of 1687 not only documents the success of the opera with which La Guerre had made her compositional debut in 1685 but also indicates that upon hearing this work Louis XIV asked her to compose a *divertissement* for the marriage of Mlle de Nantes, one of his daughters by Mme de Montespan. The dedication additionally mentions La Guerre's completion of three new operas that she hoped would interest the king.[8] Regrettably, none of these five works is specifically identified. The only known titled stage works by La Guerre are *Les Jeux à l'honneur de la victoire* and *Cephale et Procris*. The former is an undated ballet of which, unfortunately, only a manuscript copy of the libretto survives.[9] The latter is a five-act *tragédie lyrique* based on a libretto by Joseph-François Duché de Vancy. Produced on

March 15, 1694, it was the first work by a woman to be presented at the Académie Royale de Musique. The prologue extols the virtues of Louis XIV, whereas the subject matter of the tragedy is taken from the *Metamorphoses* of Ovid. Lully's influence permeates the music. Though dominated by recitatives, many with changing meters, the vocal writing also includes airs, which are generally short and in *da capo* form, as well as choruses, most of which are homophonic. The instrumental music consists of an opening French overture, preludes, *ritournelles,* descriptive *symphonies,* and dances.[10]

During the late seventeenth and early eighteenth centuries, the Italian cantata began to attract the attention of French composers, including La Guerre. In 1708 and 1711, she published two books of cantatas, each containing six pieces. These *Cantates françoises sur des sujets tirez de l'Écriture* are significant not only because they are among the earliest such compositions published in France but also because they are the first examples of the French sacred cantata. Their texts, written by Antoine Houdar de la Motte, are based on subjects from the Old Testament and the Apocrypha. The cantatas show considerable diversity in scoring. Ten are written for solo soprano, five of them with continuo accompaniment and five with continuo and obbligato instruments. Of the two remaining works, both accompanied by continuo only, one calls for two sopranos and the other for soprano and bass. The format of the cantatas is also highly variable. Only *Joseph* employs the customary six-movement scheme of three recitatives alternating with three airs. The other cantatas contain from seven to twelve movements, being enlarged by additional airs and recitatives, and—in the works with obbligato instruments—by instrumental preludes and interludes as well.

Le Passage de la Mer Rouge from Book 1, excerpts of which appear in this volume, brings into view important aspects of La Guerre's cantata writing, among them: (1) a predilection for recitatives in duple meter, whose apparent metric regularity is counteracted by a variety of rhythmic patterns in the vocal part and by an active bass line; (2) a penchant for tasteful, *da capo* airs, with vocal elaboration usually reserved for highlighting key words; (3) a colorful harmonic language—including sudden modal shifts and unexpected dissonances—that helps effect vivid text settings; (4) the inclusion of descriptive *symphonies;* (5) the incorporation of elements associated with the Italian vocal style (for example, the dramatic use of rests in the vocal part); and (6) reminiscent of the Italian trio sonata, the use of imitation, suspensions, and doubling in thirds or sixths in movements with obbligato instruments.

Sometime after 1715, La Guerre published a third book of cantatas.[11] Dedicated to Maximilian Emanuel II of Bavaria, it contains three secular works based on mythological subjects, all of which are scored for solo soprano with continuo and obbligato instruments. Of greater length than her sacred can-

tatas, these compositions allow for many different combinations of the instruments with the voice. Moreover, La Guerre increases the range of performance possibilities by indicating in the *Avertissement* that any of the airs may be performed separately with continuo accompaniment only. Following the cantatas in the volume is *Le Raccommodement comique de Pierrot et de Nicole,* a duet for soprano and bass with continuo. Although part of this duo had been heard in 1715 at the Foire Saint-Germain in Jean-Claude Gillier's production of *La Ceinture de Vénus,* the entire piece had not previously been made available to the public.[12]

As for La Guerre's instrumental music, her harpsichord compositions consist of two books published in 1687 and 1707. The first contains thirty-four pieces: three unmeasured preludes (two with measured sections in the tradition of Louis Couperin), a *Tocade* (the only piece so titled in the French harpsichord literature), and thirty dances, including a binary-rhythm gigue. The compositions divide by key into four groups. Each group builds upon an allemande-courante-sarabande-gigue nucleus that is always preceded by an introductory movement and followed by other pieces. This remarkable consistency contributed significantly to the stabilization of the French harpsichord suite during the late seventeenth and early eighteenth centuries. La Guerre's first harpsichord book is notable also for its introduction of a functionally oriented notation for unmeasured writing, one in which white notes normally indicate harmonic tones and black notes, melodic movement.

Representative of La Guerre's early keyboard pieces are three movements from the A-minor suite included here. In the Prelude, unmeasured writing and broken-chord patterns rooted in French lute music combine with Italianate passagework to create a decidedly toccatalike character. The Allemande is distinguished by its melodious expression, rhythmic subtlety, and thin, transparent texture. The Chaconne, in keeping with the prevailing seventeenth-century French practice, unfolds in *rondeau* form: featuring chromatic voice-leading and poignant dissonances, the low-lying refrain alternates with four couplets of increasing rhythmic vitality.

The fourteen pieces that constitute La Guerre's second harpsichord book form two suites. Except for the lack of an introductory movement, these suites are organized like her earlier ones. The harpsichord pieces of 1707 are especially noteworthy in that according to the title of the collection (see list of extant works) they could be played "on the violin"—presumably with the violin softly reinforcing the keyboard treble. Interestingly, the *Mercure galant* of 1687 raises the possibility that La Guerre's earlier harpsichord works may likewise have been performed as ensemble pieces.[13]

The harmonic richness, abundant ornamentation, and refined expression of La Guerre's keyboard compositions reveal her indebtedness to the traditions of seventeenth-century French harpsichord and lute music. But more progressive features like sequential repetition, suspension chains, and circle-of-fifth progressions show her regard also for late seventeenth- and early eighteenth-century Italian procedures. Although some of her pieces betray one influence more than the other, most display a skillful consolidation of both French and Italian elements. As would be expected, the harpsichord works of 1707 show a more pronounced Italian influence.

La Guerre's remaining instrumental compositions consist of six unpublished sonatas (two for solo violin, viola da gamba, and organ or harpsichord; four for two violins, violoncello, and organ) and six *Sonates pour le viollon et pour le clavecin* published in 1707 along with her second harpsichord book. The unpublished pieces date back to at least 1695 and are thus among the earliest sonatas composed in France. Together with the pioneer endeavors of François Couperin, Sébastien de Brossard, and Jean-Féry Rebel, they confirm the appeal of the Italian style in the late 1600s and, in particular, the impact of Arcangelo Corelli's music.

Like those of other early French sonata composers, La Guerre's solo and trio sonatas combine French and Italian features. Her sonatas as a whole comprise four to nine movements and are greatly indebted to the church-sonata tradition. Movements with tempo titles prevail, but arias and dances are also present. The movements contrast well but do not adhere to any particular sequence of tempos. This lack of uniformity as to number, types, and order of movements is not peculiar to La Guerre's pieces but applies also to sonatas by Couperin and Rebel, among others. Patterned after the airs in seventeenth-century French stage music, the arias in La Guerre's sonatas are especially notable for their lyrical melodies and textural shifts. The latter largely resulted from the changing role of the melodic continuo instrument, which sometimes doubles the keyboard bass, at other times provides a supplemental voice, and at still other times serves as a soloist. Bass *récits* in the sonatas additionally reflect the French fondness for using the melodic continuo instrument in a soloistic, as well as an accompanimental capacity. Distinctive aspects of La Guerre's approach to the sonata include her propensity for slow finales, her considerable variety of formal structures (binary, ternary, variation, fugal, rondeaulike, and free designs), and her love of tonal contrast as evidenced by frequent changes of mode and by an occasional incorporation of contrasting keys.

The first two movements of the D-major trio sonata printed here exemplify La Guerre's unpublished sonatas in that they unfold in a continuous, nonrepetitive manner and are contrapuntal in texture. The *Grave*, featuring rich harmonies and long, artful melodies, begins with the imitative presentation—at the tonic level—of a short motive. Thereafter, this material is subjected to continuous expansion involving brief modulations to closely related keys. The *Vivace e Presto*, a typical fast movement, relies heavily on motivic interplay enlivened by syncopations and major-minor inflec-

tions. The movement concludes with a short but harmonically rich *Adagio*.

In the year of La Guerre's death, a commemorative medal was fashioned in her honor. It bore her image and the inscription *Aux grands musiciens j'ay disputé le prix* (With the great musicians I competed for the prize). Child prodigy, celebrated performer, and versatile composer, La Guerre had indeed competed for recognition and gained the praise of her contemporaries. While many writers have chronicled her achievements, Titon du Tillet's lengthy tribute in *Le Parnasse françois* is especially illuminating. It reads in part as follows:

> She had above all a marvelous talent for improvising and for playing fantasies extemporaneously, and sometimes for an entire half hour she would follow an improvisation and a fantasy with songs and harmonies extremely varied and in excellent taste, which would charm the listeners.
>
> Madame [sic] de la Guerre had a very great genius for composition and excelled in vocal music as well as instrumental, as she made known by several works in all kinds of music that one has of her composition; . . .
>
> Surely one can say that never has anyone of her sex had such great talents as she both for composing music and for performing it so admirably on the harpsichord and on the organ.[14]

Notes

1. The year of Elizabeth's birth, long a matter of dispute, has now been determined, thanks to the discovery of a reference to her baptism on March 17, 1665 (*The Norton/Grove Dictionary of Women Composers*, s.v. "Jacquet de la Guerre, Elisabeth-Claude," by Edith Borroff). In keeping with the composer's practice, the present essay uses the spelling "Elizabeth" (rather than "Elisabeth") for La Guerre's first name.

2. *Mercure galant*, March 1687, p. 177. (Translations mine unless otherwise noted.)

3. Ibid., December 1678, p. 128.

4. Michel Brenet [Marie Bobillier], "Quatre femmes musiciennes I: Mademoiselle Jacquet de la Guerre," *L'Art* 59 (October 1894): 108–9. According to the Marquis de Dangeau, additional performances were given on July 23 and August 9 (Chantal Masson, "Journal du Marquis de Dangeau 1684–1720," *"Recherches" sur la Musique française classique* 2 [1961–62]: 198).

5. Évrard Titon du Tillet, *Le Parnasse françois* (Paris: Jean-Baptiste Coignard Fils, 1732), p. 636.

6. Ibid. Translation from Edith Borroff, *An Introduction to Elisabeth-Claude Jacquet de La Guerre* (Brooklyn, New York: The Institute of Mediaeval Music, 1966), p. 18.

7. For a fuller account of La Guerre's life and music see Borroff, *La Guerre*, and Carol Henry Bates, "The Instrumental Music of Elisabeth-Claude Jacquet de la Guerre" (Ph.D. diss., Indiana University, 1978).

8. The extant portion of the dedication is quoted and translated in Carol Henry Bates, "Elisabeth Jacquet de la Guerre: A New

Source of Seventeenth-Century French Harpsichord Music," *"Recherches" sur la Musique française classique* 22 (1984): 11–12.

9. Paris, Bibliothèque Nationale, ms. fr. 2217. Brenet suggests that this "ballet chanté" may have been the work La Guerre presented at her compositional debut ("Quatre femmes musiciennes," p. 108). Other writers, however, including Borroff (*La Guerre*, p. 12), believe that this ballet commemorated the successful conquest of Mons and therefore was composed in 1691.

10. For a thorough investigation and modern edition of *Cephale et Procris*, see Wanda R. Griffiths, "Jacquet de la Guerre's *Cephale et Procris*: Style and Performance" (Ph.D. diss., Claremont Graduate School, 1992).

11. For detailed information about this volume see Adrian Rose, "Élisabeth-Claude Jacquet de La Guerre and the secular *cantate françoise*," *Early Music* 13, no. 4 (1985): 529–41. Another secular cantata that may have been written by La Guerre is *La Musette, ou les bergers de Suresne* (now lost), which, though published anonymously in 1713, was attributed to La Guerre by Sébastien de Brossard (Rose, n. 26).

12. Other popular songs by La Guerre are identified in the list of extant works.

13. "Most of these pieces are suited for performance on a treble violin or treble viol with a bass . . ." (*Mercure galant*, March 1687, p. 179).

14. Titon du Tillet, *Le Parnasse françois*, p. 636.

Bibliography

Extant Works

Les Piéces de clavessin, livre premier (Paris, 1687). Sole source: Venice, Conservatorio di Musica Benedetto Marcello, Stampe antico 137. Facs. ed., Geneva: Minkoff (forthcoming). Mod. ed., C. H. Bates, *Elisabeth-Claude Jacquet de la Guerre: Pièces de clavecin*, Le Pupitre 66 (Paris: Heugel, 1986).

Cephale et Procris, tragédie lyrique (Paris, 1694). Selected sources: Paris, Bibliothèque Nationale, Vm^2. 124 (score); Berkeley, University of California Music Library, M1500, D42C4, Case (score).

Two unpublished sonatas for solo violin, viola da gamba, and organ or harpsichord (ca. 1695). Sole source: Paris, Bibliothèque Nationale, Vm^7. 1111^a (parts). Mod. ed., C. H. Bates, *Elizabeth-Claude Jacquet de la Guerre: Frühe Solosonaten* (score and parts; Kassel: Furore, forthcoming).

Four trio sonatas for two violins, violoncello, and organ (ca. 1695). Sources: Paris, Bibliothèque Nationale, Vm^7. 1110 (score) and Vm^7. 1111^b (parts). Mod. ed., C. H. Bates, *Elisabeth-Claude Jacquet de la Guerre: Triosonaten* (score and parts), 2 vols. (Kassel: Furore, 1993–95).

Pieces de clavecin qui peuvent se joüer sur le viollon and *Sonates pour le viollon et pour le clavecin*, 2 vols. in 1 (Paris, 1707). Sources: Paris, Bibliothèque Nationale, Vm^7. 1860 (sole copy of double volume); corrected prints of the sonatas only (score)—Paris, Conservatoire, D.6534(3), and London, British Library, Music Room f.380.q. Mod. ed. of harpsichord pieces, C. H. Bates (see

Les Piéces de clavessin above); mod. ed. of sonatas, C. H. Bates, *Elizabeth-Claude Jacquet de la Guerre: Sonates pour le viollon et pour le clavecin* (score and parts), 3 vols. (Kassel: Furore, in press).

Cantates françoises sur des sujets tirez de l'Écriture, livre premier (Paris, 1708). Selected sources: Paris, Conservatoire, D.6534(1); London, British Library, Music E.69i. Facs. ed., *The Eighteenth-Century French Cantata*, vol. 3 (New York: Garland, 1990). Mod. ed. of *Le Passage de la Mer Rouge*, Diane Guthrie (Bryn Mawr: Hildegard, 1994).

Aux vains attraits d'une nouvelle ardeur (unaccompanied duet), in the C. Ballard *Recueil d'airs sérieux et à boire* (Paris, 1710).

Cantates françoises sur des sujets tirez de l'Écriture, livre second (Paris, 1711). Selected sources: Paris, Conservatoire, D.6534(2); London, British Library, Music E.69ii. Facs. ed., *The Eighteenth-Century French Cantata*, vol. 3 (New York: Garland, 1990).

Heureux l'instant qui vous vit naître, Pour la gloire des souverains, Cédons tous aux tendres ardeurs, and *Cher favori de la victoire* (four airs for solo voice and continuo), in R. Trépagne de Ménerville's *Les Amusemens de Monseigneur le Duc de Bretagne, Dauphin* (Paris, 1712).

Semelé, L'Ile de Delos, Le Sommeil d'Ulisse, Cantates françoises aûquelles on a joint Le Raccommodement comique (Paris, n.d.). Selected sources: Paris, Bibliothèque Nationale, Vm^7. 161; London, British Library, I.298. Facs. ed., *The Eighteenth-Century French Cantata*, vol. 13 (New York: Garland, 1990). Mod. ed. of *Semelé*, S. Erickson and R. Block, in *Historical Anthology of Music by Women*, edited by J. Briscoe (Bloomington: Indiana University Press, 1987).

Les Rossignols dés que le jour commence (duet with continuo from *Cephale et Procris*), in the J.-B.-C. Ballard *Recueil d'airs sérieux et à boire* (Paris, 1721); also appeared as an unaccompanied air for solo voice in *Nouveau recueil de chansons choisies* (The Hague, 1729; 2d edition, 1732).

Entre nous, mes chers amis (unaccompanied *air à boire* for solo voice) and *Tant que je verrons ce pot* (parody on the Bourrée from *Cephale et Procris* for solo voice and continuo), in the J.-B.-C. Ballard *Recueil d'airs sérieux et à boire* (Paris, 1724).

Books and Articles

Bates, Carol Henry. "Elizabeth Jacquet de la Guerre: A New Source of Seventeenth-Century French Harpsichord Music." *"Recherches" sur la Musique française classique* 22 (1984): 7–49.

———. "The Instrumental Music of Elizabeth-Claude Jacquet de la Guerre." Ph.D. diss., Indiana University, 1978.

Borroff, Edith. *An Introduction to Elizabeth-Claude Jacquet de La Guerre*. Brooklyn, New York: The Institute of Mediaeval Music, 1966.

———. "Jacquet de la Guerre, Elizabeth-Claude." In *The Norton/Grove Dictionary of Women Composers*. New York: W.W. Norton, 1995.

Brenet, Michel [Marie Bobillier]. "Quatre femmes musiciennes I: Mademoiselle Jacquet de la Guerre." *L'Art* 59 (October 1894): 107–12.

Cessac, Catherine. "Elizabeth Jacquet de la Guerre (1665–1729): claveciniste et compositeur." Ph.D. diss., University of Paris, Sorbonne, 1993.

Griffiths, Wanda R. "Jacquet de la Guerre's *Cephale et Procris*: Style and Performance." Ph.D. diss., Claremont Graduate School, 1992.

Guthrie, Diane Upchurch. "Elizabeth-Claude Jacquet de la Guerre's *Le Passage de la Mer Rouge:* An Edition with Commentary and Notes on Performance." D.M.A. diss., University of North Carolina at Greensboro, 1992.

Masson, Chantal. "Journal du Marquis de Dangeau 1684–1720." *"Recherches" sur la Musique française classique* 2 (1961–62): 193–223.

Mercure galant, December 1678; March 1687.

Rose, Adrian. "Élizabeth-Claude Jacquet de la Guerre and the secular *cantate françoise*." *Early Music* 13, no. 4 (1985): 529–41.

Titon du Tillet, Évrard. *Le Parnasse françois.* Paris: Jean-Baptiste Coignard Fils, 1732.

Discography

Jacquet de la Guerre, Elisabeth. *Cantates bibliques* [selections from books 1 and 2]; *Pièces instrumentales et vocale* [Trio Sonata in G minor, selections from the 1707 harpsichord book, and *Le Raccommodement comique de Pierrot et de Nicole*]. Isabelle Poulenard and Sophie Boulin, sopranos; Michel Verschaeve, baritone; instrumental ensembles conducted by Guy Robert and Georges Guillard. Arion ARN 268012. Two compact discs.

Jacquet de la Guerre, Elisabeth. *Pièces de clavecin* (1687). Emer Buckley, harpsichord. Harmonia Mundi France HM 1098. LP sound recording.

Jacquet de la Guerre, Elizabeth-Claude. *Music for Solo Harpsichord* [suites I and IV of 1687; suite I of 1707]. John Metz, harpsichord. Summit Records DCD 136. Compact disc.

French Baroque Cantatas by Philippe Courbois and Elisabeth Jacquet de la Guerre [includes La Guerre's *Samson* and *Le Sommeil d'Ulisse*]. John Ostendorf, bass-baritone; Bronx Arts Ensemble Chamber Orchestra; Johannes Somary, conductor. Leonarda Productions LP1 109. LP sound recording.

Editorial Comments

Harpsichord Selections

Although the original source utilizes four clefs (treble, soprano, alto, and baritone), this edition employs only the treble and bass clefs. Except for superfluous accidentals, the original key signatures have been retained, as have the original time signatures. The original note values have also been preserved, except in a few

passages where modification helps clarify rhythmic activity (e.g., in measures 20 and 21 of the Chaconne the notation of the soprano line has been changed from ♩ ♩ ♩ ♩. ♫ ♫ to ♩ ♩ ♩♩ ♫ ♫ ♫). Because of their possible bearing on articulation, the beamings in the original source have been retained. Editorial ties are shown by dotted lines; square brackets enclose rests, notes, and markings not found in the source.

Redundant accidentals have been omitted except in a few chromatic passages where La Guerre's own precautionary signs have been preserved, and in the unmeasured Prelude where the modern convention governing accidentals cannot be applied. (In this piece an accidental affects only the note that immediately follows, not later occurrences of the same pitch.) Sharps or flats used to cancel chromatic alterations in the original source have been replaced by natural signs. Parentheses enclose "implicit" accidentals, those not present in the original source but necessitated by the change to modern notation. Accidentals supplied to correct errors or omissions in the text are placed in square brackets, and accidentals sugggested for precautionary reasons are written above or below notes.

In the original source all of the binary pieces in the A-minor suite have single endings at the close of sections. This edition has provided double endings in the Allemande in order to accommodate upbeats. Repeat signs have been modernized, with |1. ⎯⎯⎯| and |2. ⎯⎯⎯| designations added where needed.

Written in unmeasured notation without a time signature or bar lines, the Prelude in the A-minor suite is intended to be performed in a rhythmically free, spontaneous manner. The notes should be played in sequence, with careful attention being paid to those accompanied or followed by curved lines. These lines primarily set off tones that should be sustained, most often to form chords. On occasion, however, they serve instead to indicate *legato* note groupings (see system 7, top staff, notes 16–18). The various note values in the Prelude should be interpreted principally as indicators of musical function rather than of duration. White notes (whole notes) usually signify harmonic tones, whereas black notes (sixteenths, eighths, and quarters) normally denote melodic activity such as passing tones and passagework. While the various note values do indeed have rhythmic implications—the sixteenth notes at the beginning of the Prelude, for example, seem to call for a rapid execution—they primarily delineate musical function. This notational method gives the harpsichordist some interpretive guidance while at the same time allowing considerable flexibility of rhythmic flow. The performer should strive to create the effect of an improvisation. (For historical perspective as well as further information about the notation and performance of unmeasured harpsichord preludes see Howard Ferguson, ed., *Early French Keyboard Music: An Anthology*, 2 vols. (London: Oxford University Press, 1966); Davitt Moroney, "The performance of unmeasured harpsichord preludes," *Early Music* 4, no. 2 (April 1976): 143–151; Colin Tilney, *The Art of the Unmeasured Prelude for Harpsichord: France 1660–1720*, 3 vols. (London: Schott, 1991); and Richard Troeger, "The French Unmeasured Harpsichord Prelude: Notation and Performance," *Early Keyboard Journal* 10 (1992): 89–119.)

The only extant copy of La Guerre's harpsichord book of 1687 does not include a table of ornaments. The following suggested realizations of the ornaments encountered in the three suite movements included here illustrate the melodic contour of each type of embellishment. Some flexibility in the rhythmic interpretation of ornaments is appropriate. The trill, for instance, may incorporate additional repercussions and may be played at different speeds. Except for the interpretation of the *port de voix* (+), which reflects the practice of Jean-Henry d'Anglebert, the suggested realizations are based on Jacques Champion de Chambonnières's ornament renderings. (See Jean-Henry d'Anglebert, *Pièces de clavecin* [1689], ed. Kenneth Gilbert (Paris: Heugel, 1975); and J. C. de Chambonnières, *Les deux livres de clavecin* [1670], ed. Thurston Dart (Monaco: Éditions de L'Oiseau-Lyre, 1969).)

The following list of original source readings documents the few instances where editorial emendations have proven necessary.

Prelude	System 11, top staff, notes 1-4:	
Allemande	M. 3, top staff, beat 3:	4th ♪ has trill (not mordent)
Chaconne	M. 7, bottom staff:	+ on *d,* not *e*
"	M. 51, bottom staff, beat 3:	*E-D*

Trio-Sonata Excerpts

La Guerre's four trio sonatas are preserved in two different manuscripts: Paris, Bibliothèque Nationale, Vm^7. 1110, written in score format; and Paris, Bibliothèque Nationale, Vm^7. 111^b, which contains sets of parts. Although both of these sources are incomplete, together they provide a satisfactory reading of the music. Because of its greater completeness—it includes, among other things, instrumental specifications as well as a significantly larger number of tempo markings, accidentals, ornaments, and figured-bass symbols—Vm^7. 1111^b serves as the basis of this edition of the first two movements of the D-major trio sonata. When necessary, however, the edition freely incorporates material from Vm^7. 1110. The list of original source readings records all such borrowings as well as significant differences between the two manuscript readings. For more detailed information about the original sources, see pages vii and viii in the Furore edition of this sonata.

Although the principal source utilizes three clefs (French violin,

soprano, and bass), this edition employs only the treble and bass clefs. The original key and time signatures have been preserved, however, as have the original note values. Because they may bear on phrasing and articulation, beamings in Vm^7. 1111^b have also been retained despite their inconsistencies. Editorial ties are distinguished by dotted lines. Square brackets enclose editorial ornaments and other additions to the text, including accidentals supplied to correct errors or omissions. Redundant accidentals in the source have been eliminated, and sharps or flats used to nullify chromatic alterations have been replaced by natural signs. Parentheses enclose "implicit" accidentals, those not found in the source but required for modern notation. Precautionary accidentals are placed above or below notes.

The bass figuring has been moved from its original position above the keyboard bass to below the bottom staff. Bass figures that make no sense in their contexts have been eliminated and are recorded in the list of original source readings. Curved lines used in the source to indicate retention of harmony have been replaced by straight, horizontal lines.

Bass realizations have been intentionally kept simple in order to encourage accompanists to incorporate additional embellishments, increase the amount of rhythmic movement, and fill out the texture. Soloists, too, should not hesitate to add ornaments, so long as they exercise restraint in keeping with the French style. Through such extemporization, which was considered essential in the Baroque period, performers can become individually and vitally involved in the creative process. The only ornaments specified in the sonata movements included in this anthology are the *tremblement simple* and the *tremblement lié et appuyé,* which may be realized, respectively, as follows:

Unless otherwise noted, the following list pertains only to the text of Paris, Bibliothèque Nationale, Vm^7. 1111^b. The original title of the D-major trio sonata, here taken from the organo partbook, reads: "Suonata. III^a. a 2. VV. e Violoncello obligato. Con organo."

Measure(s)	Part(s)	
1–88	Violoncello	The source lacks a separate cello part for this sonata. This edition therefore patterns these measures after the organo bass. The organo partbook includes the independent cello line in mm. 81–82.
11	Organo	First figure = $5\frac{2}{4}$
18	Violino I	Note 6: naturalized in Vm^7. 1110 only
47	Organo	No tempo indication
50	Organo	$\frac{6}{4}$ in the figuring between beats 2 and 3
53	Organo, Violoncello	Note 5: naturalized in Vm^7. 1110 only
59	Organo	Figuring: ♮ 6♯ 5; changed to correspond to mm. 64 and 83
63	Organo	First figure: 6 5
83	Organo, Violoncello	Taken from Vm^7. 1110; Vm^7. 1111^b gives ♩ ♩
84	Violino I	No tempo indication
85	Organo	Note 2: ♭ in figuring
87	Violino II·	Notes 1–2: slur in Vm^7. 1110 only

Selected Movements
from the
Harpsichord Suite in A Minor (1687)

Elizabeth - Claude Jacquet de la Guerre
Carol Henry Bates, editor

Prelude

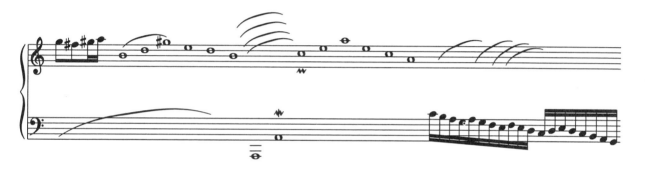

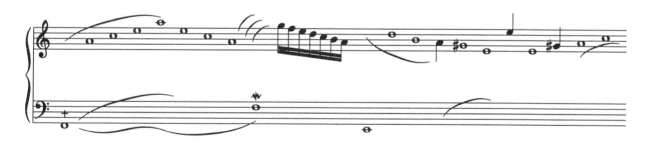

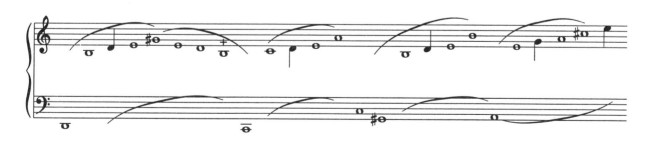

This modern edition was originally issued in *Elisabeth - Claude Jacquet de la Guerre: Pièces de clavecin* (Paris: Heugel, 1986). The present computer - generated resetting has been prepared "avec l'aimable autorisation des Editions Heugel S.A., Paris."

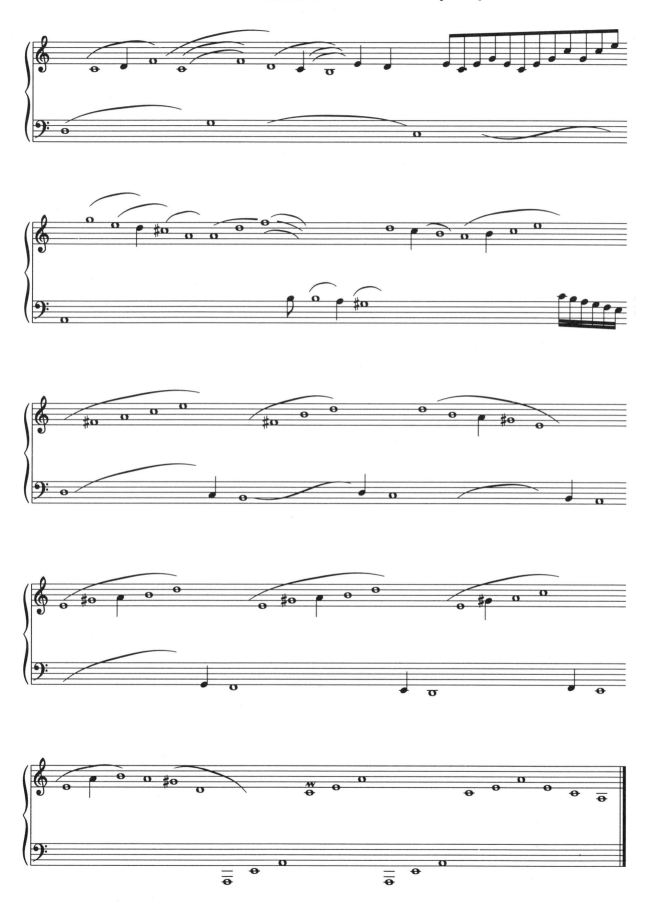

Selected Movements
from
Suonata
[D]

Elizabeth - Claude Jacquet de la Guerre
Carol Henry Bates, editor

This modern edition was originally issued in *Elizabeth-Claude Jacquet de la Guerre: Triosonaten,* Band II (Kassel: Furore, 1993).
The present computer-generated resetting has been prepared with kind permission of Furore Verlag.

The Cantatas of Elizabeth-Claude Jacquet de la Guerre

(1665–1729)

DIANE UPCHURCH GUTHRIE

Elizabeth-Claude Jacquet de la Guerre (1665–1729) was known first and foremost as a celebrated harpsichordist, both in the court of King Louis XIV and in the fashionable Parisian salons at the turn of the eighteenth century.[1] Her compositions, primarily keyboard pieces and small chamber works, were not only encouraged by the king, but the majority of them were also dedicated to her royal patron. Among her works are fifteen solo cantatas that are worthy of study and performance, not only for their own artistic excellence but because they are highly representative of the *cantate française*.

The *cantate française* appeared in the salons of eighteenth-century France as an imitation of the popular Italian chamber cantatas imported during the latter years of the seventeenth century.[2] Although cantatas and similar works were likely composed in France in the late 1600s, the first published works titled *Cantatas françoises* did not appear until 1706.[3] Nearly every French composer of the period contributed to the genre. Among the most prolific and well-known composers of *cantates françaises* were Jean-Baptiste Morin, Jean-Baptiste Stuck, Nicolas Bernier (1665–1734), André Campra (1660–1744), Louis-Nicolas Clérambault (1676–1749), and Michel Pignolet de Montéclair (1666–1737). An estimated eight to nine hundred of these small intimate works were produced before 1750.[4]

The great number of contributions by French composers to the *cantate française* during the years 1706–1750 was obviously brought about by their desire to adapt the Italian counterpart to fit the French language and musical style (*le réunion des deux goûts*).[5] The decline of Louis XIV's interest in opera and the ensuing change in musical tastes at court further contributed to the rise of the *cantate française*. It is not surprising, therefore, that La Guerre, whose close association with the musical milieu of both Paris and the French court

had already been established, was also attracted to the *cantate française*.[6] La Guerre's cantatas were, in fact, among the earliest published examples.

La Guerre's first two books, entitled *Cantates françoises sur des sujets tirez de l'Ecriture* (1708 and 1711), comprise a continuing publication of twelve cantatas based on biblical stories. In order, the six cantatas included in Book I are *Esther, Le Passage de la Mer Rouge* (The Crossing of the Red Sea), *Jacob et Rachel, Jonas, Susanne et les Viellards* (Susanna and the Elders), and *Judith*. Book II also contains six cantatas: *Adam, Le Temple rebasti* (The Temple Rebuilt), *Le Déluge, Joseph, Jephté*, and *Samson*.

A third book containing three cantatas based on mythological subjects was published by La Guerre sometime after 1715. The cantatas offered in Book III include *Semelé, L'Ile de Delos*, and *Le Sommeil*.[7]

The *Cantates françoises sur des sujets tirez de l'Ecriture* (Books I and II) are, from a textual standpoint, a distinct variety. Early in the development of the genre, the majority of *cantate française* texts were usually based on mythological and allegorical subjects and were amorous in nature.[8] Not only are La Guerre's *Cantates françoises sur des sujets tirez de l'Ecriture* among a very small group of French cantatas based on stories from the scriptures, but, notably, they were the first cantatas of the biblical variety to be published.[9] By choosing biblical subjects for the cantatas, La Guerre not only showed her originality, but she also demonstrated her keen understanding of the king's taste at that point in time. The moralistic tone of the cantatas based on subjects from the Old Testament were undoubtedly well suited to the aging Louis and his pious wife, the Mme de Maintenon. A single dedicatory letter addressed to the king in the 1708 collection serves both publications. The dedication reads in part as follows:

Sire, even if the long habit of offering my works to your Majesty had not made of it a duty; henceforth, I could not excuse myself from offering him this last work. I have made a setting of music worthy, I dare say, of Your Majesty. These are the considerable deeds of Holy Scripture that I lay before your eyes.[10]

La Guerre's *Cantates françoises sur des sujets tirez de l'Ecriture* were composed on texts written by Antoine Houdar de la Motte (1672–1731).[11] As can be observed from the titles of la Guerre's cantatas, the poet's texts deal with some of the more colorful stories of the Old Testament, which presume a more dramatic musical setting. All but three of La Motte's texts adhere to the organization of three recitative-aria pairs established by the poetic models of Jean-Baptiste Rousseau (1671–1741).[12] La Guerre's musical settings closely parallel the formal structure set forth in La Motte's texts. Occasionally, however, la Guerre intentionally varies the textual order presented in La Motte's text to set the dramatic situation more vividly. The inclusion of additional instrumental sections, some of them with descriptive titles such as *Bruit de guerres* (clamor of war), *Tempeste,* and *Sommeil* (sleep), is again indicative of her attention given to the dramatic presentation.

The cantatas in Book I and Book II are variously scored. Five of the twelve are scored for solo voice and continuo; five are scored for solo voice *avec symphonie* (with additional instruments). Two cantatas scored for two voices and continuo are included in Book II; one of them for soprano and bass, the other for two sopranos. Obbligato passages appear in both books but to a greater extent in the second.

La Guerre's musical settings of La Motte's texts illustrate the composer's expressive application of *le réunion des deux goûts* as well as her sensitivity to text and form. Consistently evident in La Guerre's style is the meticulous attention given to detail and the resourceful manner in which she employs form, texture, harmony, melody, and rhythm to express the text.

Examination of the following excerpt from the cantata *Le Passage de la Mer Rouge* (from Book I, 1708) provides an insightful study of the musical style with which La Guerre presented La Motte's adaptation of the familiar Old Testament story of Moses leading the Israelites through the Red Sea.[13] La Guerre has carefully followed the formal organization of the poetic text. The cantata, scored for soprano, violins, and continuo, includes three recitatives, and three airs with the addition of three instrumental movements as outlined below.[14] While it is not always marked in the score, the violin is clearly indicated and is presented here in brackets. La Guerre creates a variety of textures by the inclusion (or exclusion) of *symphonie.*

The short instrumental [Prélude], not named in the original publication, effectively foreshadows the uncertainty of the ensuing drama. The *incertitude* (uncertainty) is established by a variety of compositional devices: sudden unexpected

Movement	Scoring
[Prélude]	[violin] and continuo
Récitatif	voice, violin(s), and continuo
Air	voice and continuo
Ritournelle	[violin] and continuo
Air	voice, violin and continuo
Bruit de guerre	[violin(s)] and continuo
Récitatif	voice and continuo
Air	voice and continuo

harmonic alterations, the frequency of dissonances on strong beats, the prominence of first-inversion chords throughout, the irregularity of harmonic rhythm, and the angular melodic writing for the violin. The unpredictable character of the movement is straightaway perceived in the first two measures by both the angular melodic shape in the violin and by the juxtaposition of its "distorted" imitation in the viol. Harmonic uncertainty continues throughout the section by virtue of the A-flat/A-natural ambiguity (modal mixture), finally coming to a close by way of a more conventional and stable harmonic language. B-flat is not firmly established until the last two measures (mm. 12–13).

La Guerre interprets the opening recitative of *Le Passage de la Mer Rouge* with a combination of Italian *recitativo secco* and French *récitatif mesuré* styles and the addition of obbligato violin (m. 20). The resulting variety of textures and styles, in addition to La Guerre's obvious concern for colorful harmonic detail and text illustration, effectively establishes the frightening predicament into which Moses has led the Israelites. Beginning with m. 17, the bass line becomes increasingly active, finally breaking forth into a flourishing duet between the violin and the viol. The duet provides an intriguing contrast to the *secco* style of the initial statement while poignantly illustrating the *incertitude* of the Israelites' situation.

La Guerre's melodic writing is clearly concerned with declamation of the text, a factor so important in the development of the French cantata. The varying rhythms and phrasal shape exhibited in the melody of the opening recitative closely correspond to the prosody of the text, gaining momentum toward the ends of lines or caesuras where the phrase ultimately pauses either on notes of longer value or on a rest. The short melisma used in m. 24 to heighten the connotation of the word *murmures* (murmurings) is echoed and lengthened in the viol.

Ingrats que vos plaintes finissent (Ungrateful ones, if only your complaints would cease), the first air in *Le Passage de la Mer Rouge,* is characterized by a declamatory style and preponderance of dotted rhythms, both distinctively French traits. The *divisé* opening, in which the first vocal phrase is interrupted by the accompaniment before being sung in its entirety, and the *da capo* design of the aria are indicative of the composer's admiration of the Italian style as well. The break in the text line after *Ingrats* (m. 36), created by the *divisé* opening, emphasizes the inflection of Moses' address.

The declamatory style of the vocal line in section A is achieved by La Guerre's syllabic setting of the text. In La Guerre's cantatas, the use of melismas is generally limited to a few carefully chosen instances for the purposes of text illustration. In rare instances when La Guerre introduces more elaborate vocal lines, she is always faithful to the French tradition of *le bon goût* (good taste).[15] The interpretation of the word *ondes* (waves), for example, at mm. 69–72, is effectively depicted by the improvisatory-like melisma and the undulating rhythm of the bass line.

The melodic style of the vocal line in the contrasting section B is appropriately more stable as Moses reassures the people of God's watchful care. This stability is created by La Guerre's use of quarter notes and eighth notes, as opposed to the use of dotted values employed in the previous material, and by the predominating stepwise motion. The inclusion of *coulés* (passing tones between two descending notes) in m. 80 further contributes to the softened melodic line.

The excerpt of the cantata, *Le Passage de la Mer Rouge,* admirably reveals the musical vocabulary exhibited in La Guerre's cantatas. The creative treatment of harmonic language, the expressive use of textural variety, the meticulous attention given to prosody and dramatic implications of the text, and the successful application of *le réunion des deux goûts* are highly indicative of La Guerre's mature and sophisticated level of musical thinking.

Notes

1. The reader is directed to the following comprehensive sources concerning La Guerre's life and works: Edith Borroff, *An Introduction to Elisabeth-Claude Jacquet de la Guerre* (Brooklyn, NY: Institute of Medieval Music, 1966); Carol Henry Bates, "The Instrumental Music of Elisabeth-Claude Jacquet de la Guerre" (Ph.D. diss., University of Indiana, 1975).

2. David Tunley, ed., *The Eighteenth-Century French Cantata,* vol. 1 (New York: Garland, 1990), p. vii.

3. Two volumes of these works, one by Jean-Baptiste Morin (1677–1745) and the other by Jean-Baptiste Stuck (1680–1755), were published almost simultaneously by Christophe Ballard in 1706. For a comprehensive listing of the publication dates of French cantatas printed between 1706 and 1767, see Gene E. Vollen, *The French Cantata: A Survey and Thematic Catalog* (Ann Arbor: UMI Research Press, 1982).

4. Tunley, ed., *The Eighteenth-Century French Cantata,* 1:ix.

5. For more in-depth information concerning the structure and style of the *cantate française,* the reader is directed to Chapter 3: "Stylistic Traits in French and Italian Vocal Music of the Baroque Era," in David Tunley, *The Eighteenth-Century French Cantata* (London: Dobson Books, 1974), pp. 33–49. See also Vollen, *The French Cantata,* pp. 39–45 and 79–95.

6. See the article by Bates in this chapter.

7. For an excellent discussion of the cantatas in Book III, see Adrian Rose, "Elisabeth-Claude Jacquet de la Guerre and the Secular *Cantate françoise,*" *Early Music* 13 (1985): 529–41.

8. The subject matter of the *cantates françaises* fall into several categories. For a detailed discussion of these categories, see Vollen, *The French Cantata,* pp. 16–23.

9. Only two other collections of spiritual cantatas are mentioned by Tunley (1974), pp. 117–18, and Vollen, *The French Cantata,* pp. 17–18. Sébastien de Brossard (1654–1730) wrote a collection of six spiritual cantatas that exists only in manuscript. Although his cantatas are similar to those of la Guerre, they are not dated. It is, therefore, impossible to tell if Brossard's cantatas are modeled after La Guerre's or if they predate them. Two other sets of spiritual cantatas by René Drouart de Bousset (1703–1760) were composed in 1735 and 1740.

10. For a complete dedication of the letter, see Borroff, *An Introduction,* p. 50.

11. La Motte, a member of the Académie française, was a gifted poet who wrote texts for thirty-seven cantatas, among them Clérambault's *Abraham* (1715), Destouches's *Semelé,* and La Guerre's twelve spiritual cantatas. See Robert E. Wolf, "Antoine Houdar de La Motte," in *The New Grove Dictionary of Music and Musicians,* ed. Stanley Sadie (London: Macmillan, 1980), 10: 415–16.

12. *Judith* (Book I) includes four recitatives and three arias; *Le Temple rebasti* (Book II) includes four arias and three recitatives; and *Jephté* (Book II) includes five recitatives and four arias. For a detailed discussion of Rousseau's contribution to the genre, see Tunley (1974), pp. 14–19.

13. An edition of *Le Passage de la Mer Rouge* in its entirety, with a discussion of La Guerre's writing style, is offered in Diane Upchurch Guthrie, "Elisabeth-Claude Jacquet de la Guerre's *Le Passage de la Mer Rouge:* An Edition with Commentary and Notes on Performance" (D.M.A. diss., University of North Carolina at Greensboro, 1992). A performance edition, also edited by Diane Upchurch Guthrie, is offered by Hildegard Publishing.

14. The term *movement* is used by the writer only for the sake of convenience and with the understanding that the cantata, during this period, was a continuous work.

15. For an insightful discussion of *bon goût,* the reader is directed to Jean Laurent le Cerf de La Viéville, *Traité du bon goût en musique,* from the *Comparison de la musique italienne et de la musique française* (1705), selected and annotated, Oliver Strunk, *Source Readings in Music History* (New York: Norton, 1950), p. 502.

Bibliography

Bates, Carol Henry. "The Instrumental Music of Elisabeth-Claude Jacquet de la Guerre." Ph.D. diss., University of Indiana, 1975.

Borroff, Edith. *An Introduction to Elisabeth-Claude Jacquet de la Guerre.* Brooklyn, New York: Institute of Medieval Music, 1966.

———. "Jacquet de la Guerre, Elisabeth-Claude." In *The New Grove Dictionary of Music and Musicians,* edited by Stanley Sadie, 9: 455–56. 20 vols. London: Macmillan, 1980.

The Eighteenth-Century French Cantata. Edited by David Tunley. 17 vols. New York: Garland, 1990. (Volume 13 includes facsimiles of la Guerre's fifteen cantatas.)

Guthrie, Diane Upchurch. "Elisabeth-Claude Jacquet de la Guerre's *Le Passage de la Mer Rouge:* An Edition with Commentary and Notes on Performance." D.M.A. diss., University of North Carolina at Greensboro, 1992.

La Guerre, Elisabeth-Claude Jacquet de. *Cantates françoises sur des sujets tirez de l'Ecriture; à voix seule, et basse-continue; partie avec symphonie & partie sans symphonie, livre premier.* Paris: Christoph Ballard, 1708. [Source: London. British Library. Music E. 69 No. 137.]

———. *Cantates françoises sur des sujects tirez de l'Ecriture; à I. II. voix, et basse-continue; partie avec symphonie, & partie sans symphonie, livre second.* Paris: Christoph Ballard, 1711. [Source: London. British Library. E 69 No. 138.]

———. *Sémele, L'Ile de Délos, le Sommeil d'Ulisse, Cantates françoises aûquelles on a joint le Raccommodement Comique.* Paris: Pierre Ribou, Foucault, L'Auteur, n.d. m [Source: Paris. Bibliothèque Nationale. Vm.⁷ 161.]

Le Cerf de La Ville, Jean Laurent. *Traité du bon goût en musique,* from the *Comparison de la musique italienne et de la musique françoise* (1705). Selected and annotated by Oliver Strunk. In *Source Readings in Music History,* 489–507. New York: W. W. Norton, 1950.

Rose, Adrian. "Elisabeth-Claude Jacquet de la Guerre and the Secular *cantate françoise.*" *Early Music* 13 (November 1985): 529–41.

Tiersot Julièn. "Cantates françaises du XVIII siècle." *Le Mènestrel* 56 (1893): 131–33, 140–42, 157–58.

Tunley, David. *The Eighteenth-Century French Cantata.* London: Dennis Dobson, 1974.

Vollen, Gene E. *The French Cantata: A Survey and Thematic Catalog.* Ann Arbor, Michigan: UMI Research Press, 1982.

Wallon, Simone. "Jacquet und Jacquet de la Guerre. In *Die Musik in Geschichte und Gegenwart,* edited by Friederick Blume, 6: 1644–1647. 14 vols. Kassel: Bärenreiter, 1949–1987.

———. "Les Testaments d'Elisabeth Jacquet de la Guerre." *Revue de musicologie* 40 (1978): 29–49.

Wolf, R. Peter. "Metrical Relationships in French Recitative of the Seventeenth and Eighteenth Centuries." *"Recherches" sur la musique française classique* 18 (1978): 29–49.

Wolf, Robert E. "Antoine Houdar de La Motte." In *The New Grove Dictionary of Music and Musicians,* edited by Stanley Sadie, 10: 415–16. London: Macmillan, 1980.

Discography

La Guerre, Elisabeth Jacquet de. *Cantates françoises sur Sujets tirez de l'Ecriture/ Pièces instrumentales et vocales.* Performed by Isabelle Poulenard and Sophia Boulin, sopranos, and Michel Verschaeve, baritone. ARION 268012 [AAD], 1992.

Le Passage de la Mer Rouge

Récitatif

Israël dont le Ciel voulait briser les fers	Israel for whom Heaven (God)
Fuyait loin du Tiran la triste servitude; Mais il sent à l'aspect des mers	wanted to break the bondage
	Fled far from the sad servitude of the tyrant
Renaître son incertitude.	But upon looking at the sea he (Moses) feels
Moïse, entend déjà ces murmures nouveaux;	His uncertainty revive.
Devais-tu nous conduire à ces affreux abîmes?	Moses already hears some murmurings;
Et l'Egypte pour ses victimes	Did you have to lead us to these frightful depths
Eût-elle manqué de tombeaux?	And Egypt for her victims
	Had she lacked tombs?

Air

Ingrats, que vos plaintes finissent,	Ungrateful ones, if only your complaints would cease,
Reprenez un plus doux espoir;	
Il est un souverain pouvoir	Take again a sweeter hope;
À qui les Ondes obéissent.	There is a supreme power
Il s'arme pour votre secours,	whom the waves obey.
Les flots ouverts vont vous apprendre	He arms himself for your aid,
Que la main qui régla leur cours	The parting waters are going to teach you
A le pouvoir de les suspendre.	That the hand that ruled their course
	has the power to stop them (the waves).

Le Passage de la Mer Rouge

Cantates françoises sur des sujets tirez de l'Écriture

Elisabeth - Claude Jacquet de la Guerre
Diane Guthrie, editor

On reprendre l'Air Ingrats,
jusqu'au mot Fin.
D.S. al Fine

Bianca Maria Meda

(ca. 1665–post 1700)

ROBERT L. KENDRICK

As with Badalla, little is known about Bianca Maria Meda's life. She professed her vows at the ancient Benedictine house of San Martino del Leano in Pavia (south of Milan) sometime in the 1680s. The motet *Cari musici* opens her only preserved collection, the *Motetti a uno, due, tre, quattro* (Bologna: Monti, 1691). It is a fairly elaborate example of the late seventeenth-century solo motet, in this case with two violins, that was quite popular in Lombardy at this time and which were performed in north-central Italy by nuns—to judge by the dedications in collections listed in RISM 1679/1. Its florid recitatives, two strophic arias (instead of the usual one), recurring opening instrumental ritornello, and final "Alleluia," which develops a series of melodic ideas, place the work firmly in the tradition of extended motets of the period.

The explicit invocation of music and musicians marks the text of this piece as a "metamusical" cantata, music about music, of a kind well known in the contemporary secular repertory. Its placement at the opening of an *opus primum* suggests its function as a proem to Meda's entire collection, perhaps even a nun composer's view of the place of music in spiritual life. The difficulties of speech and silence for a religious woman in a contemplative order are not without parallels in other devotional literature of the *Seicento,* and the detailed focus on personalized Christology replays a theme in female devotion that goes back to the late Middle Ages. The direct address of Jesus as Spouse is appropriate not only for the individual Christian but especially for nuns, who were considered brides of Christ. Certainly, both the standard *topos*—of the unsatisfactoriness of earthly music—and the employment of music as a metaphor for the joys and sorrows of internal devotional experience suffuse the writings of Federigo Borromeo and his cloistered correspondents earlier in the century in Milan. Again, the most obvious feature of Meda's writing is the vocal virtuosity and the use of the vocal part for sheer effect (the long-held notes in the canto over repeated figures in the violins or bass). The far more frequent use of exact sequence and repetition, com-

pared to earlier works, is not untypical of the Lombard motet repertory. The eighteenth-century division between recitative and aria is not completely relevant to Meda's work, however; such passages as *Ah, quid dico,* which flowers into accompanied arioso in order to set the key turning-point of the text, highlight the relative fluidity of small-scale form in such motets.

Bibliography

Kendrick, Robert. "Four Views of Milanese Nuns' Music." In *Creative Women in Medieval and Early Modern Italy,* edited by E. A. Matter and J. Coakley. Philadelphia: University of Pennsylvania Press, 1994, pp. 562–96.

Discography

"Cari musici." On *Non Tacete.* Nannerl Records. (The liner notes, Latin text, and paraphrases for this recording are inaccurate).

Editorial Procedures

1. Time values and time signatures have been left unaltered. Any variants in rhythm or pitch found in the source are noted, using the following shorthand: [measure number].[part-name, abbreviated]. [note number (rests are prefixed with the letter *r*)]: [original reading]. Hence a given variant might be designated as: 34.CII.3–4: c♯″-b′, meaning m. 34, Canto II, notes 3–4 were originally c♯″ and b′.

2. Barlines have been supplied when missing.

3. Clefs have been modernized; key signatures (actually indications of *cantus*) are as in the source.

4. Accidentals apply to the entire measure plus any notes tied into the next measure (as in normal modern notation). Editorial *musica ficta* is given above the staff; such *ficta* apply only to the note over which they are placed.

5. Text underlay is as in the original prints or manuscript; repetitions indicated by the abbreviation *ij* have been expanded and

placed inside brackets < >. Punctuation is editorial and has been kept to a minimum.

6. All slurs are original.

7. Ligatures have been indicated by whole brackets, while *minor color* is set off by half brackets.

8. Continuo figures have been moved from above the staff to below; dashes have been added to suspensions (4–3). The continuo realization is only a guide and should be adopted to the actual chordal instrument used (organ, theorbo or chitarrone, harpsichord, all of which were played by Milanese nuns in this period). The use of a string bass (violoncello/bass violin) to double the continuo line is generally anachronistic, at least before the generation of Badalla and Meda.

Abbreviations: C = Canto or Cantus; A = Alto; T = Tenor; Bc = Basso continuo; Vln = Violin; pitch designations employ the Helmholtz system (e.g. 440 Hz = a′). Sigla for music libraries are those found in *RISM Einzeldrucke*.

Sources

Cari Musici. In *Motetti a 1–4* (Bologna: Monti, 1691)

Critical Notes

Variants: Some of the text requires expansion *languere[t]* in order to make grammatical sense. The canto part in *Quantae deli-ciae* and *Amare et silere* is written out for both strophes (cf. the note on mm. 154 and 158 below). 35.C.1: quarternote; 58.C.5: sharp missing; 67.C.4–5: 16th and 32nd; 91.C.[2nd time]: slur missing; 100.C.[2nd time]: tie missing; 113.C.[2nd time]: slur missing; 122.C.[lst time]: tie missing; 154, 158, 167, 171: see note below; 179.C.2–7: all 16ths; 186.VlnI.5–7: c″♯–c′♯–b′; 210.Bc.1: 8th; 212.Bc.1.: 8th; 232.C.2–4: all 16ths; 233.C.3: 16th.

Note on mm. 154 and 158 (Canto, both times) and 167 and 171 (VlnI): This rhythmic figure is corrupt and metrically incorrect as printed. In m. 154, the canto line for the first strophe reads: e″ (quarter-note), e″ (dotted 16th, not tied), d″, c″, b′ (all 32nds); the second strophe reads e″ (dotted quarter, no tie), e″ (dotted 16th), d″, c″, b′ (all 32nds). In m. 158, first strophe, the reading is as in m. 154, with the addition of a tie between the two e″s, while the second strophe reads: e″ (quarter-note), e″ (dotted 8th, tied), d″, c″, b′ (all 32nds). I have opted for a composite version of this measure which attempts to do justice to the varying hints of the notation and to the text underlay. The version of this figure in the Violin I part (167.VlnI and 171.VlI) reads: e″ (8th), e″ (dotted 16th), d″, c″, b′ (all 32nds).

Performance notes

The opening ritornello (mm. 1–12) should be played between the two strophes in both arias (at m. 65 and m. 174, first time through).

Cari Musici

Cari Musici, cum grato silentio
voces comprimite,
suspendite sonos,
cantare cessate,
et contemplate dilecte
Jesu amores.
Non me turbate, no, amante,
armonici chori
cantare cessate.

Aria:

1 Quantae deliciae
  quantae fortunata beant me,
  rapit meum cor ad se
  Jesus solus voce amante.

2 Quanta laetitia
  quanta me divina replet lux
  in amore verus dux
  mihi donat gaudia tanta.

Ah, quid dico! anima ingrata,
in silentio taciturno
amores sponsi audio sepelire,
ah non tacete, no,
o voces canorae,
non tacete.

Dear musicians, with pleasing silence
withhold your voices,
suspend your sounds,
cease your singing
and lovingly contemplate
the love of Jesus.
Do not trouble me, no,
harmonious choirs,
but cease your singing.

How many delights
enrich me, the fortunate one;
he seizes my heart for himself,
only Jesus, with a lover's voice.

How much joy
how much divine light fills me
with his love my true leader
grants me countless joys.

Oh, what am I saying! Ungrateful soul,
I hear them bury my spouse's love
in hushed silence;
oh, do not be silent, no
o melodious voices,
do not be silent.

Aria:

1   Amare et silere, cor,
     tentas impossibile,
     plus tormentum sit terribile
     quando curat reticere.

2   Tacere et ardere, no
     non potes tam firmissime,
     tuae pene sunt durissimae,
     si tacendo vis languere[t].

Alleluia.

Heart, you try in vain
to love and be silent,
To say nothing
were a more terrible torment.

To be silent and burn, no,
this you cannot do so strongly.
Your pain is excruciating
if by being silent your strength grows weak.

Alleluia.

Cari musici

Bianca Maria Meda
Robert Kendrick, editor

[Seconda:]

Quan - tae _____ de - li - ciae quan - tae
Quan - ta _____ lae - ti - tia quan - ta

quan - tae _____ de - li - ciae quan - tae for - tu - na - ta for - tu - na - ta
quan - ta _____ lae - ti - tia quan - ta me di - vi - na me di - vi - na

for - tu - na - ta be - ant me, _____
me di - vi - na re - plet lux _____

a) **Da capo**
il Ritornello
per la seconda stroffa.

a) i.e., play mm. 1 - 12, then go to m. 39 for the 2nd verse.

si - - - - - bi - le,
mis - - - - si - me,

a - ma - re et si -
ta - ce - re et ar -

a) *Ritornello da capo*
per la seconda stroffa.

a)*i.e., m. 1 - 12, then m.89 for the 2nd verse.*

Caterina Benedetta Gratianini

(fl. 1705–1715)

BARBARA GARVEY JACKSON

At least seven women are known to have composed oratorios in the eighteenth century in Vienna and in northern Italy, and of these at least four had their works performed in Vienna in the Imperial Chapel. The earliest of the Viennese group was Marianne von Raschenau, a nun and choir director at the convent of St. Jakob auf der Hülben. Though printed libretti survive for her works, no location is known for any of her music.

Caterina Benedetta Gratianini, however, has left two manuscript scores of large oratorios. In the *Santa Teresa* (St. Theresa) manuscript her name is spelled Gratianini, while in *S. Gemigniano vescous, e prottettore di Modona* [sic] (St. Gemigniano, bishop and protector of Modena) the composer's name is given as Catterina Benedetta Grazianini. Both works were apparently performed at court in Vienna, although dates for performances are known for only one. A note on the title page of *S. Gemigniano* reads *cantate avanti de Altezze . . . di Brunswic* [sic] *e di Modona quest anno 1705 . . . e riuscito mirabilmente* (sung before the Highnesses . . . of Brunswick and Modena, this year of 1705 . . . and marvelously received). No other information about the composer's life, career, training or personal status is known. A work of such local subject as *S. Gemigniano,* about the patron saint of Modena, might originally have been written either for a performance there or to honor state guests from that city who were visiting Vienna. Perhaps the composer herself was connected in some way with Modena. All that can be documented is that it did appear on the court calendar in Vienna in 1705 and again in 1715.[1]

One other bit of information is found on the title page, as well as at the beginning of each singer's first aria in the work: the cast list for the 1705 performance. The singers were Vienna (female soprano Vienna Mellini), Checo de Grandis (male soprano Francesco de Grandis), Luigino (male alto Luigi Albarelli), and bass D. Antonio Belugani.[2] Of these, the first three were in the service of the Duke of Modena, and on this basis and by the nature of the libretto, Wellesz speculated that the composer was Modenese.[3]

Unfortunately, there is no title page for *Santa Teresa;* the title and the composer's name appear at the top of the first page of the manuscript score, which is undated. Probably all the scores of the Vienna oratorio group survive in copyists' manuscripts rather than composers' autographs. The manuscript of *Santa Teresa* is in a far less practiced hand than the manuscript scores of works by Maria Margherita Grimani or Camilla de Rossi from the same time and place, and there are many careless errors in the placement of figured bass symbols and use of accidentals. They are not the sort of errors that the composer would have been likely to make but are those of a hasty copyist. Gratianini's oratorios call for string orchestra with continuo and four soloists.[4] In *Santa Teresa,* the title role is an alto (probably sung by a male alto), and the rest of the cast includes Angelo, soprano; Rodrigo, tenor; and Fernando, bass. There is no chorus in this work, or indeed in any of the oratorios by the women composers heard in Vienna in the early eighteenth century. The arias are *da capo,* as was standard at the time. Although some are accompanied only by continuo, often followed by a string ritornello, most are *con stromenti* (accompanied by the orchestra throughout). One aria has a fine cello solo independent from the continuo (the same instrumentation is found in an aria from *S. Gemigniano*).[5]

Both of Gratianini's oratorios, as well as those of the other women who composed for the Vienna court, are cast in a formal scheme like that used by Alessandro Scarlatti after about 1700. They consist of two large parts, the first and sometimes the second of which are introduced by a single- or multi-movement sinfonia for string orchestra. The oratorio sinfonias by Gratianini and her colleagues form a group of instrumental works that are suitable for separate performance and are worth studying. Like the opera and oratorio sinfonias of their male contemporaries, they are part of the ancestry of the later eighteenth-century symphony, though not nearly so extended in length. Therefore, the works chosen to represent Gratianini in this collection are the two sinfonias from *Santa Teresa,* which also show limited use of dynamic markings and contrast between solo and tutti passages.

The *Sinfonia* to the *Prima Parte* is in E minor and begins with a largo in triple time. There are copious, although neither complete nor accurately placed, figured bass markings. The last phrase, which echoes the preceding one, is marked *piano*. In the second section, an allegro, the first and second violins play in unison; in contrast, solos for first and second violins play independent concertino-style passages. The copyist labeled each violin part *soli* in these sections, but undoubtedly the composer intended that only one play on a part.

The *Seconda Parte* is in B minor and uses the old Dorian signature of one sharp, thus requiring the use of accidentals for C-sharps, with which the copyist had considerable trouble. It consists of two sections, both in common time: a short largo with extensive use of seventh chords in sequences and a partly imitative, rather improvisatory allegro, which ends each of its four phrases with a fermata. At the end, there is a *piano* marking, immediately followed by *piu piano*.

There are several scribal errors. In addition to the figured-bass placement—which is uncorrected in this edition—and the accidental errors, which are shown in brackets, the bass part in the sinfonia to *Parte Prima* skipped m. 40 and compensated for it by repeating m. 43. The missing measure was easily supplied editorially by comparing parallel passages.

Notes

1. Alexander von Weilen, *Zur Wiener Theatergeschichte. Die vom Jahre 1629 bis zum Jahre 1740 am Wiener Hofe zur Aufführung gelangten Werke theatralischen Charakters und Oratorien* (Vienna: Hölders, 1901).

2. The singers' full names were identified through data in Robert L. and Norma W. Weaver, *A Chronology of Music in the Florentine Theater 1590–1750: Operas, Prologues, Finales, Intermezzos, and Plays with Incidental Music* (Detroit: Information Coordinators, 1978). No further identification of the bass has been possible however.

3. Egon Wellesz, "Die Opern und Oratorien in Wien 1660–1708," *Studien zur Musikwissenschaft* 6 (1919): 16.

4. Although the works call for string orchestra throughout, *S. Gemigniano* contains one aria, *Consoli che il petto*, for alto, oboe, violins, and continuo. It is published in a modern edition in *Arias from Oratorios by Women Composers of the Eighteenth Century*, vol. 1, ed. Barbara Garvey Jackson. (Fayetteville: ClarNan Editions, 1987).

5. *Il ancor ti resto in petto*, from *Santa Teresa*, for tenor, solo cello, and continuo; and *A veder si raro oggetto*, from *S. Gemigniano vescous,* e *prottettore di Modona,* for soprano, solo cello, and continuo, are found in a modern edition in *Arias from Oratorios by Women Composers of the Eighteenth Century*, vol. 3, ed. Barbara Garvey Jackson (Fayetteville: ClarNan Editions, 1990).

Bibliography

Sources

The sole copies of both manuscript scores are in Vienna: Musiksammlung der Österreichische Nationalbibliothek. Permission to use this material is gratefully acknowledged. The composer's name in these citations is spelled as it is in the particular manuscript.

Gratianini, Caterina Benedetta. *Santa Teresa Oratorio a quattro voci con Stromenti*. Ms. score, n.d.

Grazianini, Sgra. Catterina Benedetta. *Oratorio di S. Gemigniano Vescovo, e Protettore de Modona*. Ms. score, 1705.

Books and Articles

Cohen, Aaron. "Grazianini, Caterina Benedicta." *International Encyclopedia of Women Composers*. 2nd ed. Vol. 1, 284.

Eitner, Robert. "Grazianini, Catterina Benedetta." *Biographisch-bibliographisches Quellen-Lexikon der Musiker und Musikgelehrten*. Vol. 4, 355 (lists *S. Gemigniano* as 1715).

Schering, Arnold. *Geschichte des Oratoriums*. Leipzig: Breitkopf and Härtel, 1911.

Weaver, Robert L. and Norma W. *A Chronology of Music in the Florentine Theater 1590–1750: Operas, Prologues, Finales, Intermezzos, and Plays with Incidental Music*. Detroit: Information Coordinators, 1978.

Weilen, Alexander von. *Zur Wiener Theatergeschichte. Die vom Jahre 1629 bis zum Jahre 1740 am Wiener Hofe zur Aufführung gelangten Werke theatralischen Charakters und Oratorien*. Vienna: Hölders, 1901.

Wellesz, Egon. "Die Opern und Oratorien in Wien 1660–1708." *Studien zur Musikwissenschaft* 6 (1919): 16.

Modern Editions

Consolati che il petto, *A veder si raro oggetto*, *In questo chiaro dì*, and *Dia lode il grato Core*, from *S. Gemigniano*; *Il ancor ti resta in petto*, from *Santa Teresa*. In *Arias from Oratorios by Women Composers of the Eighteenth Century*, vols. 1, 3, and 4. Edited by Barbara Garvey Jackson. Fayetteville: ClarNan Editions, 1987, 1990, 1992.

Santa Teresa
(Sinfonias to Part I and Part II)

Prima Parte

Caterina Benedetta Gratianini
Barbara Garvey Jackson, editor

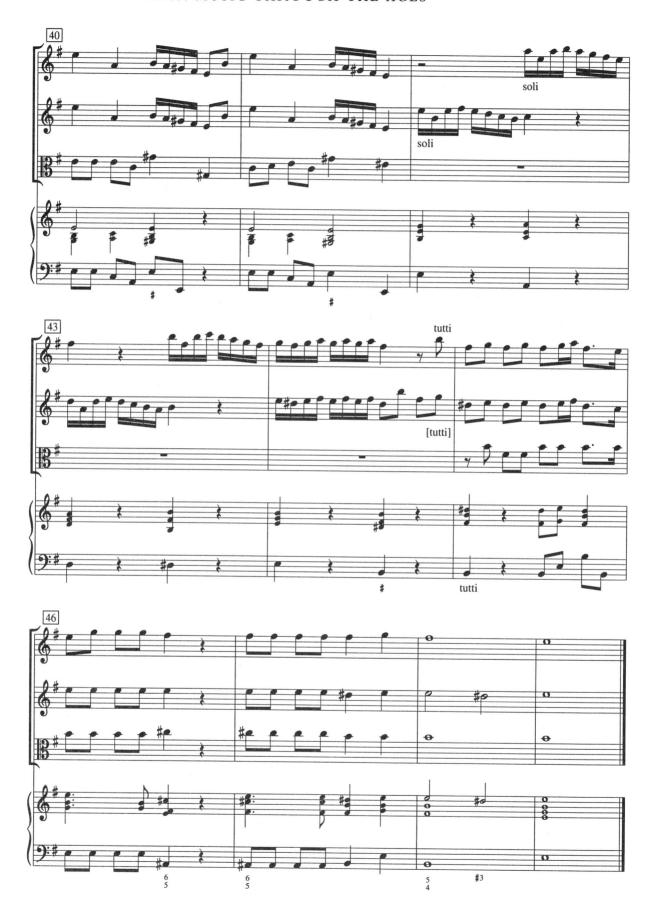

Seconda Parte

Largo

Camilla de Rossi, Romana

(fl. 1707–1710)[1]

BARBARA GARVEY JACKSON

Camilla de Rossi was one of several women in northern Italy and Austria who composed large oratorios and other dramatic works during the period between 1670 and 1725. None of them appear on court pay lists, and in most cases we know nothing of their personal lives or career status. Nevertheless, there is a record in the court calendar of the performances of many of their works. The four whose works were performed in Vienna during this period include Marianna von Raschenau, Caterina Benedetta Gratianini, Maria Margherita Grimani, and Camilla de Rossi.[2] Of the four, Camilla de Rossi has by far the largest amount of surviving music.

Nothing is known of Rossi's life except that "Romana" appears on the title pages of her manuscripts, which indicates she is of Roman origin. She wrote four oratorios for solo voices and orchestra, which were performed in the Imperial Chapel in Vienna from 1707 to 1710 during the reign of Emperor Joseph I. Single manuscript copies of each oratorio are extant in Vienna. A cantata manuscript, with no record of performance, also survives in Dresden. Rossi's name has not been found on any court pay lists of musicians in Vienna.

Each oratorio is in two large sections, usually about an hour in length, for soloists and orchestra; most include da capo arias, secco recitative, and occasional ensemble arias. No chorus is used. The word *Coro* appears in some scores, usually at the end of the work; this does not signify a chorus with singers doubling parts, but rather it refers to the ensemble of soloists.

Rossi's first dated work is the oratorio *Santa Beatrice d'Este* (1707). The libretto, written by Cardinal Benedetto Pamphili, had previously been set by the Spanish cellist and composer Giovanni Lulier, who, along with Arcangelo Corelli, was employed by Cardinal Pamphili in Rome. Lulier's setting of his employer's libretto in 1689 celebrated a visit by Cardinal Rinaldo d'Este, a member of the family to which Saint Beatrice had belonged. Camilla de Rossi's new setting of 1707 was commissioned by Emperor Joseph I, but the specific occasion for this work about a local saint from Modena that was written for a performance in Vienna is not known. Rossi's instrumentation—string orchestra, two trumpets, and archlute (which she used again for *Sant' Alessio*)—is the same as that used by Lulier.[3] Perhaps Rossi had heard Lulier's work in Rome. If she had connections with the Pamphili circle, she might also have had her musical training from one or more of the many splendid musicians there, but no documentation of her Roman years has yet been found. Rossi's *Santa Beatrice d'Este* was performed again in 1712 in Perugia, and a printed libretto from that performance survives. There is no indication of the reason for the revival there, nor do we know if the composer herself was present.

Rossi's works exhibit her keen interest in tone color. It seems clear that she was in Vienna by 1708 when she wrote *Il sacrifizio di Abramo* (The Sacrifice of Abraham), for the score calls for two chalumeaux very soon after the instruments were first heard as part of an orchestra in the operas of Giovanni Bononcini and Attilio Ariosti in Vienna (1707).[4] There are also remarkable passages for the archlute—a symbol of the innocence of Isaac—that may have been written for the composer and lutenist Francesco Conti, who was on the court pay list as a theorbist at this time.[5] Her last oratorio, *Sant' Alessio,* also features the archlute.

According to the title page of the manuscript score, Rossi wrote the text, as well as the music, for *Il figliuol prodigo* (The Prodigal Son), an oratorio written "at the command of the Emperor" in 1709. While the texts of her first two oratorios stress ideal obedience to divine will, even if it involves sacrifice of son (*Abramo*) or martyrdom and possible destruction of one's homeland (*Santa Beatrice*), *Il figliuol prodigo* deals with human love and forgiveness for the disobedient son and treats the emotions of the parents, the prodigal, and the brother with compelling realism. If the composer was able to choose her own subject, her libretto may have had particular personal significance.

Rossi's final dated work, *Sant'Alessio* (1710), is also marked by the sympathetic treatment of the relatives of the saint. Alessio repudiates worldly marriage in the pursuit of his divinely ordained mission. Although his innocent obedience is symbolized by the lute accompaniment, it is the spouse and the parents who have the most poignant and moving music—chromaticism, sigh motives, and echo effects (with *piano* and *forte* markings). An undated cantata, *Dori e Fileno*, is a sweet duet of adolescent love, for soprano and alto accompanied by string orchestra.

All Rossi's works show a sure command of instrumental writing, and her string parts—with several independent cello solo parts[6] and active and independent viola parts—suggest that she may have been trained as a string player, even though Roman girls rarely had such opportunities.[7] In her scores, bowings and phrasings are carefully marked; there is often alternation of soloists, groups of soli, and tutti passages; and dynamics (*piano* and *forte*) are indicated.

Although nothing is known about the composer herself, there are cast lists for several of her works, as for other women composers of oratorios in Vienna. All had access to the best singers in the court musical establishment: the soprani Maria Landini (the wife of the lutenist Francesco Conti) and Kunigond (La Sutterin), for example, sang Rossi's music, although some female roles were sung by the castrati Salvatore Mellini and Gaetano Orsini. Whether or not there was more than one female character, there was never more than one female singer cast in any work by Rossi, Grimani, and Gratianini, for whom cast lists survive. Young men, whether innocent or not—Isaac, Sant'Alessio, and the Prodigal Son—were sung by male altos, while tenors Silvio, Carlo Costa, and an unnamed singer in *Il sacrifizio di Abramo* sang the roles of fathers and counselors. In all of Rossi's works there is only one bass role, the villain in *Santa Beatrice d'Este*, which was sung by D. Giovanni Batta. The cast of *Il figliuol prodigo* consisted entirely of male singers: the Father was the tenor Silvio; the Mother, the male soprano Vincenzo; the Prodigal, the male alto Gaetano Orsini; the Brother, male soprano Domenico Tollini; and the Musician, who sings at the festivities when the Prodigal returns, a boy soprano named Timer, who a few years later was listed as a tenor on a court pay list. Whether or not there was any special reason for this all-male cast is unknown.

The work included in this anthology is the opening section of *Il figliuol prodigo*, in which a discussion between the parents and the Prodigal sets the stage for the story. The son has clearly announced his intention to depart before the oratorio begins—one could almost say "before the curtain rises" as this oratorio is so well-paced for staging that it could easily be acted. The pattern of interchange of recitative and brief recitative duet in this opening section occurs again at the end of the work, although greatly expanded, in the dramatic reconciliation of the Prodigal, his parents, and ultimately his brother. Throughout the work, the language

of Rossi's libretto has the ring of timeless truth for the dramatic situation; if the oratorio were staged in the twentieth century, it would even work in modern dress.

Camilla de Rossi's works designate very few figures to bass parts, as demonstrated by this excerpt. Elisions in the text are marked by arcs that connect elided vowels below the text. The spelling and capitalization of the original text has been maintained. Titles and other references are modernized in the prefatory notes.

Notes

1. No biographical material has been found for Rossi other than the dates of the Vienna performances, which determine her period of greatest activity.

2. Other composers included Maria Barbieri, a singer active in Bologna and Modena and the composer of the parts of two operas in the 1670s (the other composers who contributed sections to the works were G. B. Vitali, G. P. Colonna, and Francesco Prattichista); Angiola Teresa Muratori (married to Scannabecchi and later, to Moneta) who flourished as a painter and composer of oratorios from 1662 to 1708 in Bologna, but whose music to four oratorios is lost (only the libretti survive); and Caterina Benedetta Bianchi, Countess (in Lucca?), who composed one oratorio, *San Leopoldo*, in Lucca in 1724. Later in the century, the Viennese composer Marianne von Martinez wrote two oratorios to texts by Metastasio.

3. Lulier's setting, with an overture and sinfonia added by Arcangelo Corelli, was performed at Modena in the fall of 1689 and was heard again in the same city in 1701. In the Roman performance, a huge orchestra of more than eighty players was used. See Michael Talbot, "Corelli, Arcangelo," *The New Grove Dictionary of Music and Musicians,* vol. 4, 771.

4. Emperor Joseph I was also interested in the chalumeau at this time and used it in his scoring of the aria *Tutto in piano,* which he composed in 1709 to be inserted into Marc' Antonio Ziani's opera *Chylonida,* written for the birthday of the Empress Amalia Wilhelmine, April 21, 1709.

5. The four-movement Sinfonia for archlute solo and strings from *Il sacrifizio di Abramo* illustrates her knowledge of the instrument. See discography.

6. See, for example, the two arias for tenor, strings, cello (or celli), and continuo from *Il figliuol prodigo, Rompe il morso* and *Lascia, o Figlio, il tuo dolore,* in *Arias with Continuo and Cello Obbligato,* vol. 3 of *Arias from Oratorios by Women Composers of the Eighteenth Century* (Fayetteville, Arkansas: ClarNan Editions, 1990).

7. If she grew up in Rome, as the designation *Romana* on the title pages of her scores suggests, the opportunities for hearing or performing as a string player would have been far more restricted by Papal puritanism than would have been the case had she been a Venetian. In Rome, for example, most oratorio performances were for male audiences only, and many celebrated musicians performed in cardinals' households, to which women had little access. In Venice, on the other hand, the famous conservatories did train girls in music, and their performances were heard by mixed audiences. There were even day students at these institutions. See Jane L. Bal-

dauf-Berdes, *Women Musicians of Venice: Musical Foundations, 1525–1855* (Oxford: Clarendon Press, 1993).

Bibliography

Source

Il figliuol prodigo [Libretto by composer]. Ms. score, 1709. Vienna Österreichisches Nationalbibliothek, Mus. Hs. 19.122. Orchestra string parts Mus. Hs. 19.123. Printed libretto [also includes German translation as *Der verlohrne Sohne*. Permission to use this material was granted by the music collection of the Österreichisches Nationalbibliothek.

Books and Articles

Cohen, Aaron. "Rossi, Camilla de." *International Encyclopedia of Women Composers.* 2nd ed. Vol. 1, 601.

Eitner, Robert. "Rossi, Camilla de." *Biographisch-bibliographisches Quellen-Lexikon der Musiker und Musikgelehrten.* Vol. 8, 321.

Jackson, Barbara Garvey. "Oratorios by Command of the Emperor: The Music of Camilla de Rossi." *Current Musicology* 42 (1986): 7–19.

Schering, Arnold. *Geschichte des Oratoriums.* Leipzig: Breitkopf & Härtel, 1911.

Weaver, Robert L. and Norma W. *A Chronology of Music in the Florentine Theater 1590–1750: Operas, Prologues, Finales, Intermezzos, and Plays with Incidental Music.* Detroit: Information Coordinators, 1978.

Weilen, Alexander von. *Zur Wiener Theatergeschichte. Die vom Jahre 1629 bis zum Jahre 1740 am Wiener Hofe zur Aufführung gelangten Werke theatralischen Charakters und Oratorien.* Item nos. 575, 593, 604, and 614. Vienna: Hölders, 1901.

Wellesz, Egon. "Die Opern und Oratorien in Wien 1660-1708," *Studien zur Musikwissenschaft* 6 (1919): 16.

Modern Editions

Dori e Fileno [cantata]. Edited by Barbara Garvey Jackson. Fayetteville, Arkansas: ClarNan Editions, 1984.

Il Sacrifizio di Abramo [oratorio]. Edited by Barbara Garvey Jackson. Fayetteville, Arkansas: ClarNan Editions, 1984.

Santa Beatrice d'Este [oratorio]. Edited by Barbara Garvey Jackson. Fayetteville, Arkansas: ClarNan Editions, 1986; with revised preface and translation, 1993.

Quanto, quanto mi consola, Qui dove il pò . . . Poiche parmi di sentire, and *Sono il fasto, e la bellezza,* from *Santa Beatrice d'Este; Strali, fulmini, tempeste, procelle,* from *Il Sacrifzio di Abramo; Cielo, pietoso Cielo* and *Sonori concenti,* from *S. Alessio; Rompe il morso, Lascia, o Figlio, il tuo dolore,* and *Quella nave, che riposa,* from *Il figliuol prodigo.* In *Arias from Oratorios by Women Composers of the Eighteenth Century,* vols. 1–4. Fayetteville AR: ClarNan Editions, 1987, 1990, 1990, 1992.

Other Works

Santa Beatrice d'Este. [Libretto by Cardinal Benedetto Pamphili] Ms. score, 1707. Vienna: Österreichisches Nationalbibliothek, Mus. Hs. 17.312. Orchestra string parts for the arias, Mus. Hs. 17.313. Printed libretto, Mus. Hs. 19.122. The printed libretto for the Perugia revival in 1712 is in Bologna: Civico Museo Bibliografico Musicale, shelf mark 4613.

Il sacrifizio di Abramo. [Libretto by Francesco Dario] Ms. score, 1708. Vienna: Österreichisches Nationalbibliothek, Mus. Hs. 17.306. Printed libretto [also includes German translation as *Das Brand-Opfer des Abraham*], Vienna Österreichisches Nationalbibliothek, COD 406 745-BM.

Sant'Alessio. [Librettist unknown] Ms. score, 1710. Vienna: Österreichisches Nationalbibliothek, Mus. Hs. 17.307.

Cantata à 2. Canto, e Alto. Frà Dori, e Fileno. Ms. score. Dresden: Sächsische Landesbibliothek, Ms. Mus. 2382-L-1; second copy lost in World War II.

Discography

Sinfonia from *Il Sacrifizio di Abramo* [to Seconda Parte]. For solo lute and string orchestra. In *Baroquen Treasures* [CD and cassette]. Bay Area Women's Philharmonic, JoAnn Falletta, lutenist and conductor. Newport Classics, 1990.

Il figliuol prodigo

Recit.

Padre: Figlio, Prodigo Figlio, credi al mio crin canuto. Ti pentirai di non aver creduto.

Father: Son, Prodigal Son. Trust my grey hair. You will be sorry not to have believed me.

Aria.

Per Salire ad erto monte Porge l'ali a nobil core generosa la Virtù.
Ma bagnar non vuol la Fronte di sudore neghittosa gioventù
Per Salire ad erto monte . . .

A noble heart, generous virtue, gives wings to climb the steep mountain.
But lazy youth does not want to bathe the brow with sweat.
A noble heart, etc.

Recit.

Madre: Udisti Figlio.

Figlio: Intesi.

Padre: E pur non credi.

Figlio: Ciò, che me diè Fortuna, a me concedi.

Padre: È la Fortuna un nome Il Mondo inganno.

Madre: Gioventude un baleno lieve Fior la bellezza.

Padre: Larve sono gli onori.

Madre e Padre: È son le Gemme, egli ori, a chi Senno non hà gradi al periglio.

Figlio: Gemme, ed oro vi chiedo, e non consiglio.

Padre: È Gemme, et oro avrai pur mendico Sarai Prodigo Figlio.

Aria.

Figlio Prodigo: Augeletto di tenere piume si contenta di Selva romita.
Fatto adulto, poi cangia costume per godere più libera Vita.
Augletto di tenere piume . . .

Mother: Listen Son!

Son: I'm listening.

Father: And yet you don't believe.

Son: Grant me that which is my fortune.

Father: Fortune is a name, the false world.

Mother: Youth, a flash of lightning; beauty, a trifling flower.

Father: Honors are phantoms.

Mother and Father: And [so] are the jewels he would ask for, he for whom wisdom has no degrees of peril.

Son: Treasure, and now, I demand of you, and not advice!

Father: It [advice] is treasure, and now you will really be a pauper. You will be the Prodigal Son.

Son: The little bird of immature feather is satisfied with the lonely forest.
Having grown up, then I change habits to enjoy a freer life.
The little bird, etc.

Il Figliuol Prodigo

(Beginning of the first scene: Padre, Madre, and Figlio Prodigo)

Camilla de Rossi

Barbara Garvey Jackson, editor

Lyrics under the music:

13 mon - te Por - ge l'ali a no - bil co - re,_ por - ge

16 l'ali a _ no - bil co - re ge - ne - ro - sa la _ vir - tù.

20 Per Sa - li - re ad er - to mon - te, por - ge

24 l'ali a no - bil co - re ge - - ne - ro - sa, ge - - ne -

do - re ____ ne - ghit - to - sa, ne - ghit - to - sa gio - ven -

tù, ma ba - gnar non vuol la fron - te di Su -

do - re ne - ghit - to - sa gio - ven - tù, ma ba -

gnar __ non vuol __ la ____ fron - te ne - ghit - to - sa Gio - ven - tù.

Dal 𝄋

Recit.

U-dis-ti Fi-glio. In - te-si. e pur non cre-di. Ciò, che mi diè for-

tu - na, a me con-ce-di è la For-tu - na un no-me Il mon-do in-

Gio-ven tu-de un-ba - le-no lie-ve Fior la bel - lez-za

gan-no. Lar-ve so - no gli o-

è son le Gem-me, egli ori, a chi Sen - no non hà gradi al per-

no-ri è son le Gem-me, egli ori, a chi Sen - no non hà gradi al per-

Maria Margherita Grimani

(fl. 1713–1718)

BARBARA GARVEY JACKSON

Music by Maria Margherita Grimani was performed in Vienna on several occasions during the reign of Emperor Charles VI. Although her family name is that of a very famous Venetian family, and although Pietro Grimani was the Venetian ambassador to Vienna in 1713, during which year two works by Maria Margherita Grimani were performed there, her relationship, if any, to the ambassador's family has not been established.[1] Nothing is known of the composer's life except the surviving music—all of which was performed in Vienna—and a note on the score of her opera of 1713 that it was "dedicated from Bologna, April 5, 1713." That opera, *Pallade e Marte, componimento dramatico* (Pallas and Mars, dramatic composition), was the first piece of her music known to have been performed in Vienna. It was written to celebrate the name day of the emperor, an important occasion and a prestigious commission, if it was indeed ordered by the emperor. It was performed on November 4, 1713. It may be significant that such an important performance was given to a composer named Grimani shortly after Pietro Grimani had negotiated the treaty that allied Venice and the emperor against the Turks.[2]

There does seem to be at least a coincidental relationship between the activities of specific women composers of large-scale dramatic music and the reigns of the emperors in whose courts they worked, although only in the case of Grimani is there a possible family connection with a political figure. Marianne von Raschenau (ca.1651–ca.1710 or 1714), a Viennese nun, wrote during the reign of Leopold I, a very religious emperor who was also a patron of music and a composer whose works included oratorio, opera, and liturgical music. Raschenau's works, for which all the music has been lost, included two oratorios—*Gli infermi risonati dal Redentore* (The Sympathic Suffering of the Redeemer), of 1694, and *Le sacre visioni di Santa Teresa* (The Sacred Visions of St. Theresa), of 1703—and two secular works that were probably operas, *I tributi del tempo all'augustissima Casa d'Austria* (1696) and *Il consiglio di Pallade, componimento per musica*

(1697).[3] A work like "The Tributes to the Epoch of the Most August House of Austria" might not have been unusual from the hand of a male cleric but seems an unusual subject for a nun; "The Counsel of Pallas [Athena]" would be an even more surprising subject. Yet the women composers who followed Raschenau used two of the same themes she had used—Gratianini wrote a Santa Teresa oratorio and Maria Margherita Grimani wrote an opera on Pallas Athena and Mars. When the reign of Leopold I ended in 1705, no more music at court appears from Raschenau although she continued to be active as *Chormeisterin* (Choirdirector) at her convent and her music was probably still being composed and performed there.[4] It is possible that 1705 was the year of the last court performance of a work by Gratianini, although since her *Santa Teresa* is undated, we do not know for sure.

Camilla de Rossi's music was performed in Vienna only during the short reign of Joseph I. He was also a musician, and before his accession to the throne he was active in the court theater as a singer and dancer. He seems to have been well acquainted with the music of Alessandro Scarlatti and perhaps encouraged the use of Scarlatti-like forms as found in the oratorios of Gratianini, Rossi, and Grimani. He himself composed several arias, and his interest in the chalumeau seems to have been shared by Rossi. At the end of his reign, no more of Rossi's works appear at court and no other trace of her activities has been found.

Grimani's works all appear in the reign of Charles VI, and the series of women dramatic composers for Vienna ends with her. It is possible that the political problems faced by the Empress Maria Theresia—including the War of the Austrian Succession and the low state of the treasury after the end of Charles's extravagant reign—made the focus on music that had characterized Maria Theresia's predecessors impractical, even impossible, to continue. Salary and personnel cuts had to be made in the musical establishment at court when she came to the throne. In Grimani's case, one might speculate that she could have returned to Italy when a family member was no longer in Vienna as a diplomat. Since her personal status—single, married, or nun—is unknown, there is not even an indication as to whether her surname was a birth name or a married name.

Maria Margherita Grimani's surviving works include the aforementioned opera and two oratorios—*La visitazione di Santa Elisabetta* (The Visitation of S. Elizabeth) and *La decollazione di S. Giovanni Battista* (The Beheading of Saint John the Baptist). All are for soloists and orchestra; no choruses are used, although the term *Coro* is applied to the ensemble of soloists at the end of *La visitazione* and a duet for the two soloists ends *Pallade e Marte*. *La visitazione* was heard in 1713 and revived in 1718; *La decollazione* was performed in 1715. Single manuscript copies of each of her works are in the Austrian National Library.

The opera is by far the shortest of her works, merely sixty-five pages of manuscript. It is scored for soprano and alto voices, with solo cello, oboe, and theorbo, and strings and continuo; with the exception of the theorbo, the scoring is the same as that of the later oratorio *La Decollazione*. The oboe seems to have been a favorite instrument of Grimani's, as there are three arias in her works that use it. *Pallade e Marte* opens with a short three-movement sinfonia. Soloists sing alternating arias: one accompanied by string orchestra, one for continuo that concludes with a string rittornello, two arias with independent obbligato parts (one for cello and one for oboe), and a closing duet. Even this short work does not match Klein's description of "usually with continuo accompaniment only," for in this work alone, there are many more types of arias than continuo ones. Moreover, Klein is inaccurate in describing the accompaniments of Grimani's other works as exhibiting "extreme simplicity of descriptive techniques and . . . renunciation of dramatic effects." Klein considers the recitatives "schematic and uninteresting"—which could of course be said of much of the *secco* recitative of the period and would in no way be distinctively characteristic of Grimani.[5] Despite the fact that Schering,[6] as early as 1911, considered that Grimani's work showed "impressive command of the art of expression," there was no further interest in her work until the renewal of interest in women composers in the late twentieth century. The sinfonias of all her works—as well as two arias from one oratorio and the closing Coro from the other—are now available in modern editions.

The cast of singers for *La visitatione* is known: La Contini (female soprano, Maria vergine), Gaetano Orsini (male alto, Santa Elisabetta), Pietro Cesari (male alto, Santa Anna), and Bigoni (bass, San Giuseppe). As was the case in other oratorios for which the cast is known, even though there was more than one female role, all but one of the treble roles were sung by castrati. Unfortunately, the cast page of *La decollazione* lists the names of only the characters, not the singers. San Giovanni Battista (St. John the Baptist) is an alto role; Erode

(Herod), a bass; Erodiade (Herodias) and Salome are soprani; and Un Confidente d'Erode (Herod's Confidant) is a tenor.

The passage selected for this anthology is from Part II of *La decollazione di San Giovanni Battista*. It is scored for a string orchestra with continuo, to which an oboe was added for San Giovanni's aria *S'hò fra nodi,* which ended Part I, and Salome's aria *L'esser fida* in Part II. The passage begins Salome's campaign to incite Herod to kill John the Baptist and reveals two contrasting characterizations: the first aria presents a conventional characterization of Herod as bombastic and vain, accompanied by repeated sixteenth-note chords in *stile concitato*. Salome, pretending naiveté, answers with the dance tune that was introduced by the orchestra. She sings in unison with violins only, a most unusual procedure. After the passage included in this anthology, as Part II progresses, she eventually dances, and the Confidant and Herodias respond. Salome's aria, accompanied by the oboe, is more openly seductive. After a chilling recitative, she demands the head of John the Baptist as payment. In the concluding aria of the oratorio the saint declares that for the innocent heart, death is the beginning of life.[7]

Notes

1. Rudolph Klein, "Grimani, Maria Margherita," *The New Grove Dictionary of Music and Musicians,* vol. 8, p. 733; and *Die Musik in Geschichte und Gegenwart,* vol. 5, pp. 922–923.

2. The Grimani family had many musical interests, among them ownership of several opera theaters, including the Teatro San Giovanni Crisostomo, in which Handel's first Italian opera, *Agrippina,* was a great success in 1709. The libretto is by Cardinal Vincenzo Grimani, viceroy of Naples. The family had great political power as well—Pietro Grimani eventually became the doge of Venice.

3. Klein considers Grimani's *Pallade e Marte* to be the first opera in Vienna by a woman composer. However, these two secular works by Raschenau are probably operas and predate Grimani's work by nearly two decades.

4. In the *Visitationsprotokolle* of the Diocesan Archives in Vienna, April 1, 1710, the visitors noted that fifty-nine-year-old Raschenau was *Chormeisterin* and had lived in the convent of St. Jakob auf der Hülben for thirty-eight years. This information was provided by Dr. Rudolf Heilinger of the catalogue department of the Österreichische Nationalbibliothek (letter to Jackson, April 21, 1981) and Dr. Peter Csendes, archivist of the Wiener Stadt- und Landesarchiv (letter to Jackson, May 7, 1981). They also cite Eva-Maria Hantschel, *Das Augustiner-Chorfrauenkloster St. Jakob auf der Hülben in Wien, 1301–1783* (phil. Diss., Vienna, 1969) and Felix Czeike, *Das grosse Gröner Wien-Lexikon* (Vienna: Molden, 1974), p. 554.

5. See Klein's *New Grove* article.

6. Arnold Schering, *Geschichte des Oratoriums* (Leipzig: Breitkopf & Härtel, 1911), p. 111.

7. Modern editions of *L'esser fida* (The faithful creature) and of *A un core innocente* (To an innocent heart) are found in: *Arias from*

Oratorios by Women Composers of the Eighteenth Century, vol. 1, ed. Barbara Garvey Jackson (Fayetteville, Arkansas: ClarNan Editions, 1987).

Bibliography

Eitner, Robert. "Grimani, Maria Margherita." In *Biographisch-bibliographisches Quellen-Lexikon der Musiker und Musikgelehrten,* vol. 4, pp. 378–79.

Jackson, Barbara Garvey. "Maria Margherita Grimani (fl. ca. 1713–1718)." In *Historical Anthology of Music by Women.* Bloomington: Indiana University Press, 1987.

Klein, Rodolph. "Grimani, Maria Margherita." In *The New Grove Dictionary of Music and Musicians,* vol.7, p. 733. Based on his article in *Die Musik in Geschichte und Gegenwart,* vol. 5, pp. 922–23.

Schering, Arnold. *Geschichte des Oratoriums.* Leipzig: Breitkopf & Härtel, 1911.

Weilen, Alexander von. *Zur Wiener Theatergeschichte. Die vom Jahre 1629 bis zum Jahre 1740 am Wiener Hofe zur Aufführung gelangten Werke theatralischen Charakters und Oratorien.* Vienna: Hölders, 1901.

Wellesz, Egon. "Die Opern und Oratorien in Wien, 1660–1708," *Studien zur Musikwissenschaft* 6 (1919):16.

Source

Single copies of manuscript scores of all Grimani's surviving works are in Vienna at the Musiksammlung der Österreichischen Nationalbibliothek. I acknowledge with gratitude permission of the library to publish this excerpt.

La decollazione di San Giovanni Battista. Oratorio. Ms. score, 1715. Mus. Hs. 17.666.

Manuscripts

La visitazione di Santa Elisabetta. Oratorio. Ms. score, 1718. Mus. Hs. 17.668. [Apparently, the copy of the score used for the revival in 1718 rather than that of the first performance in 1713].

Pallade e Marte. Ms. score, 1713. Mus. Hs. 17.741.

Modern Editions

L'esser fida and *A un core innocente,* from *La decollazione di San Giovanni Battista.* In *Arias from Oratorios by Women Composers of the Eighteenth Century,* vol. 1. Fayetteville, Arkansas: ClarNan Editions, 1987.

Ogni Colle, final *Coro* from *La visitazione.* Louisville, Kentucky: Editions Ars Femina, 1992.

Sinfonia [for strings and continuo], from *Pallade e Marte* [facsimile of the manuscript]. In *Historical Anthology of Music by Women,* edited by James Briscoe. Bloomington: Indiana University Press, 1987.

Sinfonia to *La decollazione.* Louisville, Kentucky: Editions Ars Femina, 1992.

Sinfonia to *La visitazione.* Louisville, Kentucky: Editions Ars Femina, 1992.

Sinfonia to *Pallade et Marte.* Louisville, Kentucky: Editions Ars Femina, 1992.

Discography

Sinfonie [sic] by Maria Grimani. In *Women's Orchestral Works,* performed by the New England Women's Symphony; concertmaster, Jean Lamon. Galaxia Women's Enterprises, 1980. The jacket notes incorrectly state that the longer work introduced by this sinfonia has been lost and that no figured bass is indicated.

La decollazione de S. Giovanni Battista

Recit.

Erode: Gradisco i vostri auspici di preghiere si Liete, che per farmi felice as Ciel porgete. Se per me gl'Astri amici arrideranno a vostri prieghe ardenti godrò solo per voi Lieto i contenti. Or preparisi intanto per degno applauso al mio giorno vitale con superbo splendor danza Reale.

Aria.

Erode: Sù, sù risuonino Stromenti armonici pe'l Ciel rimbombino Le glorie splendide del mio Natal.

Festeggi il Popole il Regno giubili e l'alme mostrino a tanta nascita il gaudio egual.

Sù, sù risuonino Stromenti armonici . . .

Herod: I gratefully accept the protection of such joyful prayers, that you offer to heaven to make me happy. Now meanwhile prepare the Royal dance with proud splendor for worthy applause to the day that gave me life.

Herod: Up, up, let the harmonious instruments resound, to let heaven reverberate to the splendid glories of my birthday.

The people celebrate, the kingdom rejoices, and let the spirits display equal joy at such a birth.

Up, up, let the harmonious instruments, etc.

Recit.

Erode: Tu Salome diletta avanti al Real soglio movi le prime danze: io cosi voglio.

Herod: Thou, beloved Salome, dance the first dance before the Royal throne: I wish it so. [Dance music sounds in the orchestra. Salome sings to the accompaniment of the tune alone, but does not yet dance.]

Aria.

Salome: Anche col piede a te la fede vuò tributar.

A'un Rè si degno col mio danzar un fido pegno Saprò donar.

Anche col piede . . .

Salome: I would like to pay tribute to you faithfully also with my feet.

To a King so worthy I will know how to give a faithful token with my dancing.

I would like to pay tribute, etc.

La decollazione di S. Giovanni Battista
(Scene between Erode and Salome)

Maria Margharita Grimani
Barbara Garvey Jackson, editor

Aria

tal.   Sù, sù ri-suo – ni-no   Stro-men-ti ar-mo – ni-ci

pe'l Ciel rim-bom – bi-no   le glo-rie splen – di-de   del mio Na-tal _____

Le glo-rie splen - di-de

del mio Na-tal, del mio Na- tal.

Recit. [48] Erode

Tu Sa - lo-me di - let - ta av - anti al Re - al

[50]

so - glio mo - vi le pri - me dan - ze: io co - si vo - glio.

Aria [53] **Allegro**

Vln.

Vla.

Soprano (Salome)

B.c.

An - che col oie - de a te la fe - de

vuò tri - bu - tar, _____ vuò tri - bu - tar.

A'un Rè sì deg-no col mio_ dan -

[Fine]

Biographies of Editors

Sylvia Glickman, a New York-born musician, holds bachelor's and master's degrees in performance from the Juilliard School of Music where she was a piano student of Beveridge Webster. As a Fulbright Scholar, she was awarded an L.R.A.M. in Performance from the Royal Academy of Music in London where she worked with Harold Craxton in piano and Manuel Frankel in composition and received the Hecht Prize in Composition. She also studied composition as a child with Mark Brunswick in New York. She won the Loeb Prize, the highest award for excellence, from Juilliard and was among the first group awarded a solo recitalist grant from the National Endowment for the Arts in 1981. Glickman has performed to critical acclaim throughout the United States and in Europe, Israel, and Africa. Her concert programs reflect her interest and research in the music of women composers and contemporary composers as well as American music. Women's Way of Philadelphia honored Ms. Glickman in May 1986, for her "exceptional talent as a musician and teacher, and for her unique contributions to women's music history" and the New York Women Composers, Inc. gave her its annual award for "Distinguished Service in Support of Concert Music Composed by Women" in 1995. Ms. Glickman's anthology *Amy Beach: Virtuoso Piano Music* was published in 1982 by Da Capo Press; her *Anthology of American Piano Music from 1865–1909* is volume 4 in *Three Centuries of American Music* (G. K. Hall, 1990). Her Performance Edition of Piano Sonatas by Alexander Reinagle (1756–1809) was prepared as a companion to her recording of the sonatas, which were the first keyboard sonatas written in America. Ms. Glickman is a regular reviewer for *Choice: Books for College Libraries* and edited the keyboard section of the annual *Books for College Libraries* in 1987. She was on the music panel of the Pennsylvania Council on the Arts from 1989–91. Glickman is founding president of the Hildegard Publishing Company, a press devoted to furthering the music of women composers, past and present. She is the president of the Hildegard Institute, devoted to research on music by women, and artistic director of the Hildegard Chamber Players, a group devoted to playing this repertory. She was editor of the *Journal of the International Alliance for Women in Music* from 1995–6 and made several contributions to *The New Grove Dictionary of Women Composers* (London: Macmillan, 1995).

Martha Furman Schleifer, a graduate of Temple University, received a Ph.D. in musicology from Bryn Mawr College. She is a member of the music history faculty at Temple University and is senior editor of Hildegard Publishing Company. Schleifer was coeditor of *Three Centuries of American Music* (Boston: G.K. Hall, 1986–1992), a twelve-volume anthology of music by American composers. She is a series editor for *Composers of North America*, a series in continuous publication by Scarecrow Press, and was the author of *William Wallace Gilchrist (1846–1916)*, first book in the series. She is coeditor of the *Biographical Dictionary of Latin American Classical Composers*, published in 1995 by Scarecrow Press, for which she also functioned as an independent free-lance editor. Schleifer is the author of *American Opera and Music for the Stage—Eighteenth and Nineteenth Centuries* and of *American Opera and Music for the Stage—Early Twentieth Century*, volumes 5 and 6 of *Three Centuries of American Music*. She co-edited the *Cumulative Index for Three Centuries of American Music*, which is included in volume 12. Author of numerous articles and papers on music and musicians in Philadelphia, she has also made several contributions to *The New Grove Dictionary of Women Composers*, London: Macmillan, 1995. She has been the Review Editor for the *Journal of the International Alliance for Women in Music* since 1995.

Biographies of Contributors

Carol Henry Bates holds a Ph.D. in musicology from Indiana University and teaches in the Honors College of the University of South Carolina in Columbia. Her primary research interests are French harpsichord and chamber music of the late seventeenth and early eighteenth centuries. She has published modern editions of Elizabeth Jacquet de la Guerre's instrumental music and is the author of articles and reviews in *Early Music, Recherches sur la Musique française classique, MLA Notes, Early Keyboard Journal,* and the Garland *Encyclopedia of Keyboard Instruments.*

Jane Bowers, professor of music history and literature at the University of Wisconsin-Milwaukee, has been researching women in music for over twenty years. Co-editor of the Deems Taylor-ASCAP award-winning book *Women Making Music: The Western Art Tradition, 1150–1950* (University of Illinois Press, 1986) and the author of numerous articles, she first specialized in Italian women composers of the late sixteenth and seventeenth centuries and then went on to study women in music cross-culturally. She is currently working on a biography and repertory study of Chicago blues singer Estelle ("Mama") Yancy, and she has on the back burner a book about women's traditional musical roles and repertories relating to important stages of the life cycle (birth, puberty, marriage, and death). Her other scholarly interests include the history of the flute, flute music, and flute making.

Stewart Carter is professor of music at Wake Forest University in Winston-Salem, where he teaches music history and theory and directs the Collegium Musicum. He has published many articles and reviews in journals, including *Early Music, MLA Notes,* and *Historic Brass Society Journal.* His edition of *Isabella Leonarda, Selected Compositions* was published in the series *Recent Researches in the Music of the Baroque Editor.* He is executive editor of *Historic Brass Society Journal* and former editor of *Historical Performance.* An active performer on recorder and sackbut, he performs regularly with the Wake Forest Consort. He is codirector of the annual Early Brass Festival at Amherst, Massachusetts, and also teaches annually at the Amherst Early Music Festival.

Claire A. Fontijn is a musicologist, baroque flutist, and singer. She earned degrees in French, historical performance practices, and musicology from the University of Orléans in France, Oberlin College, the Royal Conservatory of the Hague, and Duke University. An assistant professor of musicology at Wellesley College, she is writing a book about Antonia Bembo.

Karl Wilhelm Geck, born in Bonn, studied music history and English and American language and literature at the University of the Saarland in Saarbrücken and the University of Georgia in Athens. He earned a degree in library science at the College of Library Science in Cologne. He received a Dr. phil. in 1992. In 1988 he became librarian at the University of the Saarland and since 1991 has been academic librarian at the Saxony State Library in Dresden.

Diane Upchurch Guthrie, a native of Raeford, North Carolina, received her bachelor of music degree from Queens College in Charlotte and a master of music in vocal performance from Florida State University. She earned the Doctorate of Musical Arts at the University of North Carolina in 1992. Her dissertation, "Elizabeth-Claude Jacquet de la Guerre's *Le Passage de la Mer Rouge*: An Edition with Commentary and Notes on Performance," culminated in three performances of the edition. She was formerly on the music faculty at Methodist College in Fayetteville, N.C., but now resides in Winston-Salem, N.C., where she is associated with the Salem College School of Music. Dr. Guthrie continues to perform as a recitalist and soloist throughout the Southeast.

Barbara Garvey Jackson, born in Normal, Illinois, is an emerita professor of music history from the University of Arkansas at Fayetteville. She is an editor and publisher of ClarNan Editions, publishing historic music by women composers. She plays violin and early keyboards. Ms. Jackson holds a B.M. degree from the University of Illinois, an M.M. from the Eastman School of Music, and a Ph.D. from Stanford University.

Robert L. Kendrick received a B.A. degree from the University of Pennsylvania and a Ph.D. from New York University. He is currently assistant professor of music at Harvard University.

Thomasin LaMay teaches in the music and women's studies departments at Goucher College. Her publications include articles on Monteverdi, Berlioz, French Revolutionary opera, and Italian virtuose of the seventeenth century. She is currently working on a book that deciphers methods of coding, storytelling, and structure in the music of late Renaissance women composers.

Sally Catlin Park earned her Ph.D. in music at Bryn Mawr College. Her professional activities have been in the areas of church music and the musical education of children. A specialist in the seventeenth century, she has worked with original keyboard manuscripts, including German tablatures, interpreting historical questions posed by the vast quantity of anonymous and undated compositions that survive. Park holds an administrative position in development at Columbia University.

Lisa Urkevich is a Ph.D. candidate in musicology at the University of Maryland. She holds degrees in ethnomusicology, music education, and historical musicology and has been involved with music editing and computer graphic design for the C. P. E. Bach Edition. Her dissertation explores the history and content of the so-called Anne Boleyn music book, Music MS1070 of the Royal College of Music, London.

Randall Wong received his Doctor of Musical Arts degree in historical performance from Stanford University in 1992. He has been among the forefront of American singers specializing in "historically informed" performance, editing early printings and manuscripts for his own and other musicians' use. He has created a number of new operatic roles for the Houston Grand Opera and the New York City Opera, and is a frequent collaborator of the composer Meredith Monk. His recordings include operas of Hasse, Jomelli, Meredith Monk, and Stewart Wallace.

Index